Warring Navies

INDIA & PAKISTAN

Commodore Ranjit B. Rai (Retd.)

with Joseph P. Chacko

Copyright © 2014 Ranjit Bhawnani Rai / RR Consultancy

ISBN 13: 978-8193005545 , ISBN 10: 81-93005546

All rights reserved.

Ebook & International Rights for

Frontier India Technology
No 22, 4th Floor, MK Joshi Building, Devi Chowk, Shastri Nagar,
Dombivli West, Maharashtra, India. 421202
http://frontierindia.biz

The views expressed in this book are those of the authors and not at all of the publisher. The publisher is not responsible for the views of the author and authenticity of the data, in any way whatsoever. Cataloging / listing of this book for re-sale purpose can be done, only by the authorised companies. Cataloging /listing or sale by unauthorized distributors / bookshops /booksellers etc., is strictly prohibited and will be legally prosecuted. All disputes are subject to Thane, Maharashtra jurisdiction only.

IN REMEMBRANCE

We would like to pay homage to the Shaheeds and Shahudas who gave their all in the wars, and with a fervent hope that we do not have to fight another fruitless war.

CONTENTS

	A Salute to Admiral S. M. Nanda - The Bomber of Karachi	I
	Introduction by General Ved P. Malik	1
	Preface and Overview of Contents	5
1	All the Wars - Military Leadership	14
2	Operation Vijay - Liberation of Goa 1961	31
3	The Navy does Sweet Fanny Adams in 1965	42
4	The Pakistan Navy History upto 1965	50
5	Dramatis Personae of the 1971 War	58
6	The Order of Battle (ORBAT - 1971)	72
7	The Mukti Bahini's War for Bangladesh	82
8	Prologue to Victory in the War of 1971	97
9	The War Diary 1971	114
10	America's Anti-India Pro-Pakistan Tilt	140
11	Osa Missile Boats' Nylon Necklace	154
12	The IAF - Indian Navy Attacks on Karachi	159
13	PNS Ghazi goes to a watery grave	172
14	INS Khukri falls prey to PNS Hangor	184
15	Forgotten Heroes - Roy Chou and Aku Roy	191

16	Pakistan War Stories – 1971	200
17	Operation Lal Dora - Mauritius 1983	208
18	"Flowers Are Blooming" - Seychelles 1986	223
19	Operation Pawan - Sri Lanka 1987 – 1991	231
20	Nuclear Sub INS Chakra-1 - A Near Miss	252
21	Views by Gen. Muqeen Khan and other Authors	257
	India's Maritime Perspective by Admiral Vishnu Bhagwat	267
	Regional Security by Lt. Gen. Satish Nambiar	274
	Epilogue The Mental Map Matters	279
	Appendix 1: Other Operations of the Indian Navy	285
	Appendix 2: The Future Indian Navy in the 21st Century	291
	Appendix 3: Simla Agreement and the Hamoodur Report	297
	Pictorial Section with images from naval history	303

DEDICATION

To my ever supportive wife, Praveena, my anchor, and the wonderful families of
my two sons, Raul and Ritin.
I am because we are.
And to the fine Indian Navy
I had the privilege to serve.

-- **Ranjit B. Rai**

To my every smiling wife - Shami. She has been through thick and thin,
as I turned my passions into businesses.

-- **Joseph P. Chacko**

A Salute to **Admiral S. M. Nanda** PVSM AVSM
"The Bomber of Karachi"

PRIME MINISTER

No.312-PMH/71

New Delhi,
December 22, 1971.

Dear Admiral Nanda,

The Navy's exploits in these fourteen days of fighting will long be remembered. The achievements of our Naval Forces have thrilled the nation. Your leadership and the daring and the skill of our Fleet have made singular contribution to the success of the war on both fronts. I should like to express the gratitude of the Government and the people of India to you and to your officers and men.

None of this would have been possible without the most exacting leadership and dedication at all levels. In this, your role has been crucial. No words can be a better recompense for your labours than the people's admiration and India's success.

With kindest regards,

Yours sincerely,

(Indira Gandhi)

Admiral S.M.Nanda,
Chief of the Naval Staff,
New Delhi.

"The faint hearted do not win wars!

In 1971, we 'dared' and our Navy entered the enemy's den to inflict a decisive defeat. With this, our countrymen realised the importance for a 'great nation' to have a 'great Navy'. I have been more than happy to see the Navy growing ever since, into an even finer fighting force.

My congratulations to Ranjit Rai for finally bringing out this book which is very well written and which I would recommend strongly to all those in the Service and Civilian walks of life, to whom the call of the sea has some interest and mystery."

ADMIRAL S M NANDA, PVSM AVSM
Chief of Naval Staff, Indian Navy, during 1971

"Ideals are like stars, we never reach them.
But like Mariners of the Sea,
We chart our Course by them."
— Michael Lewis

INTRODUCTION

By
General Ved P. Malik PVSM AVSM, Former Chief of the Army Staff

I have great pleasure in introducing my batch-mate and colleague in arms, Commodore Ranjit Bhawnani Rai, the author of this book.

Ranjit and I joined the prestigious National Defence Academy (NDA) in July 1955. This newly built tri-service institution in Khadakwasla near Pune, with its imposing buildings in an exclusive, spread out estate, was our home for the next three years. Ranjit was a naval cadet; I was to join the army. For two years, we studied, played and trained together. In the third year, the military training part got separated to enable us to pursue our respective service subjects.

Ranjit was good in academics and debates. He passed out as Battalion Cadet Adjutant, a senior appointment usually reserved for those who could bully other cadets. I did not have to suffer, as I was part of another battalion and a Cadet Sergeant Major myself!

Ranjit went on to have an outstanding career in the navy. He won the Best Cadet award on the naval training ship INS Tir, a National Bronze Medal in Yachting in 1974, and became Deputy Director Naval Training (Officers) in 1975.

Except for odd course get-togethers, our paths did not cross till we were posted in New Delhi in 1987; Ranjit as Director of Naval Intelligence and I as Deputy Director General, Military Operations in Army Headquarters. Our offices were in the same corridor. Very often, we had to work together on joint plans for operational contingencies and events within and outside India. His intelligence inputs and assessments were always to the point and very useful.

Two major operations in which both of us were deeply involved were Operation Pawan (Sri Lanka) and Operation Cactus (Maldives). I have covered decision making aspects of these joint operations in my book, India's Military Conflicts and Diplomacy (Harper Collins 2013).

After his New Delhi tenure, Ranjit went away as India's Defence Adviser in Singapore, with accreditation to Philippines and Thailand. He played an important military diplomacy role for India in organizing annual joint exercises SIMBEX and military to military cooperation in several other fields.

Ranjit took premature retirement from the Navy in 1993 but has continued to take more than usual interest in India's strategic and maritime affairs. He has been writing regularly on these and mercantile shipping matters in the print media and attending international conferences and seminars all over the world.

His latest book, WARRING NAVIES - India and Pakistan, is a sequel to 'A Nation and Its Navy at War' (Lancers 1988) in which he had covered Indian Navy's operations in the 1971 war between India and Pakistan. Since then, he has visited Pakistan to be able to carry out a more objective review of the naval operations in the 1965 and 1971 wars.

According to Michel Eyquem Montaigne, "The only good histories are those that have been written by the persons themselves who commanded in the affairs whereof they write; rest is hearsay." Ranjit's book, therefore, will be an authentic and useful addition to the actions of the Indian Navy in war and peace and our maritime history. It would be of great interest to lay persons as well as specialists interested in India's national security. He tells me that it is also an attempt to get India and Pakistan closer through the seas and the navies. I hope it succeeds in such a mission.

Ranjit has asked me to add a few words in this introduction on how I view India's geo-strategy, particularly its maritime dimension. A brief attempt, in accordance with his wishes, is given in these succeeding paragraphs:

'India has a 7683 km long coastline, nearly 600 islands (very few inhabited) and an over 2 million sq km Exclusive Economic Zone. Its location acts as a bridge linking Western, Southern and South East Asian regions along the Indian Ocean. Its size, situation and potential obliges it to function as a stabilizing force in the region.

Till a few decades ago, despite naval actions in 1965 and 1971 wars, our strategic thinking was mostly ground based. In the mid 90s, we realised that due to dominating strategic location overlooking the Indian Ocean, our maritime capabilities were essential and played an important role in our grand and military strategies. Unless perceived in due measure, and made an integral part of our strategic thinking and planning, our national security efforts will remain unsatisfactory. That thinking made us give an important role to the Navy in the 1999 Kargil war, had it escalated.

The 26/11 terrorist strikes in Mumbai imparted a welcome tactical dimension to our coastal security. But there is still inadequate strategic maritime vision.

It is well known that China is emerging as a major economic and military power and gradually extending its influence among the Indian Ocean Rim nations. The current heavy traffic of oil tankers, merchant ships and navies of the Rim nations and major powers passing through the Indian Ocean is expected to increase further, and become competitive. Recently, the United States of America has decided that instead of thinning out its naval presence in the Asia-Pacific region (as earlier decided), it will work for a graduated naval surge and by 2020, 60 per cent of the US naval fleet will be moving around this region.

Our maritime strategy must be dynamic, befitting an aspiring power that faces a multitude of threats ranging from the security of island territories, mainland coastline, the EEZ, to the shipping sea lanes in the region. It should be capable of covering threats and challenges - from pirates to inimical navies - in a major part of the Indian Ocean.

We need to spell this strategy and doctrine unambiguously after identifying all possible contingencies and available options.'

In the end, I wish to extend my best wishes to Ranjit and his latest book.

V P Malik

PREFACE AND OVERVIEW OF CONTENTS

This book amplifies the author's previous 'A Nation And Its Navy At War' on the 1971 War, and has Joseph P. Chacko's kind assistance. It takes a fresh look at Indo-Pak wars with emphasis on their Navies. This Preface provides a brief overview of the contents. India is stodgy in declassifying historical documents and encourages a statist historiography. Hence the authors' findings, research & analysis, rely on interviews, books, articles and reports, with all this evidence juxtaposed to help the reader get a larger context, while unravelling the sequence of events and examining controversies. There is a focus on the naval operations.

The author has researched the interesting times of the three "Gung Ho Chiefs", under a young impetuous Prime Minister Rajiv Gandhi as Defence Minister and his bright Rhodes Scholar ex- corporate aide Arun Singh. This gives an inside look at workings in the labyrinths of South and North Blocks that control India. The politicians were wet behind the ears on matters military, and the Chiefs were over ambitious. As Director of Naval Operations and Intelligence (DNI), the author witnessed this in career interactions, especially closely in the Khalistani rising in Punjab, Op Pawan, Op Brasstacks (bringing India close to war with Pakistan), and Op Chequerboard (which rattled the Chinese). Intelligence has been India's Achilles heel in all wars and operations and it so continues, deserving attention.

This book therefore is more about the originally British trained professional Indian and Pakistan militaries and the ethos that propels them. The Indian Armed Forces have come out with credit for their devotion to the nation. Despite poor politico–military direction, the Armed Forces have kept India as one, as a glue factor not recognized by many.

An Overview of the Contents

To understand India and Pakistan today, we must recall events leading to their sudden formation in August 1947, amidst bloodbaths and the largest migration known in history. Decades of hostility over Kashmir, instigated by Pakistan, began with the war of 1947-48, mentioned in the book to set the scene. The Navy and the Air Force were kept out, except for the IAF transport of Army troops, led by namesake Lt. Col. Ranjit Rai (MVC posthumous), just in time to save Srinagar. The other wars, including the unsuccessful 1962 war to stop China in the Himalayas, were all tactically fought as reactive responses out of necessity.

Then followed the intermittent wars, including the 17-day bitter war of 1965. The Navy was asked to keep clear (Chapter 3). Vice Admiral S.M. Nanda vowed that if war came again, the Navy would be an avenging participant, and kept his promise in 1971 as its Chief! The 1971 Indo-Pak war saw the Indian Navy rising to support the war of liberation that helped create Bangladesh. The 1971 war is covered in some detail as it was a landmark war that introduced missile warfare from the seas, taking the Pakistan Navy by surprise. Pakistan showed it had a capable submarine-operating Navy with the sinking of the INS Khukri.

The kaleidoscopic actions of both navies, includes the 4 December 1971 morning attack by the IAF Hunters on Karachi's Kemari oil tanks by happenstance, uncovered after 35 years by the author. The Indian Navy's brilliant missile attacks on Karachi, on 4th night (Op Trident) and again on 8 December night (OP Python) when the fires at Kemari had just been doused by the Pakistanis, are described. The heroic actions of Mukti Bahini are recounted.

The author is convinced all the wars the two nations

have fought, except the 1971 war, were stalemated. India won the 1971 war in the East, mainly due to Mukti Bahini's full support to the Army as navigators, and to the Indian Navy for clandestine operations in East Pakistan. PM Mrs. Indira Gandhi permitted Army Chief Gen. S.H.F.J. Manekshaw MC (later Field Marshal) to act as a Chief of Defence Staff (CDS), and his leadership proved critical to success.

Other chapters bring alive the Navy's operations in Op Vijay in Goa, 1983's Op Lal Dora in Mauritius, 1987's Op Flowers are Blooming in Seychelles, 1988's Op Cactus in Maldives, and Op Pawan (1987-91) in Sri Lanka, with mention of Mrs. Indira Gandhi's Op Buster. Under PM Rajiv Gandhi, India's only military Peace Keeping operation, from 1987-90, code named Op Pawan, to assist beleaguered Tamils and the government of Jayawardene in Sri Lanka, turned out to become a war against the LTTE with loss of 1400 Army souls and hundreds of maimed bodies. The fine Indian Army retreated in 1990, leaving Sri Lanka in no better a situation. It caused India's Foreign Exchange Reserves (FFE) to plummet. In her time Mrs Indira Gandhi had kept Sri Lanka in check using other means. President Rajapaksha later decimated the LTTE.

In May 1998, India and Pakistan went nuclear and many thought peace would descend on the two countries. PM Atal Behari Vajpayee took a bus journey across the Wagah border to Lahore in 1999. His was a magnanimous peace offering, to get Pakistan to resolve all issues including Kashmir. PM Nawaz Sharif received India's Prime Minister with warmth, Pakistani's hall mark when they receive guests. India believed that a new Indo-Pak era of peace was dawning.

But in 1999 May, a war in Kargil erupted, pre-planned by Pakistan's Chief of Army Staff (later President) Gen Pervez Musharraf, to cut India's link between Kashmir and Ladakh. Indian Chief of Army Staff Gen V P Malik in

Kargil - Surprise to Victory, 'to put the record straight', recounts the valiant fight 'with what we had'. He brings out the lacunae in Intelligence and higher defence management. The Kargil war was doused when the Indian Navy assembled both Eastern and Western Naval Fleets under Rear Admiral Suresh Mehta, poised to blockade Pakistan (Op Talwar). While war raged on the inhospitable heights of Kargil, Pakistan's PM Nawaz Sharif rushed to Washington. President Clinton received Sharif on 4 July, USA's Independence Day, and warned him to back off or face a blockade by India, which could have brought Pakistan to penury.

Despite terrorism, two years of peace followed, and India's economy strengthened. But the high-profile attack by Lashkar-e- Taiba's five terrorists and Jaish-e-Mohammed on the Indian Parliament on 13 December, 2001 led to the death of a dozen people. The gunmen drove into the parked car of the Indian Vice President Krishan Kant and began firing. Luckily all ministers and MPs escaped unhurt. The Indian Armed Forces were mobilized to teach Pakistan a lesson in Op Parakaram, which lasted a year. The Government of India, lacking a mechanism for swift security decision making, got cold feet. Both nations being accepted nuclear nations, the USA cautioned India. The Armed Forces remained mobilized for almost 11 months, and the Navy, ready for war, operated with weapons and missiles loaded.

On 26 November 2008, ten trained suicide-ready LET terrorists from Pakistan landed on Mumbai's Colaba beach and caused havoc for 3 days. The aftermath of the '26/11 Mumbai attack' saw a beefing up of India's coastal security and adding of assets to the Indian Navy and Coast Guard. But infrastructure lags. The Indian Navy's ambitious acquisition programme is discussed in an Appendix.

Wounds still fester amongst Pakistan's military, ever since the creation of Bangladesh, with single-minded fervor to avenge the 1971 defeat. The perpetual dispute over Kashmir has contributed to destabilizing the security environment of South Asia. Pakistan, to shield itself against India, and aided by China, is aggressively pursuing nuclear devices, even at sea. It has attracted international attention and sympathy in the dispute over Kashmir. Nehru in his time rejected a 'No War' pact by Pakistan, asking, "No war against whom?"

A No War pact deserves revival. It was entered as a clause into the Simla Agreement (1972), when 93,000 Pakistani prisoners of war (POWs) were returned after months in Indian camps without consulting the Armed Forces Chiefs. But no final commitment to convert that clause into a treaty took place. It was Bhutto's stab in India's back. Mrs. Gandhi and her advisers could not have been so naïve as not to follow up. Research into official papers if they exist, may uncover more to it.

Lastly, we explore the maritime future in the Indian Ocean Region (IOR). The sub-continent is referred to as "the most explosive region in the world." Another war between India and Pakistan cannot be ruled out. If that happens, it may lead to the splintering of Pakistan along the Pashtun, Sindh and Baluchistan lines. The future is most uncertain, as the USA and ISAF are set to withdraw from Afghanistan in 2014, leaving a vacuum in the region. Regional nations are watchful, and the Taliban looks to retake the political control it tasted earlier.

"It is obvious that the Indian Ocean will be one of the major challenges of the future. The security it has enjoyed for over 150 years (since 1864) has been completely shattered by events of the last few years. With major powers developing in the area, ...America, China, and perhaps Russia, will have access to the seas in a manner totally different from what the Europeans had in the centuries that followed Vasco da Gama's arrival." This extract is from 'India and the Indian Ocean'by historian Dr K.M. Panikkar in the mid-20th Century, and is being played out now.

In this scenario, a rising China plays its game by calling Pakistan it's all weather friend, higher than the mountains and deeper than the seas. The Indian Ocean Region has become the world's strategic playground with vested interests, as Mahan and KM Panikkar had predicted for the 21st century. The sea routes in the IOR and the energy outflow from the Persian Gulf sustains the economy and energy needs of the world, and Pakistan knows that it controls the exit of the gulf and has access to the Central Asian Republics (CAR), coveted by India. Iran has nuclear ambitions, presently controlled.

Geography is the handmaiden of strategy. India's maritime position is prime. Mrs. Indira Gandhi as PM was on the cusp of getting an Indian Ocean strategy into play with grips on the Indian Ocean island nations and friendship with all countries along the India's Oceanic rim. But years of UPA's foreign policy (2004-2014) dictated by local coalition politics, has wasted many efforts in the IOR states to which the Indian Navy had contributed much. The same can be said of India's economy, with the UPA coalition compulsions abetting corruption during the same period, to the neglect of the Armed Forces' needs.

India-US relations improved in 2006 when India signed a one-page defence framework as a prelude to the historic nuclear deal (sans a damage liability clause). Indian Navy's Maritime Military Strategy aims to be the policeman of the Indian Ocean with nuclear deterrence, and ability to guard the critical choke points on Mahanian strategic lines of power play. China, with serious unresolved border issues with India, is irked by this, and has set in motion its cheque-book diplomacy to build a garland of vassal ports to surround India, referred to as 'China's String of Pearls,' since pearls in a garland can be added or removed, as in the Chinese board game of surround called Weiqi (GO). China seeks a security architecture in which it is a component in the IOR. India would like to checkmate this. The USA, Japan and Australia would like to strategically partner with a reluctant India, still steeped in Non-Alignment and now an undefined policy of Strategic Autonomy (from its Hindu DNA), to be the bridging power between rising China and the rest of the world. (See last chapters).

This book is primarily the story of the Indian and Pakistan Navies, daughter navies of the Royal Navy after 1947, and their strategies and violent actions, and gains and losses at war (1965 and 1971, with the activities of Mukti Bahini). The 'naval tars' on both sides came off well with flying, or shall we say, sailing colours, with decorations of Vir Chakras and Maha Vir Chakras and Nishan- e-Haiders … but also with widows and fatherless children, who are now forgotten. Aptly is it written:

"God and a Soldier people adore
In time of War, not before;
And when war is over and all things are righted
God is neglected and an old Soldier slighted."

We are grateful to those many who took the trouble to speak about their experiences and the courage of the officers and sailors of the naval services, who inspired us to complete this book. It is a starting point for military researchers to delve further. The author has stuck to facts, yet omissions are unavoidable. As a seasoned naval officer, and a researcher assisting in authorship, we have tried to convey the spirit of both the Navies in the 1971 and other wars. It has been our objective to portray the futility of wars between two peoples which once were one in Hindustan.

Rightly, Navy Day in India is now celebrated nationally on 4 December, commemorating the Indian Navy's first daring attack on Karachi in 1971. It is also for Indians to ponder over its maritime force, and in return, for the Service to reaffirm its loyalty and dedication to the defence of the nation. Pakistan Navy must seek to avoid another confrontation on the seas, and lead the way for an understanding.

With changes in maritime strategy and the scramble for the seas in the Indian Ocean, facing the enemy will not be a new thing for either the Indian or Pakistan Navy, which now claims to have taken an area nuclear missile to sea. A tradition of competence has been established. We hope younger generations of both Navies will look back upon 1971 and other wars with a sense of pride, inspiration but also regret to see where our shared destinies can lead us. This book is so dedicated to many a memory.

Acknowledgements and Thanks

The author is grateful to term-mate and friend Gen. Ved P Malik, PVSM AVSM, former Army Chief in the Kargil war, for readily providing an introduction. He has written widely on the Kargil war and higher defence management in his book, India's Military Conflicts And Diplomacy (Harper Collins 2013). He has added a brief prognosis for the future. Many thanks, to Admiral Vishnu Bhagwat, PVSM AVSM, our term mate and former Chief of Naval Staff, for giving his insightful views on India's Maritime Perspective.

Padma Bhushan Lt. Gen. Satish Nambiar, PVSM AVSM VrC, former Commander of the UN Forces in Yugoslavia and former Deputy Chief and Director of the USI, having been on the committee to re-organise the UN, has kindly provided his view from the top on the regional scenario.

The late Admiral S.M.Nanda, PVSM AVSM, provided much encouragement through his appreciative note.

David Brewster from the ANU, who has been a co-author in articles, and the author of India - A Pacific Power, has assisted the author in the Epilogue.

Thanks also to Praveena Rai, Meena and Teddy Noronha, and Alok Chandola, for reading through and providing valuable inputs.

We acknowledge the kind permission accorded by Captain Bharat Verma of Lancers to the use of extracts from the book 'A Nation and Its Navy At War' (Lancers 1988); excerpts from the "Sentinels of the Sea' and 'Bubbles Of Water' compiled by Rear Admiral Mian Zahir Shah for the Pakistan Navy Book Club, references to the Indian Navy's publications, and 'From Transition to Triumph' and 'The Story of the Pakistan Navy' compiled by the history section of the Pakistan Navy; and Cmde Vijay Jerath's 25th Missile Boat Squadron (Prakash Books). Our gratitude goes to them all, and to the many others who recalled events, including contributors and friends.

The views expressed in the chapters of this book are the author's, arising from a sincere wish to appreciate and improve. This is an effort to bring understanding between India and Pakistan; so that they strive mightily to put peace first.

Shan No Varunah.
May the Lord of the Seas bless the Indian Navy.
Commodore (Retd.) Ranjit Bhawnani Rai with Joseph P. Chacko.

April 2014, New Delhi   ranjitrai123@gmail.com
www.indiadefenceforum.com

CHAPTER 1
ALL THE WARS - MILITARY LEADERSHIP

The purpose of war is peace. Sun Tzu in Art Of War (760 AD) Military Leadership needs to be guided by 'Enlightened Direction'. Defence is a bucking horse. It needs corralling and good riding to deliver. - Author.

Military leadership reflects a nation's psychological ethos. The ancients of India gave warriors pride of place. Epics like the Ramayana and Mahabharata glorify a righteous war.

The 15th century strategist Chanakya (also called Kautilya) wrote a treatise on statecraft, economic policy and military strategy called "Arthashastra" in which military strategy was intrinsic to polity and statecraft. Modern Indian leaders, with few exceptions, appear unappreciative of how national strategy is conducted. India's first National Security Council was established in 1998, 51 years after independence and after major wars. This lack of a cohesive national strategic guiding body was a serious debility. The government is undecided over many critical issues like the role of its armed forces in policy formation, the bureaucracy - military divide, and a Chief of Defence Staff.

This goes back to India's historical legacy. Former NSA J.N. Dixit, in his book Makers of India's Foreign Policy, describes India's political tradition as a conflict between (King) Ashoka, who stood for uncompromising morality, and Chanakya, who accepted the demands of realpolitik. Ashoka the Great, after successfully conquering and consolidating all of India around the first century, renounced war. In recent times, Mahatma Gandhi and Nehru both advocated Ahimsa or non-violence. India has high achievements in the fields of religion, philosophy, wisdom and spirituality. The dilemma is whether we should give credence to military history and leadership with little to glorify, or relegate them to the sidelines and preach our spirituality. Only Subhash Chandra Bose, Sardar Patel, Lal Bahadur Shastri, P. V. Narasimha Rao and Mrs. Indira Gandhi are counted in Chanakya's camp. India has no record, but for a brief period of the Chola rule, of any conquest outside of its shores. It has lacked prowess in warding off conquerors - Portuguese, French and British and Muslims - and was colonised by foreigners.

India has fought four major wars. A brief recounting of these could enlighten the reader on India's military leadership of the day.

Indo-Pak War 1947- 1948: The first war over Kashmir

After Partition in 1947, India and Pakistan inherited a core of reasonably well-trained mid-level officers with experience of World War II, and a small military in the ratio of two to one. Then began the accession into India or Pakistan of princely states. Sardar Patel, as Home Minister, persuaded most contiguous states to join India. Two exceptions were Jammu & Kashmir and Hyderabad, both predominantly Muslim. J&K Maharaja Hari Singh, with a small state army of a few battalions, desired to remain neutral and independent. Lord Mountbatten wanted J&K with its 85% Muslim population to join Pakistan, but deferred to the wishes of the Hindu ruler, labeling him a fool in private. Mountbatten insisted that the Andaman and Nicobar Islands be part of India, going against the recommendation of Whitehall, which wanted one island go to Pakistan, as a staging post between East and West Pakistan, and the rest to British Malaya.

Mountbatten assumed J&K would go to Pakistan some day, but Pakistan violated the status quo. In October 1947, abetted by British C-in-C, Gen Frank Meservy, it organised tribal raids into various parts of J&K. By 24 October a full scale offensive in the valley of J&K was launched by Pakistan, under the guise of a tribal uprising. Hari Singh turned to India for help, which was delivered on 26 October, after J&K formally acceded to India. Indian appeals to Pakistan to desist went ignored leading to the first India Pakistan War. Interestingly British officers were in charge of armies, navies and air forces on both sides. Aware of Mountbatten's sympathies towards Pakistan, the C-in-C's of India Gens. Robert Lockhart (till 27 November 1947) and Roy Boucher, left matters to Gen Dudley Russel of the Western Command in Simla who was directly in charge of the operations to quell any offensive.

While British officers in Pakistan had no restrictions, those on the Indian side were termed mercenaries and barred from the fighting zone by British edict, though they advised on operations with a pro-Pakistan tilt. Major O.S. Kalkat in the North West Frontier, managed to see a plan for Op Gulmarg addressed to Brigadier C.P. Murray by the C-in-C Pakistan General Meservy. He escaped to Delhi and revealed it to the British Staff Officers, who withheld it from PM Pandit Nehru and the Defence Minister Baldev Singh.

A day after J&K accession, on 27 October 1947 300 soldiers from Indian Army's 1 Sikh under Lt. Col. Dewan Ranjit Rai flew in IAF Dakotas and secured Srinagar airfield. Lt Col Rai died during defence of Baramulla, and was awarded the Maha Vir Chakra. Major Som Nath Sharma (whose brother became Chief of Army Staff after Gen K. Sundarji) led his company of 4 Kumaon but died defending Srinagar against 700 tribesmen disguised as Kashmiris. Maj Gen (later Lt Gen) Kulwant Singh had just taken command of the valley before Srinagar fell; a day later, would have been disastrous. Brigadier (later Lt Gen) L.P. Sen arrived with 161 Inf Bde, and the tide turned in India's favour.

However progress was slow due to non-military factors. Indian plans were leaked by its British officers to those on the Pak side. A Maj Brown learning of state forces weaknesses at Gilgit and Skardu overran these vitally strategic posts, now Pak held. On 20 January 1948, Lt Gen K.M. Cariappa took over Western Command from Gen Russell with timely, and now legendary, leadership. He learnt that General Roy Boucher C-in-C Indian Army regularly spoke to C-in-C Pak Army Sir Douglas Gracey and leaked plans made by Gen Cariappa. Pleas to pull up the British General were of no avail but Nehru permitted Gen Cariappa to keep Ops Orders from their British C-in-C. The tolerance of British treachery by Indian leaders shows the psyche of complete acceptance by military leadership of civilian control, despite their blunders.

By early 1948, Maj Gen K.S. Thimayya, DSO, an ex Burma campaign veteran, arrived with his new 19th Division to plan for an early summer offensive. Maj Gen Bhagwati Singh (whose son Admiral Madhvendra Singh was my shipmate and became CNS), led three Brigades to capture Thana Mandi in a see-saw battle.

The Indian Army spent 1948 fighting to regain territory from Pakistani regular and irregular forces. Pakistan inducted its 9 Inf Div under Gen Nazir Ahmed. By September, the Poonch, Kargil and Zojila line had to be taken. Famous battles were fought in Op Bison, despite Gen Roy Boucher's advice to desist, since Gen Cariappa knew that snowfall in November would prevent operations. Some 90,000 troops and the Air Force transport were engaged. Defence Minister Baldev Singh was prepared to commit the Navy in J & K, if needed.

A UN resolution for ceasefire lay cleared since 13 August 1948, which Pakistan had rejected but accepted on 1 January 1949, after the capture of Kargil by India on 23 November 1948. A ceasefire line came into being, not defined in the snow bound northern area called Siachen. Indian Army losses were 1500 killed, 3500 wounded and

1000 missing in action. Pakistan's casualties were larger, including tribesmen. Pakistan did not commit its Air Force, ensuring a limited war, and called it an uprising. Thus began the Kashmir problem where one third is Pakistan-occupied Kashmir (POK).

In September 1948, the Nizam of Hyderabad was contemplating accession to Pakistan. Indian Army units under Maj. Gen. J.N. Chaudhuri took control of that state, which then acceded to India. Gen. Roy Boucher warned against the operation for fear that the Nizam would use his Air Force to bomb Delhi and Bombay. Gen Boucher continued as C-in-C till 15 January 1949, when Gen. K.M. Cariappa took over, even though Nehru felt he was too anglicised.

There is not much analysis of military direction or lessons of this war. The military was downgraded and salaries of the forces were reduced, a fallout of Nehru's socialist stance. Defence budgets saw annual decline and this affected morale and quality of the troops in the next decade. The cumulative effect and lack of a military-political decision-making co-ordination resulted in defeat in the 1962 India China War. UN observers kept peace along the ceasefire line which became the 'Line of Control' in 1971. The Northern area of Siachen is still not demarcated beyond NJ 9542 and is an icy area of conflict, occupied by the Indian Army.

Indo China War 1962 - A Geo-political Military Debacle

When Gen. Cariappa as C-in-C wished to define the Armed Forces' role, he was told it was to defend national borders from the threats of a third rate power, implying Pakistan. Nehru with his Hindi Chini Bhai Bhai (India and China are brothers) policy never imagined a threat from China. The British had left the Indo-Tibet border vague. China took control of Tibet in 1950.

The border was considered to run along the McMahon Line of water-shed in Assam. The Assam Rifles, a paramilitary force under the Home Ministry, was responsible for the Indian border with Tibet and Burma and de facto for the border with China. The Ministry of External Affairs should have been concerned with this subject, but it was dealt with by Assam's Governor. With IFS officials not willing to serve there, a NEFA service was mooted with volunteers from other services.

Doyen diplomat K.P.S. Menon, India's Ambassador in China since 1945 and later Foreign Secretary, was a one man repository cum executive on this subject, guided by Pt. Nehru, an over-trusting philosopher. Gen. Cariappa retiring as C-in-C in 1952, to become High Commissioner in Australia, offered to be the Governor of Assam to attend to border issues, but Pt. Nehru would not dislodge an affable stalwart Sindhi Congress leader Jairamdas Daulatram (known to my family). For 17 long years, Nehru was PM and Minister of External Affairs. An inadequate Sardar Baldev Singh was Defence Minister, whose amusing subservience to Nehru was legendary. Krishna Menon, the stormy petrel of Nehru's indulgence, took over Defence. A Minister of State for Defence Gopalaswami Ayyangar died in harness after a few months, followed by Dr. K.N. Katju who quit. Nehru took over Defence and Mahaveer Tyagi appointed Minister of Defence Organisation, a subject unaddressed since. No serious importance was attached to the Defence portfolio under a busy Nehru.

In China, life was repressed and unreal in the 50's under Mao Tse Tung's megalomaniac movement, with his long March and the Red Guards. Sardar Patel, a month before his death in 1950, futilely warned Nehru to defend India's China border. While China built the Aksai Chin Road (finished in 1957), India was propagating non-alignment and friendship, with Zhou En Lai visiting India in 1954. As a young lad, I remember waving Indian and Chinese flags screaming Hindi Chini Bhai Bhai i.e, Indians and Chinese are Brothers. India recognized Tibet as a region of China, giving up territorial rights that the British exercised at a 1914 Darjeeling meeting. On 28 April 1954, a trade agreement that Nehru proposed for 25 years, was signed by Zhou for 8 years. Nehru still dreamed of a utopian world in the East led by the two oldest civilizations.

By 1958, the Chinese were nibbling into Indian territory. They intruded into UP in the Barahoti area, occupied Karnah forts and areas near Chushul in Eastern Ladakh, and entered NEFA. Their maps claimed 50,000 square miles of Indian territory. China took over Aksai Chin. Nehru did not reveal this to the nation. With the accent on looking west, Indian Intelligence of the area was pathetic. In 1959 the Dalai Lama fled Tibet and was given funds and sanctuary in Mussoorie and then Dharmsala, angering the Chinese. Mao had suffered internal reverses, and looking to re-excite mass fervour, used the opportunity provided by India's pro-Tibet policy.

In 1961, when diplomacy failed to dislodge the Portuguese, Op Vijay liberated Goa in 72 hours. A minister spoke for the swollen heads in Parliament by saying: "If the Chinese will not vacate our territory, India will have to repeat what it did in Goa." As a young subaltern in INS Mysore, I took part in Op Vijay in Goa - an exciting experience (see chapter 2).

China's nibblings were worrisome. Gen. K.S. (Timmy) Thimayya, a Coorgi like Cariappa, had taken over as Chief of Army Staff in 1959. CGS Gen. B M Kaul was looking for glory. Family friends with Nehru, he cultivated Defence Minister Krishna Menon. Nehru's handling of the British uniformed leadership in the 1947-48 war with Pakistan showed his military innocence. His judgment of the inadequate intelligence provided to him on China's military designs was also poor. Nehru was too taken up by Zhou En Lai with whom he corresponded regularly. B.N. Mullick, powerful head of the Intelligence Bureau (prior to

R.A.W.) gave Nehru information of China's intrusions but was unable to provide any foreign intelligence indicators, a task left to the MEA. Mullick failed to appreciate how deeply the Chinese agents had infiltrated NEFA, which was along the Indian border. Nehru ignored the West's resentment to India's policy of non-alignment, while supporters of Mao's march were generating hysteria in China. No ambassador dared report all this to Nehru who was deaf to it. Mullick soured military civil relations by reporting that Gen. Thimayya was planning a military takeover on 30 January 1961. [In mid-January 2012, the routine move of an army unit to Delhi was cancelled when the Government imagined an alleged coup by Gen. V.K. Singh].

Military indicators were ominous on the India-China border. Gen. Chang Ko had prepared Tibet with roads to launch an offensive and inducted eight Divisions. India had sent 113 protest notes on aerial intrusions. In 1958, a Chinese military delegation under Marshal Yeh Chiang Ying studied Indian army operations. The 4th Division demonstrated its operations with Maj. Gen.B.M.Kaul as its Commander. This very Division faced China in the war under Lt. Gen. Kaul, now it's Corps Commander. The Chinese must have eked enough information on Indian preparedness to decide that the Indian Army was trained for war against Pakistan, not China. The Chinese army was battle-hardened by the Korean War.

In 1959, Sandhurst-trained Lt. Gen. S. P. Thorat as GOC Eastern Command prepared a plan of Defence against the Chinese in event of attack. As a subaltern, I had met this close friend of my father. Posts were to be set up near the McMahon Line of watershed, but battle engaged with ease at lower areas like Bomdila, by vacating forward posts. It was the classic military plan to fight on ground of your choosing, prepared by a bright military tactician copying Gen Slim's World War II tactics. With Thimayya's retirement and Thorat's transfer, the plans disappeared.

Crisis management, and pleasing Pt. Nehru with family friend Kaul's help, influenced the actions of Gen. P.N. Thapar the new Army Chief. Lt. Gen. L. P. Sen had taken over Eastern Command. Civilian dictate ruled with a policy to set up forward posts, and these were being ordered on China's border, without the military assessing their tenability. In January 1962, the Dhola post was established on Namka Chu. Its tenability in winter was never examined.

China objected and built up for an attack. On 8 September 1962, the Chinese surrounded that very post. Brig. JP Dalvi the Brigade Cdr. was on annual leave and Pt. Nehru was in London for a Commonwealth Meet. The Chinese also occupied the Thagla Ridge. Morarji Desai the Foreign Minister was abroad. Gen. Kaul was on leave and Krishna Menon left for a U.N. session. Nehru was to return to India via Nigeria.

Krishna Menon and the I.B. chief Mullick visited Tezpur, where an uncle of mine Air Commodore A.S.M. Bhawnani was the Station Commander. He was later witness to the onslaught of the Chinese from the night of 19/20 October and saw the civilian officials evacuate the area. The Indian Army fought heroic battles at all forward posts and at Namka Chu, Tangdhar, and Tawang. The next month saw a planned strategy of Chinese advances in NEFA and Chushul in Ladakh. After humiliating India, they retreated to posts of vantage of their choosing and unilaterally ceased fire on 20 November 1962. Thus ended a brief India China war with defeat for India. The border dispute is still to be resolved and the line of control is called the line of peace and tranquility.

Major General D. K. Palit who was the Director of Military Operations, in 'War in the High Himalayas' writes, "Finally it was not the massiveness of the Chinese forces that caused the debacle but the lack of strength of ours. We had placed men and weapons in adequate numbers, but without the ammunition or provisions to keep them going. The defeat left Nehru a broken man and Krishna Menon resigned." The lessons are that Indian military plans are personality oriented and there is no national security planning body. Think tanks are shunned. The Henderson-Brooks committee report ordered to go into the causes of defeat was held back by MOD but has been made public by Neville Maxwell in 2014.

The 1965 Indo-Pak War

The Indo-Pak War that erupted on 9 April 1965 in Kutch and sporadically lasted till the 23 September ceasefire, was an extension of the 1947-48 Indo-Pak war over Kashmir. The Indian side lost around 2800 officers and men, 8000 were wounded and 1600 were taken as POW's. At its end, the Indian Army held some 500 sq. miles of area in Kargil, Tithwal, Uri, Lahore, Mirpurkhas and Sialkot. Pakistan held a little more in Akhnoor, Khem Karan and Fazilka. This war was planned by Pakistan to nibble at Indian territory in the South and make another unsuccessful grab for J&K.

The leadership in Pakistan in 1965 was militarily led. President Gen. Ayub Khan (of Christine Keeler fame), his Army C-in-C Gen Musa Khan and Senior Generals who fought on the front like Lt. Gen. Yahya Khan, felt they could strike at India and gain ground. The 1962 India China War had humbled India and Indian military morale had sagged. Indian political leadership refused to accept blame. Generals Thapar and Kaul resigned. A much saddened Nehru died in 1964. Diminutive Lal Bahadur Shastri, a fine leader but lacking the charisma of Nehru, became PM.

The Pakistan Army had revamped its military on the largesse offered by US supplies, especially some 400 Patton Tanks, augmenting their Chaffee tanks and F 86 Sabre Jets. Pakistan had 6 Divisions and 14 Air Force Squadrons versus India's 19 Divisions (only 180 Centurion

Tanks), Hunters, SU-7's and 25 Air Force Squadrons. Indian forces were spread widely to the East (now Bangladesh) and the West against Pakistan, and in the North against the Chinese. Pakistan had built artificial obstacles in the Punjab Sector like the Ichogil Canal and embankments to stop Indian forces advancing there. Their intelligence in J&K had been beefed up.

The Indian Army under Gen. J.N. Chaudhari, an armoured corps officer of Hyderabad fame was still consolidating, post India-China War, when surprised by the Pakistan Army. The attack came in the Rann of Kutch (a low lying area), aimed at isolated BSF posts on the border with Gujarat and Rajasthan. On 6 April 1965, the Pakistan Army overran Indian posts in the Kutch sector as it was easily accessible. India's response was slow, but it was a stroke of luck. No armour was committed to that area as Pakistan expected, and these units were later to save the situation in the North. Indian Intelligence on the border in Kutch, Punjab & J&K was also poor. Indian Army and police posts were surprised by the new Armoured Units of the Pakistan Army, used in the South. Their route to these posts was easy and Pakistan's 51 Inf. Brigade had a regiment of heavy tanks. The Indian Army decided to strengthen the Punjab- Lahore sector.

No Air Force was committed in this phase, it being suggested later that Air Chief Marshal Arjan Singh and his Pakistani counterpart ACM Asghar Khan, as friends, had an unwritten pact not to engage their Air Forces. Having penetrated 16 to 32 km into Indian territory in Mirpur Khas on 1 July 1965, Pakistan proposed a ceasefire, via the British PM. The Rann of Kutch issue was put to the International Court of Justice. But Pakistan was preparing a bold operation codenamed Gibraltar for an infiltration into Kashmir with 15,000 raiders, Razakars and Azad Kashmir troops under a fiery Maj. Gen. Akhtar Hussain Malik, 12 Inf. Div. Cdr. at Murree.

Ceasefire line violations increased. Crossings of borders

by civilians was a common problem but accepted feature in some areas, especially on festive occasions or weddings. On 8 August 1965, under guise of celebrating the festival of Pir Dastgir Sahib, hordes of infiltrators entered Kashmir and harassed the Indian Army with a just 'below war' situation. With disorganisation in J&K, the Defence Secretary requested the Army to take over the state and even declare Martial Law. Army Chief Gen. J. N. Chaudhuri who was in Jalandhar, refrained from taking over. He informed the District Magistrate that the Army had enough on its plate defending the 470 mile border, than to attend to civil duties. It was a decision which saved the future militarily. By 13 August, clashes escalated to war. Major battles were fought at Haji Pir on 28 August, in Poonch Area on 5/6 September and Kishanganga in the ensuing days, when the IAF responded. A ceasefire came into being and the second India-Pakistan war ended.

It ended in a military stalemate and it was the Soviet Union that helped solve post war issues at Tashkent. India's PM Lal Bahadur Shastri died of a heart attack there the night he signed the Tashkent Agreement in exchange of territory. He was forced to return the Haji Pir salient to Pakistan. The line of control (LOC) in Kashmir came into being from the old cease fire line.

The 1971 War for the liberation of Bangladesh

A concatenation of circumstances found India at war with Pakistan for 14 days in 1971.This conflict demonstrated its power and potential with glory, both in the inventiveness of its officers and the gallantry of its men. Mrs. Indira Gandhi, India's Prime Minister since 1966, provided superb political leadership and Mr. Jagjivan Ram an astute administrator as Defence Minister made it possible for the military leadership to shine. Credit goes to Sam Manekshaw (later Field Marshal) the Parsi swashbuckling General from the Gurkha regiment, who as

Chairman Chiefs of Staff led as a CDS, and streamlined the planning of the three Services. He was ably supported by Admiral S. M. Nanda and Air Chief Marshal Pratap Lal. The genesis of the war lay in the repressive policies of the West Pakistani leaders to subjugate East Pakistan with atrocities when they tried to assert their political rights. This war proved that given right leadership, Indian forces can rise to the occasion.

The Gung-Ho Chiefs who got together

The period 1985-88 was definitely an interesting phase of economic, military and allied manoeuvrings for adventures in India's defence policy. Rajiv Gandhi was Defence Minister for periods, but he held that portfolio in name. He had delegated powers to his friend Arun Singh, with whom he was to fall out later on what came to be the 'Bofors Scandal'.

The three Chiefs of the period were seasoned seamers in cricket terminology. Admiral R. H. Tahiliani was Chairman Chiefs of Staff Committee. He exceeded the Naval Budget and pushed through a Pay Commission to get the Chiefs a pay equal to the Cabinet Secretary. He tampered with promotions, some leading to cases in court. He dealt body liners to Defence Secretary S.K. Bhatnagar, who he later replaced as Governor of Sikkim. Gen. K. Sundarji was the flamboyant Army Chief, and Air Chief Marshal Denis La Fontaine was an affable but proficient Air Chief. The trio were a force to reckon with.

To quote some weird actions during 1986-87, Tai Ming Cheung, a Far Eastern Economic Review correspondent, has interesting comments on Indian Defence in the magazine dated 27 July 1989.

Discussing the undeclared war with Pakistand in the heights of the Siachen glacier where more Indian soldiers die of weather than fighting, he reported "Another example of a more gung ho military posture is the holding of elaborate exercises, to test the new operational concepts, provocatively close to the country's borders with Pakistan and China. Operation Brasstacks in the winter of 1986-87 was the largest ever army exercise involving 150,000 troops and 2,500 tanks operating not far from the India Pakistan border. Another war game codenamed Operation Falcon, involving three Divisions was conducted in Arunachal Pradesh near the Sino Indian border. Senior Indian generals said these operations were intended to show to a belligerent neighbour, the power and strength of India's Armed Forces."

The bane of India's military cum political problems is the lack of an organized system of command and control, which could have overseen these exercises. Again to quote the Far Eastern Economic Review : "Another worry among both proponents and critics of this build up is the ad hoc nature of defence planning. Critics say that the lack of coherent overall strategy to define the use of these capabilities will make it easier for some policy makers to abuse the armed might. Says one Western military attache in New Delhi - The build-up is not of concern, but the intent is. The Indians do not seem to have any clearly defined game plan for these capabilities. That is what is unsettling."

Defence Policy 1985-88. Was Rajiv Gandhi gullible?

Critics point to such controversial figures as Gen. K. Sundarji, Army Chief from 1986-88, as one of the chief architects in revamping the army into a more offensive force. They charge that it is he who convinced Rajiv Gandhi of the need for such a bold display of Indian military might. Sundarji's ambitions were to follow Brasstacks and Chequer Board into a national exercise Brassboard, without weighing the political and economic costs of such ventures. In Op Pawan (chapter 19), Sundarji got his own way, and the Indian Army got mired in Sri

Lanka. The Chairman Chiefs of Staff Committee Admiral Tahiliani could not exercise his leadership. For now, the situation persists and each service guards its own turf.

Till the three services are merged under one head for joint functions, as done the world over, and till a security formulating body is formed, India's defence policy may proceed rudderless. India has never balanced the needs of the three services and hence squabbles have led to an extra cost for defence, even as economic challenges force defence budgets down. To quote the honest opinion of Defence Minister of Bahrain, Sheikh Khalifa Bin Ahmed Al Khatiya, when asked how he balances service needs: "You must know what Service Chiefs are like, always so greedy! When you ask them what they want, they always want all emphasis on their own forces. But any development programme has to be based upon threat priorities, capabilities and other factors - it cannot be based upon a 'wish list'. The other major reason is the government. It has other priorities - roads, schools, hospitals, and so forth." (ADJI July 1992).

Sadly, Indian Defence has not contributed to national development. In S.E.Asia, one observes that in Singapore 'Total Defence' has contributed to instilling national pride and discipline. In Indonesia, Dwifungsi (dual function of defence and development) and ABRI Masuk Desa (Armed Forces enter villages) as tenets of defence policy have done much to help uplift those nations. In Malaysia the police and services, guided by Mahathir Mohamad, contributed to education. In Thailand the King has directed the armed forces to help stability and development. This subject needs national debate.

Need for a Policy Framework

To explain India's politico-defence mechanism, one can do no better than quote India's doyen defence columnist, the late K. Subrahmanyam, who was an IAS officer and an academic: The harsh truth is what George Tanan has said and Gen. Sundarji recorded, "The best kept secret of India is the political and bureaucratic establishments have no policy framework and no tradition of strategic thinking." Soon India will have to decide where it is going even in defence. Downsizing the army and bringing the three services under one cohesive command will be the starting block if we are to be a power to reckon with in the East, commensurate with our size.

In 1999 in the Kargil war, the weaknesses of intelligence (which has burgeoned in India with additional agencies and no Intelligence Director), and shortfalls in inter-service co-ordination showed up in the early stages in May when the Army was surprised by the Pakistani intrusion. The Air Force dithered to act on the call of the Army, fearing it would lead to war, and did not know how to approach the Government till matters came to a head. In the two month war, the Indian Air Force in Op Safed Sagar lost two MiG-21s and an M1-17 helicopter while the Indian casualty figures were 527 dead and 1,363 wounded. The casualty figures on the Pakistani side were more.

The Indian Navy came off well. In Op Talwar it assembled both fleets fully armed off the Pakistani coast to blockade all shipping. On 4 July, President Clinton in the Oval Office warned PM Nawaz Sharif that Pakistan could be starved of supplies (oil) if it did not retreat from Kargil. It is less known that this was the classic "Naval Manoeuvre" described in the Royal Naval Doctrine Book Of Reference 8.

In the 2004 tsunami, the Indian Navy sailed thirty two ships and bested the US Navy with alacrity to provide succour in the Andaman Nicobar islands, Indonesia, Sri Lanka and Maldives. Since then the Government has been supportive of navy's plans to induct platforms, and 44 ships are on order in Indian yards, mainly in Defence PSUs. The acquisition of aircraft carrier INS Vikramaditya, lease of nuclear Akula INS Chakra, the building of nuclear submarine INS Arihant and ships and planes, are transforming the Indian Navy into a fine Blue Water Navy but it should not become the swan song of India's maritime strategy, discussed in the ending chapters.

There is more to maritime strategy than platforms. The fine Navy and the Government needs to take full advantage of this asset of the nation for its future in the region. A navy is for war, but it is also the best vehicle for the insurance of peace.

CHAPTER 2
OPERATION VIJAY - LIBERATION OF GOA 1961

Even after Indian independence in 1947, the Portuguese continued to maintain sovereignty over the districts of Goa, Daman and Diu, Dadra and Nagar Haveli - collectively known as the Estado da Índia Portuguesa. The French retained Pondicherry. Goa, Daman and Diu covered an area of around 1,540 square miles (4,000 square km) and had a population of 637,591 (61% Hindus, 36.7% Christian - mostly Catholic). Most spoke Portuguese and lived a harmonious Portuguese way of life with fondness for music and dance. The Goan diaspora was estimated at 175,000 (about 100,000 within the Indian Union). Goa saw an economic boom through exports of iron ore and manganese. Many rich Goan families like the Dempos and Chowgules flourished.

When India became a Republic on 26 January 1950, France gave up her sovereignty over Pondicherry retaining some rights there for its citizens who had French passports. However, despite negotiations to merge enclaves, António de Oliveira Salazar, Prime Minister and dictator of Portugal, claimed that these enclaves were not colonies but an integral part of Portugal. The US Ambassadors in Delhi, particularly Ellsworth Bunker and John Kenneth Galbraith who were both pro India, proposed for India to purchase the Portuguese enclaves and accept a verdict of accession through the United Nations. This was sympathetically considered by Pandit Nehru who was averse to the use of force but Portugal had the support of the US Secretary of State, Dulles, an 'India hater'. He encouraged Portugal to hold on to the territories, as an integral part of Portugal, with the possibility of using it as a NATO base.

Resistance to Portuguese rule in the 20th century was pioneered by Tristão de Bragança Cunha, a French-educated Goan who founded the Goa Congress Committee in 1928. Da Cunha released a booklet called 'Four hundred years of Foreign Rule' which Indian leaders including Pandit Nehru supported. Sensing this mood, Pt Nehru closed down the Indian Legation at Lisbon in June 1953. The Portuguese consulate in Bombay and Goa remained open. Dadra was liberated on 27 July 1954 by the United Front Of Goans. Nagar Haveli rose in revolt and overthrew the Portuguese regime in August 1954. On 15 August 1955, about 4000 unarmed Indian activists attempted to enter Goa at six border locations and were violently repulsed by Portuguese police officers. The resulting two dozen deaths built public opinion in India against the presence of the Portuguese in Goa. On 1 September 1955, India shut its consul office in Goa. In 1956, Portuguese Ambassador to France, Marcelo Duarte Matias, along with the Portuguese dictator, argued in favour of a referendum in Goa to determine its future, which was wisely rejected by the Indian Cabinet.

Portugal's appeal to the International Court of Justice, in the 'Case Concerning Right of Passage over Indian Territory over the territories of Dadra and Nagar Haveli', was ruled in favour of the Portuguese, stating it was a sovereign right. The Portuguese took no action to reoccupy the enclaves. Dadra and Nagar Haveli enjoyed de facto independence until the invasion of Goa in 1961, when the Indian Government executed their official integration into India.

The Spark for the Liberation of Goa

On 24 November 1961, a passenger steamer SS Sabarmati making passage between the Portuguese-held island of Anjidiv, south of Goa and Karwar (where the Indian Navy now has a naval base INS Kadamba for the aircraft carrier INS Vikramditya), was fired upon by Portuguese ground troops from the island and resulted in injuries to its chief engineer and the death of a passenger. The Portuguese feared that the boat carried a military landing party intent on storming the island. The Portuguese troops used to take pot shots at boats passing the channel. The incidents fostered widespread public support in India for military action in Goa, and this issue was raised in Parliament.

Vice Admiral R.D. Katari, the first Indian naval officer to take over as the first Chief of Naval Staff in 1958, had strained relations (as did the other Chiefs Gen. Thimayya and Air Marshal Subroto Mukherjee), with the Defence Minister Krishna Menon, who summoned Katari and stormed "I want the Navy to take over Anjadiv island." In his autobiography, A Sailor Remembers, Katari writes "My reply was that, if ordered, it could be done but I reminded him that this would be deemed a war like act against Portugal. I suggested that if we are prepared to virtually declare war on the country, it would be simpler and less expensive in men and money, to take Goa from the landward side. After that Anjidiv would fall. Menon's reply was 'Oh I see. I shall consult the Prime Minister, but in the meanwhile make your plans for taking Anjidiv'."

This author, as a Sub Lieutenant on INS Mysore and officer in charge of the Triple 6 Inch 'A' Gun Turret, learnt that some gunnery sailors who were good marksmen were sent to Gunnery School in Cochin to train under Lt Cdr Arun Auditto for a landing on Anjadiv. At the end of November, the Flag Officer Indian Fleet (FOCIF) Rear Admiral B. S. Soman on Flagship INS Mysore held meetings with his Fleet staff and Fleet Captain Kulkarni. Fleet Operations Officer Cdr. Colaco and the Secretary Cdr Satyindra Singh, a Supply officer, invited me to the wardroom as Flag Sub Lt. to Soman. I sensed activity and an increase in checks by gunnery officer Lt. Cdr. Ranjit Chaudhri.

A mandate was given to the military to be ready to capture Portuguese occupied territories. Lieutenant-General Mucho Chaudhari, the Southern Army Commander in Pune, was nominated overall commander. Major-General K.P. Candeth of the 17th Infantry Division and 50th Parachute Brigade were tasked to prepare for Operation Vijay. The Operation Orders for that invasion are a professional treat to read, compared to the vague and brief orders for Operation Pawan, the IPKF foray into Sri Lanka (chapter 19). The assault on the enclave of Daman was assigned to the 1st Maratha Light Infantry while the operations in Diu were assigned to the 20th Rajput and 4th Madras battalion and INS Delhi.

Air Vice Marshal Erlic Pinto of Western Air Command was appointed Air Component Commander for Goa operations from Pune and tasked as follows:

• The destruction of Goa's lone airfield in Dabolim, without causing damage to the terminal building and airport facilities. India's largest naval base INS Hansa is now located there.

• Destruction of the wireless station at Bambolim, Goa (now an Army Signals training centre).

• Denial of airfields at Daman and Diu, not to be attacked without prior permission.

• Support to advancing ground troops.

On 10 December 1961, nine days prior to the invasion, Nehru told the press that "Continuance of Goa under Portuguese rule is an impossibility." American response was that, if India took armed action in Goa, it would be brought to the U.N. Security Council, and India could expect no support from the U.S. delegation. The Indian Ambassador in the USA kept 'Foggy Bottom' posted.

The armed action, codenamed Operation Vijay, involved air, sea and land strikes for over 36 hours, and was a decisive victory for India, ending 451 years of Portuguese colonial rule in Goa. Twenty two Indians and thirty Portuguese were killed in the fighting. The brief conflict drew a mixture of worldwide praise and condemnation. India called it liberation of its historic territory, while Portugal viewed it as an aggression against its national soil.

Portuguese War Preparations and Actions

Portuguese began preparing for a military contingency in 1954, prompted by an Indian economic blockade. Three army battalions were shipped to Goa, raising Portuguese military presence to 12,000 men. In 1960, the Army undersecretary of State, Costa Gomes, surveyed Goa and proposed a reduction in the military grouping bringing the strength to around 3,500. At the time of war, Portuguese ground forces consisted of 3,995 men, including 810 Indian soldiers (Indo-Portuguese). The Indians were ill trained and were primarily for targeting those persons the Portuguese considered extremists. There were over 1000 police officers and 400 border guards.

A Portuguese Navy frigate the NRP Afonso de Albuquerque was present in Goa at the time of the invasion, with four 120 mm guns capable of two rounds per minute, and four automatic rapid firing guns. Portuguese Navy also had three light patrol boats (Lanchas de Fiscalização), armed with 20mm Oerlikon guns.

Portuguese air presence was limited to a Douglas DC-4 Skymaster of Portuguese India Airlines and a Lockheed Constellation of Portuguese international airline (TAP). Portuguese Air Force tried to send ten tons of anti-tank grenades in two DC-6 aircraft from Montijo Air Base. But with lack of stop over permissions from USA (Wheelus Air Base in Libya) and other countries, it was aborted.

Lacking permission, TAP chartered a plane to evacuate Portuguese civilians, which arrived with half a dozen bags of sausages and female paratroopers. For air defence, Portuguese smuggled in few obsolete air defence guns under the guise of soccer equipment.

The Portuguese divided the territory into four defence sectors to delay the advance of Indian liberation forces with the Plano Sentinela (Sentinel Plan). Capt. Carlos Azavedo, who was stationed in Goa during the war, told a Portuguese newspaper 'Expresso' on 8 December 2001, "It was an unrealistic and unachievable plan."

The Indian Naval Preparations and Actions

As a precaution, the Indian Navy deployed two warships, INS Rajput, an 'R' Class destroyer, and the INS Kirpan, a Blackwood class anti-submarine frigate off the coast of Goa and Anjadiv. The actual attack on Goa was delegated to four task groups: a Surface Action Group comprising five ships: INS Mysore (Flag), Trishul, Betwa, Beas and Cauvery; a carrier group INS Vikrant, Kuthar, Kirpan, Khukri and Rajput; a Minesweeping Group consisting of M18, including INS Karwar, Kakinada, Cannanore and Bimlipatam; and a support group which consisted of the INS Dharini, which became the Flagship of the Naval Officer In Charge Goa, Commodore Agate.

The storming and taking of Anjidiv Island was assigned to the INS Trishul with Bofors and 4.5inch guns, and INS Mysore with Bofors, 4 inch side turrets and nine 6 inch guns. This writer was witness to the action from the forecastle of Mysore and supervised the lowering of one of the whaler boats and motor cutter with a Gunnery landing party while the Army was moving into Goa. The IAF carried out raids by six Hawker Hunters, who targeted the wireless station at Bambolim and Dabolim airfield with rockets and gun cannons, as the Army advanced.

The first two boats from INS Mysore and one from

INS Trishul with armed landing teams, communication sets, supplies and a National Flag chugged along smoothly towards the island. The sharpshooters were seen with helmets bobbing in the sun. White flags of truce were flying on the island and INS Mysore in VHF touch with boats pre-supposed it would be an unopposed landing. Just when the first wave had landed and were walking onto the beach and the second boat was near the beach, massive 'ratatatat gun fire' opened up from the Island and from the large Church on the hill, felling many sailors, with bodies dropping into the water. Others crouched across the beach into the thicket, and took position.

Flag Officer Indian Fleet Rear Admiral B. S. Soman watched in surprise. Medical officers and the standby landing party were rushed in boats from INS Mysore and Trishul, which were a few miles away. This second landing, under covering fire from the ships' Bofors, and odd 4 inch shell, stormed the island and engaged the Portuguese defenders. They took position at night and next day hunted out all the Portuguese officers and men. The Portuguese defences were overrun after careful shelling on call from shore, and the survivors taken as POWs. The second morning Cdr. Colaco decided to land and took me along to help Cdr. P. S. Neogi a Supply officer to hoist the tricolour, after the island was secured by 14:00. Two officers and 5 sailors died, with 19 wounded. Lt. Kelman, a brave Anglo Indian S.D. Officer was injured and later decorated. The POWs and civilians were taken on board INS Mysore.

INS Betwa cripples NRP Afonso de Albuquerque

On the morning of 18 December, the Portuguese frigate Afonso de Albuquerque was anchored off the expansive bay of Mormugão. Three Portuguese patrol boats were present at Goa and Daman and Diu. Besides facing Indian naval units, the Afonso de Albuquerque was to provide artillery battery support to defend the harbour, and provide vital radio communications with Lisbon after shore radio facilities at Bambolim was destroyed in Indian airstrikes.

At 09:00, three Indian frigates led by the INS Betwa under Cdr. R.K.S. (Russi) Ghandhi took up station off the harbour, awaiting orders to attack the NRP Afonso and secure access to the port. At 11:00, Indian planes bombed Mormugão harbor. At 12:00, upon receiving clearance from NHQ, INS Betwa, accompanied by INS Beas entered the Goa harbour limits and opened fire on the NRP Afonso with their 4.5-inch guns which had the British FPS 5 analog computer system and kept transmitting requests to surrender in morse code between shots. In response, NRP Afonso raised anchor, and headed out towards the enemy and returned the fire with her 120 mm guns.

Besides being outnumbered, Afonso was also at a severe disadvantage since it was in a confined position that restricted its maneuverability, and also because its four 120 mm guns were capable of only two rounds a minute, as compared to the 60 rounds per minute cadence of the guns aboard the newly acquired frigates. A few minutes into the exchange of fire, at 1215, Afonso took a direct hit on its bridge, injuring its weapons officer. At 12:25, an anti-personnel shrapnel shell exploded directly over the ship, killing its radio officer and severely injuring its commander, Captain António da Cunha Aragão, after which the First Officer Pinto da Cruz took command of the vessel. The ship's propulsion system was also badly damaged in this attack.

At 12:35, she swerved 180 degrees and was run aground and beached at the Bambolim beach. At that time, against the commander's orders, a white flag was hoisted under instructions from the sergeant in charge of signals. But the flag coiled itself around the mast and as a result was not spotted by the Indian ships who continued their barrage. Many said this was a Nelsonic act by flamboyant gunnery specialist Cdr. Russi Ghandhi, who was trained at HMS Excellent at Whale Island in the U.K. and ADC to Lord Mountbatten in 1947.

At 12:50, after firing nearly 400 rounds at the Indians, hitting two of the Indian vessels, and suffering severe damage, the order was given on NRP Afonso to 'abandon ship'. Under heavy fire, directed both at the ship and the coast, non-essential crew made their way ashore. At 13:10, the rest of the crew, with their injured Captain, disembarked onto the beach after setting fire to the ship. Captain Aragão was transferred by car to the hospital at Panaji.

NRP Afonso suffered 5 dead, with 13 wounded in action. The frigate's crew formally surrendered with the remaining Portuguese forces on 19 December 1961 at 20:30 hrs. As a gesture of goodwill, the captains of INS Betwa and INS Beas visited Captain Aragão, recuperating in bed in Panaji. NRP Afonso was opened to the Navy and this author visited the ship. Afonso was renamed Sarasvati by the Indian Navy with skeleton crew as she lay grounded near Dona Paula, until 1962 when it was towed to Bombay and sold for scrap. Parts of the ship were preserved and are on display at the Naval Museum in Mumbai.

International reactions to the liberation

The United States' official reaction to the invasion was delivered by Adlai Stevenson in the UN Security Council. He condemned the armed action by India and demanded that all Indian forces be unconditionally withdrawn from Goan soil. To express its displeasure, the US Senate Foreign Relations Committee tried, over objections by President Kennedy, to cut the 1962 foreign aid to India by 25 percent. Referring to Western perception, that India had previously been lecturing the world about the virtues of nonviolence, President Kennedy told the Indian ambassador L. K. Jha, "You spend the last fifteen years preaching morality to us, and then you go ahead and act the way any normal country would behave. People are saying, the preacher has been caught coming out of the brothel."

The USSR vetoed a U.N. Security Council resolution condemning the Indian invasion of Goa. The Soviet head of state, Leonid Brezhnev, visiting India at the time, applauded the Indian action, urging Indians to ignore Western indignation as it came "from those who are accustomed to strangle the peoples striving for independence and from those who enrich themselves from colonialist plunder." Nikita Khrushchev telegraphed Nehru that there was "unanimous acclaim" from Soviet citizens for "Friendly India".

Long after the action in Goa, Peking stressed the support of the Chinese government for the struggle of the people of Asia, Africa and Latin America against "imperialist colonialism". China neither condemned nor applauded the invasion, despite Portuguese rule of Macau at the time. China was enjoying cordial relations with India, though the Sino-Indian War would begin the next year in 1962.

The liberation of Goa was the Indian Navy's first involvement in any conflict and its role in Operation Vijay against the Portuguese Navy was stellar. Three Portuguese frigates, NRP Bartolomeu Dias, NRP João de Lisboa and NRP Gonçalves Zarco deployed to patrol the waters off Goa, Daman and Diu, along with several patrol boats (Lancha de Fiscalização) fled before the hostilities and only NRP Afonso de Albuquerque saw action. The actions in Diu were of little significance and landing parties ensured the takeover.

Postscript : On the second evening, 19 December, FOCIF Soman, learnt that a surrender was taking place ashore, took his barge from Mysore and this author accompanied him to land at a jetty in Marmagoa. The jawan there pointed his rifle at us and shouted, "Kon hai. Kahan jata hai. Code bole." (Who Goes There. Shout Code). I explained that the Admiral was on board, but he wanted the code word. I was flummoxed. He called a JCO. I told him Anjidiv was captured and the Admiral needed to go ashore. He looked at his list and said, "It says Navy will be allowed only after D-Plus 2; I cannot allow anyone without the code word." The Admiral decided to land the next day.

Admiral Katari writes in a tailpiece that the Chief of General Staff Lt. Gen. B.N. Kaul marched into Goa with the victorious Indian Army troops and this provoked Lt. Gen. J.N. Chaudhuri to inquire of Army Chief Gen. K. S. Thimayya in Delhi whether the Chief did not trust him. Katari also writes about strained relations between the Chiefs and Menon and about how Gen. Timmy Thimmaya was made to withdraw his resignation. Nehru had favourites and it became clear that Gen Kaul, a family friend, was being groomed for operational posts. He was made the Corps Commander in the 1962 Indo China war.

CHAPTER 3
THE NAVY DOES SWEET FANNY ADAMS IN 1965

The Indian Navy was never involved in the 1965 war because the Indian Government, lacking precedents or experience, had no strategy for a naval war. PM Lal Bahadur Shastri and his Cabinet, getting intelligence inputs that Indonesia was coming to Pakistan's aid, played safe. The protection of the Andaman and Nicobar Islands was thus given priority in Cabinet meetings. - Author.

Pakistan President Gen. Ayub Khan's military eyes were on planned incursions in Kashmir. On 9 April 1965 India was taken by surprise by a large Pakistani attack on Border Security Force's Sardar Point in Kutch (Op Desert Hawk) to grab the non- demarcated areas, assess the use of US military hardware, and then move the war North. The land skirmishes continued till August when Pakistan executed Op Gibraltar, infiltrating army and civilians across the Kashmir border. It was all out war by 1 September. The IAF on Army request went into action in Chamb-Akhnoor sectors. Indian AMX tanks were no match for Pakistani Pattons. A ceasefire was declared on 23 September 1965.

The Pakistani Navy sailed PNS Ghazi to patrol off Bombay and attack large naval warships, while the Pakistan Fleet under COMPAK made a defensive "cordon saintlier" around 150 miles from Karachi, a brilliant move.

(As an aside, this author as CNS Pakistan Navy to C-in-C Pakistan Lt .Gen. V. N. Sharma (later COAS) in Ex Brasstacks employed this same naval strategy in a war game conducted by D. G. Military Training Lt. Gen. S.F. Rodrigues. India's largest war game was played out at the

Palam Parade Ground in 1987 before the ground exercise. It was the brain child of Chief of Army Staff General Krishnaswamy Sundarji who wished to mechanise and modernize his Army. Western Army Commander Lt. Gen. P.N. Hoon, called Brasstacks a mobilization of the entire Indian army.

Pakistan military regarded this war game as a threatening exhibition of "overwhelming conventional force".

The Navy brass in 1987 headed by CNS Admiral Ram Tahiliani and Vice Chief J. G. Nadkarni treated the exercise Brasstacks lightly, so when the author presented the PN plans as C-IN-C, to the VIP closed door gathering at Palam which included PM and Defence Minister Rajiv Gandhi, Minister of State Arun Singh, Service chiefs and Foreign Secretary A.P.Venkateswaran (who resigned later), Admiral Tahiliani stopped the presentation half way, stating operational information was being disclosed. Nadkarni was to view the rehearsal but did not. Rear Admiral S M Lakhar, Western Fleet Commander, was the Indian opposition at sea. The author was dressed down and ordered to play the operational game meekly. Brasstacks was basically an Army game, with the aborted Exercise Brassboard, a national war game that was to follow. It was a blatant display of turf keeping, with no CDS to oversee joint operations.)

The Pakistan Air Force Chief's Depiction

In 1965, the Pakistan Navy seems to have conducted its defensive role well. Yet remarks by Air Marshal Nur Khan, who took over midway from Air Marshal Ashgar Khan, show the chaotic conduct of the war in Pakistan as no different from India. It is now confirmed that Indian Air Chief Arjan Singh who knew his counterpart Ashgar Khan well, had agreed not to involve their Air Forces in the early phases. MOD in India appears to have nodded.

The Chief of Naval Staff in Pakistan Vice Admiral M. R. Khan and Chief of Naval Staff Vice Admiral B. S. Soman were friends since training days and had worked together in New Delhi in South Block in the committee appointed in June 1947 to divide the naval resources. When war broke, the Navy was set to act, but was kept out by a note from H.C. Sarin, Joint Secretary (later Defence Secretary) in the MOD. An explanatory letter of 29 January 1988 from Admiral B. S. Soman to Admiral S. N. Kohli explains it all:

"As far as I remember, it was the morning after the evening of the start of the war that I got a file from the Ministry signed by Sarin then Joint Secretary, saying that "The Navy is not to initiate any offensive action against Pakistan at sea and is not to operate above the latitude of Porbunder except in pursuit of Pakistan Navy offensive action." If I remember correctly Defence Secretary P.V. Rao was not in Delhi. I immediately contacted the Minister Mr. Y.B. Chavan. In our meeting I strongly protested against this order and said in any case I cannot accept it from a Joint Secretary in the Ministry. If I remembered correctly, he initialed it and asked me if that would do and I replied that in that case I would like to see the Prime Minister. On his assurance that it was a Cabinet decision – I am not sure whether the PM too initialed the file – I accepted it on the understanding that should I consider it necessary, I may be allowed to see the President of India as the Commander in Chief. I was not much worried about Pakistan, and was most concerned about the possible actions of Indonesia in the A&N area, the defence of which was the sole responsibility of the Navy at the time, ever since the 1962 catastrophe".

(B.S.Soman, was a regular commissioned officer, and superseded Admiral S.G. Karmarkar, a seasoned Dufferin trained merchant navy Captain who joined the RIN as a Volunteer Reserve Officer in the war and was the first

Indian to command British officers on INS Cauvery. This author served as Flag Lt.to both. Soman completed 3 years as Chairman Chiefs of Staff Committee in January 1965, handing over to Gen. J. N. Chaudhuri].

"Sweet Fanny Adams"

This British sailors' 18th century bawdy euphemism for "sweet nothing", during the Raj, naturally got colloquial usage in the Indian Navy, given its Royal Navy pedigree and customs. The phrase saw excessive use in the 1962 war, as the Indian Navy did Sweet Fanny Adams in 1965.

A poorly prepared Indian Army suffered a traumatic defeat at the hands of the Chinese in 1962, demoralizing the nation and weakening a sad Pandit Nehru. In 2012, veteran journalist Inder Malhotra unearthed US declassified information on the Indo-China war. There were shockingly desperate letters from Nehru, requesting President Kennedy for urgent military aviation help to quell the Chinese. Defence Minister Krishna Menon had not even contemplated using the professional, well equipped, even lethal IAF.

After the war, U.S. support was sought by a forceful young Orissa politician Biju Patnaik. A daring pilot, knowing Armed Forces needs, he set up Kalinga Airways and with his own daring flying example, sustained Indian Army troops in forward areas with air drops of food and supplies in Dakotas, when the IAF could not.

As a personal aside, one of many in this book, for which the reader's indulgence is sought, this author's father looked after Biju Patnaik's iron ore and manganese mines in Orissa in Barbil, and "Uncle Biju" would drive the author to school in St George's College Mussoorie with his daughter Gita (now Gita Mehta, the author of Karma Cola). Uncle Biju advanced Rs 1500 for the author to join NDA as a cadet in 1955.

The Indian Navy story in 1965 displayed poor tri-service thinking in political minds that still persists. The Navy had suffered budgetary neglect since 1962 and only a few new ships and the aircraft carrier INS Vikrant (Ex HMS Hercules 1961) had joined the Fleet. Except for sanctioning foreign cruises, Government provided little guidance. The Navy had to lean on the other two services for maritime reconnaissance, transport, victuals, stores, medical and ordinance supplies. When Pakistan boldly moved to the brink of war in the Rann of Kutch in April 1965, the Cabinet was without the one-man decisions of Pandit Nehru. India's War Book was neglected, lacking in directions for war since the British left, with no contingency planning to employ the Navy. It was called the 'Cinderella Service', fraternizing with Bombay gentry and film stars, in prohibition days.

The Pakistan Army had been armed by USA with new M47 Patton tanks and F-86 Sabre planes. The Ministry of Defence, the Chiefs of Staff Committee and the Service HQ were suddenly faced with the procedural realities of war, and overly worried about its international ramifications. The diminutive Lal Bahadur Shastri, made Prime Minister in 1964, and Defence Minister Y. B. Chavan had no precedents to go by. India had no CDS for single source advice. The Constitution (Article 53) stipulates the President is the Supreme Commander but has only a ceremonial role. All decisions are taken collectively by the Cabinet, under the Prime Minister (Article 74). Hence decision making and responsibilities are diffused. The Cabinet was confused on how to respond to the incursion.

The Rann of Kutch is a sparsely inhabited expanse of marshy terrain, where tides rise and fall hugely. The land border along the sea and the creeks, especially Sir Creek, and inlets recede, and boundary pillars are submerged. About 200 miles long and 50 miles wide in south western India, Kutch has easier access from Pakistan. In 1965, the area's maps were British legacies, with the sea boundary in dispute since 1947 till today. Peasants, speaking the Sindhi Kutchi dialects, used to cross over. Stray incidents took place in January 1965. Pakistan aggressively claimed the entire Rann saying that Sindh was one of its erstwhile provinces, and it had always exercised administrative control over the area during the British period.

Early in 1965, the Indian Fleet ships had called at Bahrain and Kuwait in a flag-showing cruise. Aircraft carrier INS Vikrant, with Seahawk fighters and Alize anti-submarine aircraft, had carried out a brief exercise with the Army in the Kutch area, next to Pakistan. Story of The Pakistan Navy cites this, as India showing its teeth to Pakistan. In September 1964, PNS Ghazi (USS Diablo) had joined as a strictly training submarine under Lt.Cdr. K.R.Niazi's command. CNS Vice Admiral A.R. Khan made plans for submarine action.

Since no naval encounter occurred or was anticipated in 1965, the Navy was not even kept in the loop with intelligence feeds. The Cabinet, unfamiliar with the political challenges of war, did not involve Navy or Air Force top brass in meetings. It felt the Army could do the fighting if push came to punch and the other services would be confined to defensive action, within geographical limits. Why air power was not deployed in the Rann for reconnaissance and to support the Army, or the Navy not alerted to patrol Kutch, are vexing questions. Politico-military contingency planning is a subject given importance in Staff Colleges abroad but largely neglected in India.

The Army was moved to the border but in June, a cease-fire was made effective from 1 July 1965. If ministerial talks did not produce a compromise, the Kutch issue would be referred to a World Court tribunal to demarcate the boundary. The ministerial meeting never took place. Pakistan did not reply to India's communications. A tribunal was appointed, which upheld by 2 to 1 Pakistan's claim to the northern half of the Rann and awarded 10 percent of the disputed territory to

Pakistan. At August end, the Pakistan Army launched the third phase of Op Grand Slam, a large- scale attack across into the Chamb area to capture Akhnoor and cut India's only road link with Kashmir. A similar intrusion in Kargil in May 1999 again surprised India, with lack of intelligence or patrolling on the heights.

An official of the time writes "The attempt on our part was to keep the whole thing confined to a local conflict, rather than assume the character of an Indo-Pak War. This as in the past was the prime objective of our policy". The Indian Fleet sailed for the Bay of Bengal in end June. There was no directive from the Government to prepare for war. A British submarine was arranged at some cost off Madras in July, for anti submarine training, after which ships of the Fleet were to visit the Andamans, Calcutta and Visakhapatnam, the routine of naval operations to avoid the south- west monsoons.

At Naval HQ at Delhi, it was a challenging situation for planners. With all operational ships in the East, resources in Bombay were meagre. Fleet programmes used to be conveyed to MOD. Soman on more than one occasion had suggested that the Fleet return to Bombay but was told that it should adhere to its programme of visiting the Andamans. No wonder PNS Ghazi found no large targets off Mumbai.

Air Marshal Ashgar Khan, President Ayub Khan's envoy in Peking, met PM Chou En Lai on 10th September 1965 and President Soekarno in Jakarta. In his book 'The Fourth Round', he records the latter's generosity: "Your dire need, is our dire need". Soekarno loaned two W class Soviet submarines Nagarangsang (Lt. Y.H. Malik, later C-in-C) and Bramaastra (Lt. Basuki) who sailed them to Pakistan after the war, undetected by India. National interests evidently overrode Soekarno's pledges to Nehru of Non-alignment or Panchsila.

By end August, heavy Pakistan troop and tank movements took place in areas under India's continuous observation in the South. Few saw it as a diversion, and most expected the attack from further North. Pakistan's thrust at Chamb on 1 September 1965 was a surprise in its exact location and intensity. The Navy was not involved. Adm. Soman's letter to Adm. S.N. Kohli (quoted above) is self explanatory.

The Navy kept vigil with Naval Control of Shipping (NCSO) pilots. The IAF flew Maritime Reconnaissance (MR) sorties from Pune in Liberators on Form Greens (Naval requisitions) but could not differentiate warships from merchant ships. This author with another officer proceeded to Pune Lohegaon air base to lecture on ship recognition and recall the three MR sorties flown. The Captain of the bulky Liberator would ask me to be in the rear gunners pit, and when it approached a contact, call me to the cockpit, traversing a gangway in high lashing winds, or while the plane was banking. An IAF navigator named Soni was our contact, and the differences in dining customs in the mess, informality in squadrons and Air Force language, especially the word 'panga' (fight) were revealing. To see a pilot officer not salute a flying officer was strange.

In the 70s, the Navy requested Maritime Reconnaissance (MR) takeover from the IAF which led to a bitter 'panga' that the Navy won, and got the 4-engine Super Constellations (ex-Air India). The IAF hoped the Navy would not succeed. It is to his credit that then Rear Admiral Ram Tahiliani, who was Deputy Chief of Naval Staff, posted the Navy's best pilots, including fighter pilots like Arun Prakash (later CNS Admiral), who succeeded beyond expectations.

Today the Indian Navy has a fleet of over 50 new P8i Boeing 737s, aging IL-38s, TU-142 s, Dorniers 228s and six Medium Range MR planes and ShinMaywa US-2 are in the pipeline. The Coast Guard has a large fleet of Dorniers and helicopters and an expansion plan for MR but lacks submarines.

CHAPTER 4
THE PAKISTAN NAVY - HISTORY UPTO 1965

The actions of the Pakistan Navy, in 1965 and after, speak of a level of professionalism bred over decades. Its leaders understood the crucial challenges of defending two naval fronts with limited assets. Full authority was exercised by the C-in-C PM Vice Admiral A R Khan, whom this author met on a Dufferin get-together in India, introduced by a family friend Cdr Iftikar Ahmed.

The Book Club and Educational Services (NES) of Pakistan Navy have done yeoman service by recording stories of the personnel who gave their all - called 'Shaudas' - in the book Sentinels of the Seas, with a chronology. The author is grateful for copyright permission granted.

Sentinels of the Seas - The Pakistan Navy (1947-1997)

Cmde Md. Alavi has documented the role of Muslim sea power in history. He describes Muslim rule as deriving strength from the seas, which cover most of Earth. One of the 23 verses about the seas in the Koran states, "It is God who hath subjected the sea unto you, that His Ships may sail therein at His Command, and that you may gain unto yourself by Commerce, of His Bounty, and you may give Thanks." The Arabs (Moors) and Turks ventured to rule Europe and Spain - called the Andulus of the Arabs.

Gen Tariq Bin Ziyad landed in Gibraltar and the Sultans of Turkey were finally defeated at the battle of Lepanto. Arab sailors migrated to Africa, Ceylon, Malaysia, India (Moplas) and Indonesia. Moghul ruler Akbar also had maritime ambitions and sailed ships for Haj to Mecca but on being intercepted off Aden, he had to discontinue. The Royal Indian Navy had a large complement of Muslim sailors, many from Ratnagiri.

Vice Admiral Haji Md. Siddiq Choudri (C-in-C 1953-1959) has traced the Pakistan Navy history to 1959, from the pre-1947 Aiyengar Nationalization Committee, and the Navy Partition Committee, where he along with Cmde Mumtaz and Capt Bhaskar Soman worked to divide naval assets, and states that Jinnah took personal interest. The PN began in 1947 with 92 commissioned officers, 63 Executive, who formed its core.

Lord Mountbatten's views on the birth of the Royal Navy's two daughter navies includes such tidbits as HMIS Godavari F-52 being renamed HMPS Sind. This author contributed to the history of the Royal Indian Navy in Daring to Dreadnought (Naval Review 2013 Seaforth - Peter Hore) and includes the pre-partition period. PN chiefs went to the USSR in the 1960s and were offered Osas, but the USA came up with better military aid and P-3 Orions. Cdr H H Ahmad covers the role of the Pak Navy in the 1965 war and the Dwarka raid in 'Destroyers at Full Ahead.'

The Dwarka Raid

On 5 August 1965, between 26,000 and 33,000 Pakistani soldiers crossed the line of control (LOC) dressed as Kashmiri locals and headed for various areas within Kashmir. Indian forces were tipped off by the local populace, around 15 August. On 6 September, Pakistan NHQ at Karachi learnt that the Indians had attacked across the international border in the Lahore area. Orders were given to PN forces to proceed to their war stations. They were well prepared having embarked fuel, stores and ammunition, and fuelled at sea continuously till 27 September. The Naval Control of Shipping Organisation (NCSO) declared an embargo on all merchant ships carrying stores for India. The Inland Water Transport Authority (IWTA) sealed off all river routes used by Indian steamers transiting through East Pakistan and to seize such vessels. These measures caused losses to India of valuable cargo, ships and river craft.

On 7 September, with the ships on patrol, Naval Headquarters sent this signal: "Task group comprising Babur (Capt M.A.K.Lodhi), Khaibar (Capt A. Hanif), Badr (Cdr I.H.Malik), Jahangir (Cdr KH Hussain), Alamgir (Cdr I.F.Quadir), Shahjahan (Cdr S.Z. Shamsie), and Tippu Sultan (Cdr Amir Aslam), are to be in position 293 degrees - 120 miles from Dwarka Light House by 071800 E/Sep with maximum power available. Task group to carry out bombardment of Dwarka about midnight, using 50 rounds per ship. Force is to retire from bombardment area by 0800 30 Sep." PNS Dacca (Cap RM Aziz) was off Karachi sustaining the 'cordon sanitaria' and PNS Ghazi (Cdr KR Niazi) was off Bombay looking for prey.

The Pakistan Navy could carry out an offensive against Dwarka (site of the Hindu Somnath Temple) without hindrance from the Indian Navy. Morale in the Pakistan Navy was high with PNS Ghazi inducted and Daphne submarines under order in France. India did not have submarines and was concentrating on anti- submarine training in challenging tropical waters, with varying bathy conditions, reducing ranges at which a submarine could be detected.

Pakistan's version: The Indian Navy, with considerable numerical superiority, was bottled up in harbour, due to our submarine's (PNS Ghazi) presence." On 8 September, Pakistan Navy's C-in-C Vice Admiral Afzal Rehman Khan, a Dufferin and Dartmouth term mate of Indian officers, sailed a task group towards Dwarka at high speed. The ships carried out bombardment of the coast, hoping to re-live Mohamed Ghazni's attacks on the Somnath temple. Lt Cdr Rashid Ghaznavi and Captain Amir Aslam have recounted the foray The 4.5 inch shells landed on the shore and killed a cow! Pakistan falsely claimed that INS Brahmaputra, a Type 15 with 4.5 inch guns with FPS 5 gunnery system and Controllable Pitch Propellers was sunk. Indian media lapped it up. The Navy denied it.

In September 1965, PAFs Air Marshal Ashgar Khan was offered MiG-15s by Indonesia's Air Chief Omar Dani. Its Navy's C-in-C Admiral Martadinata asked: "Do you want us to take over the Andamans? They are an extension of Sumatra and in any case lie between East Pakistan and Indonesia. What right do the Indians have to be there?" Since Pakistan could not assist in this, he offered to patrol the approaches to those islands and carry out aerial reconnaissance missions. He backed up his words with action.

Air Marshal Nur Khan's interview on the 1965 crisis Revealing excerpts from retired Brig. A.R Siddiqi's interview: C-in C, PAF, AM Nur Khan: The thing to remember about the '65 war is that it was never planned. I assumed command of the PAF on 23 July 1965, nearly two weeks before the Op. Gibraltar, which till then the Air HQ was totally unaware of. I myself flew to Rawalpindi to see General Musa, who confirmed that Op Gibraltar was planned for 6 August. General Akhtar Malik in Muree briefed me. I informed him that this would mean war. Even if the infiltration of 8,000 men succeeded, within days they would be crying for supply drops, and the only aircraft for the job was the transport's C-130. I conveyed to Field Marshal Ayub Khan that all pretence to show a local conflict would end, and Indians would have every right to attack the bases from where the aircraft operated. Air drops were deferred. The PAF was brought to readiness on its own with no government orders. But by 23August, the calls from troops across the Cease Fire Line were so desperate, we took the risk. This was the first and most hazardous PAF operation, due to extremely inhospitable terrain and tricky weather up north.

The Field Marshal ordered that we could only retaliate and not cross into the Indian airspace even after the Chamb operation on September 1st. The fear was that India might launch a pre-emptive strike. Any cooperation between the Army, Navy and Air Force was out of goodwill and convenience, rather than to any plan. From 6 September onwards, we were on the defensive against the Indian invasion and each arm worked on its own. To sum up:

(a) There was no plan for a joint, overall strategic conduct of the war. There was no discussion of any operational plans at any level – Government or Joint Chiefs. The Government functioned as at peacetime, right up to the Indian invasion.

(b) We blundered from a localized operation into a general war, and let the initiative go to the Indians. Given the lack of coordination, it was remarkable for the armed forces to end up in an honorable stalemate, holding more of India's POWs and territory. In East Pakistan our extremely small Air Force (one squadron only) kept the skies clear of intruders throughout. We destroyed more of the enemy aircraft on the ground there than anywhere else.

PAF had been logistically supplied entirely by the US with 120 combat aircraft (F-86 Sabers, F104 Star fighters, and B-57 Bombers); only two fixed radar stations – one in north at Skiwear, the other at Badin. There were only three operational airfields at Peshawar, Sargodha and Karachi. This deployment was hardly adequate for offensive action. However, mastery of the air over Pakistan allowed the army to operate without serious interference, and to call on the air force for close support. Over-reliance on the US - made replacement of certain types of heavy equipment and ammunition uncertain. We exposed our weakness in the worst manner. India became more alert than after the China adventure. It re-armed at a feverish pace. Even though the PAF inducted ove 200 combat aircraft in the next 2 years compared to about 150 over the previous 10 years, five more radar stations, additional forward airfields, we paid for all the hardware from our own budget.

Different sources of supply and types of aircraft posed fresh problems. From 1965, maintaining our armed forces in top operational gear became difficult, and the balance tilted in India's favor. We got into the 1971 crisis as thoughtlessly as in 1965.

If any cohesive system of transferring power existed, martial law may not have been unnecessary. Once imposed, the responsibility for the 1971 crisis lay with the inept leadership. Service chiefs never at any time met together to discuss the imposition of martial law. On 20 February 1968, General Yahya, Admiral Ahsan and I were called to the President's House. A number of Cabinet ministers were also present. The Field Marshal explained that since the political situation was getting out of hand, he intended to impose martial law in major towns of east and west Pakistan. I argued against martial law being used as a solution for a political problem and that martial law would spread to the rest of the country. I suggested a political solution, by introducing some of the reforms the public had been demanding. The Field Marshal was taken aback and could have overruled me but did not. The meeting adjourned without a decision. Admiral Afzal Rahim Khan, Defence Minister and Home minister, Mr. Ghaisuddin, were there. Admiral Ahsan and I were asked to wait at General Yahya's house while others stayed back with the President. Gen Yahya joined us to say that the President wished me to take over as the Governor of West Pakistan. I informed Yahya that I would be willing to accept, and resign as service chief provided I had the assurance that martial law would not be imposed and I would be allowed to carry out the necessary reforms. On 21 February, the Field Marshal informed us that he had decided not to stand for the Presidency and that he was going to hold parlays with political leaders. It was to his great credit that he did listen to a different point of view and also acted upon it.

On 25 March, Admiral Ahsan and I were invited to

General Yahya's house with Ghiasuddin and shown the Field Marshal's letter handing power to the Army Chief. and it was a fait accompli. I and the naval chief could resign or accept the responsibility. About three days later, I was informed with three service chiefs and General Hamid, to carry on the administration of the country.

Haider's revelations

Another interesting set of views comes from the 30-year colourful veteran Air Commodore Sajad 'Nosey' Haider, culled from his book "The Flight of the Falcon", which provides facts, dates and names, in 'Demolishing myths of Indo-Pak wars of 1965 and 1971'. Haider talks of how long and deep American influence ran in the Pakistan Air Force, and about the induction of four squadrons of F-86 Sabres in the PAF. Haider recounts the shooting down of a Canberra over Pakistani territory on the day of Eid-ul-fitr in 1959: "The Indian leadership thought that on this sacred day at the end of the holy month of Ramadan, the PAF would either be rejoicing, sleeping or in the mosque." He claims the PAF had been used in anger against 'Afghan mercenaries' as far back as 1965.

Haider explains why neither the IAF nor the PAF played a role in the Rann of Kutch action in early 1965, though the IAF could have done so with air superiority. He claims PAF Chief Asghar Khan called IAF Air Chief Arjan Singh, and requested him not to commit his aircraft. Arjan Singh believed wrongly, that the PAF was in the vicinity. An Indian Canberra over Pakistan in May 1965 was not shot down because President Ayub Khan "had the jitters" and refused permission. In contrast, on 10 August 1999 after the Kargil war, Sqn Lt P.K. Bundela, the leader, and Flt Lt S Narayanan, in a MiG-21bis, with an R60R Infrared missile. on the Rann of Kutch border shot down a Pakistani Naval Air Arm Breuget Atlantique, piloted by Lt Cdr Mehboob Alam and Lt Farasat Ali, killing all 18.

Haider is critical of Gen Ayub Khan and his Army Chief Gen Md Musa for failing to fulfill achievable objectives and claiming a "contrived victory" in the 1965 war. Haider quotes Ayub's directive to his C-in-Cs, "As a general rule, Hindu morale would not stand more than a couple of blows delivered at the right time and place. Such opportunities should therefore be sought and exploited." Haider describes unhealthy inter-services rivalry and envy in Pakistan, charging its Army with "micro-minds" for keeping the PAF out of the war plans. Haider led the PAF attack on Pathankot early in the 1965 war, destroying MiG-21s. He lauds the Koranic ritual before raids like Pathankot as a morale booster. Haider is critical of the PAF's leadership and its mishandling at the Sargodha air base.

Between the 1965 and 1971 wars, Haider states that the PAF got 70 fighters from China, and also acquired 70 F-86 Sabres from Germany flown in via Iran despite US opposition. Pakistan signed a deal for 3 Daphne submarines and X craft (midgets) on 25 February 1966 with France and received 4 patrol craft from Brooke Marine UK. Vice Adm A R Khan C-in-C Pak Navy became Defence Minister, and Vice Admiral S M Ahsan, an experienced officer who has served in SEATO staff in Bangkok, took over as C-in-C. The Ghazi was due for a refit and was sent to Turkey.

Haider tops off his book with an expose of the extreme corruption that has gripped Pakistan. The first hint of kickbacks to middlemen in Pakistan comes early on in the book when a wealthy Pakistani middleman was present for the trials of Hispano-Suiza rockets by the PAF in the late 1950s. But Haider singles out the Zia ul Haq regime and the period after that for its extreme corruption where kickbacks were "received on every commercial deal".

CHAPTER 5
DRAMATIS PERSONAE OF THE 1971 WAR

"The play's the thing." - *Hamlet, Act II, Sc 2.*
"All the world's a stage, And all the men and women merely players; They have their exits and their entrances."
- *As You Like It, Act II, Sc 7.* - *William Shakespeare.*

Late MRS INDIRA GANDHI
Prime Minister. Priyadarshini to friends.

She was Prime Minister during 1971, the Indo-Pak War. Her pivotal role is comparable to that of the legendary Winston Churchill. She was clear that the objective of the armed forces was "to help liberate Bangla Desh at any cost, hold West Pakistan at bay and, if possible, give it a telling blow, to ensure that it never seeks war again." She set these goals after failing to get a diplomatic settlement for the refugee problem. The morning briefings by General Manekshaw and her approval of action for the day, in concert with Defence Minister Jagjivan Ram, enabled victory. Her failure was to release 93,000 POWS in the Simla Agreement with nothing in return. She was honoured with the highest national award, the Bharat Ratna.

Late Shri JAGJIVAN RAM
Defence Minister. Jaggu Babu to friends.

His astute brain, administrative capabilities, total commitment to the Prime Minister's objectives, and motivated handling of the Service Chiefs, came to the fore during this brief war. He delegated authority for financial and autonomous actions during the war and eliminated bureaucratic delays. He got along with Finance Minister, Y.B. Chavan, and Foreign Minister, Swaran Singh. He fell out with Mrs. Gandhi later and joined the opposition.

Late General S.H.F.J. MANEKSHAW
Later Field Marshal. Chief of Army Staff. Sam Bahadur to friends.

A swashbuckling, jovial, down-to-earth, much loved soldier's general who almost retired as a Major General, but rose to be the leader the Army needed in 1971. His self-assumed role as spokesman for the Navy and the Air Force during high level briefings was like a Chief of Defence Staff. His ability to resolve inter-Service issues at his level spoke well of his leadership. He looked his men in the eye and boosted Army morale no end. A Parsi, he lived like a Gorkha—the regiment that nurtured him and looked after him in his retirement. To them, he was willing to give his all. Awarded Padma Vibhushan.

Late Admiral S.M. NANDA
Chief of Naval Staff. Charles to his friends.

A shrewd manager of men and resources, and a Captain's ideal Admiral. He masterminded clear-cut operational orders, which when read by his lower Commanders and Captains at sea, left no room for doubt. His vision of the Navy's objectives ensured that the Navy came out with flying colours. He saw to it that Manekshaw and Lal gave this small Service a chance. He overruled nervous views to implant his bolder ones. "No risk, no gain" was his motto. His knowledge of Karachi, wide experience in command of INS Mysore, Western Fleet and Command, and as Vice-Chief made him most suited for the post. Adm. Gorshkov the old sea-dog of Russia, was an admirer. Awarded Padma Vibhushan.

Late Air Chief Marshal P.C. LAL
Chief of Air Staff. PC to Friends

This serious soft-spoken intellectual, an ace pilot, applied modern management to take the Indian Air Force to levels of efficiency never attained before. Losses did not deter him from supporting the Navy in its Karachi raids. He worked closely with the other two Chiefs against many odds, in the war which the Indian Air Force faced with distinction. Awarded Padma Vibhushan.

Late Vice Admiral SURENDRA NATH KOHLI
Flag Officer Commanding-in-Chief West. Known as Takarmar Kohli. Later Admiral, Chief of Naval Staff 1973-1976.

As a Captain, his ship suffered a hat-trick of collisions but he came out unscathed to be given Western Naval Command in 1971. Guided by his Chief during the war, each day saw him take bolder stances and greater responsibility for action in the Western theatre. The loss of Khukri saddened him immensely and he spent many pensive hours wondering how he could have avoided this catastrophe. He dedicated Sea Power and the Indian Ocean to those who lost their lives in the Indian Navy's 1971 actions. Awarded Padma Vibhushan.

Late Vice Admiral N. KRISHNAN
Flag Officer Commanding-in-Chief (East). Tubby Krish to friends. Later Chairman, Cochin Shipyard.

Rotund, sharp-talking and truly brilliant, Krishnan commanded INS Delhi in the 1960 Goa Operations and INS Vikrant with grit. Brain power and command of the language helped him formulate the Indian Navy's plans and his brilliant deployment of INS Vikrant speaks volumes for his tactical foresight. A forceful personality some found difficult to get along with. Awarded Padma Bhushan.

Rear Admiral V.A. KAMATH (Retired)
Flag Officer Commanding South. Vasu to friends. Later Vice Admiral, Vice Chief of Naval Staff

A pipe-smoking, quiet and tradition-conscious officer. He commanded the Southern Naval Area and carried out his functions without much fuss. Awarded PVSM

Late Rear Admiral E.C. KURUVILLA
Later Vice Admiral. Chandy to friends. Chairman and Managing Director, Mazagon Docks Ltd.

A six-feet-two, broad-shouldered Admiral with specialist gunnery training from HMS Excellent. A brawny Admiral who rode horses and drove ships hard. With command experience of INS Kistna, INS Trishul and INS Vikrant, he leaned a lot on his pride and his operational staff when confronted with the intricacies of war at sea and paid scant regard to advice from shore. Awarded PVSM

Late Rear Admiral SRIHARI LAL SARMA

Flag Officer Commanding - Eastern Fleet. Shri to friends. Eastern Fleet Commander formed in October

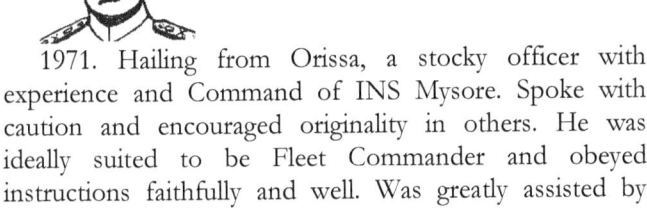

1971. Hailing from Orissa, a stocky officer with experience and Command of INS Mysore. Spoke with caution and encouraged originality in others. He was ideally suited to be Fleet Commander and obeyed instructions faithfully and well. Was greatly assisted by Captain Suraj Prakash Flag Captain. Awarded PVSM.

Captain R.K.S. GHANDHI

Later Vice Admiral, retired. Russi to friends. Chairman SCI.

A Whale Island trained officer at HMS Excellent and also Flag Lieutenant to Admiral Mountbatten, who had commanded INS Cauvery, Betwa and Trishul with seagoing élan. He was Kuruvilla's Flag Captain in Command of Mysore. Two Gunnery heads, the Flag Captain and Cdr G.M. Hiranandani, another gunnery specialist, as Fleet Operations Officer, contributed much to what happened at sea during those 14 fateful days. Awarded Vir Chakra

Late Captain S. PRAKASH
Commanding Officer INS Vikrant. Suraj the Navigator. Later Vice Chief and Director General Coast Guard.

A quiet, cool, painstaking specialist navigating officer with command experience of INS Khukri. Learnt his onions as Nanda's navigator. One can picture him with a toothpick, sitting in his Captain's chair of Vikrant as Flag Captain, and dealing the cards of war in the East, which was spearheaded by the carrier. Awarded Maha Vir Chakra.

Captain M.P. AWATI
Commanding Officer INS Kamorta (P 31). Manohar to friends. Later Vice Admiral—Flag Officer Commanding-in-Chief West.

A bearded, imposing quintessential 'old seadog'. He held sway with his abounding vocabulary, booming voice and military gait. With command experience of INS Betwa, this communication specialist came to grips with handling the lively Petya squadron he commanded with distinction in the Bay in 1971. Awarded Vir Chakra.

Late Captain M.N. MULLA
Commanding Officer INS Khukri and F 14. Masterji to friends.

A brilliant Naval officer from a family of lawyers. Targeted by a Pak submarine torpedo attack, he went down with his ship, smoking his last cigarette in the old traditions of the Navy, made famous by Melville de Mello on radio. A loved Captain for his Urdu, replete with slang. The way he dealt cards at bridge will long be remembered with nostalgia. Awarded Maha Vir Chakra posthumously.

Late Cdr B.B. YADAV
Badru to friends. Later Cmde.

This lucky Commander of the 25th Missile Boat Squadron took his well worked up boats to Karachi. He went on to win a Maha Vir Chakra for his support in this now famous attack on Karachi. The other missile killers The reader will encounter are Jerry Jerath, I.J. Sharma, Kavina and Omi Mehta who all went to Karachi with courage and scored hits. All awarded Vir Chakra

Late Captain M.K. ROY
Later Flag Officer Commanding-in-Chief East. Mickey to friends. Director Naval Intelligence in 1971.

This Royal Navy-trained Naval Observer commissioned the Cobra Alize Squadron 310 in 1961 in the UK. With his Bengali background and astute brain, he made a valuable contribution to improve the Navy's Intelligence set-up in 1971 and in providing assistance to the Mukti Bahini. Awarded PVSM.

Lieutenant Commander S.K. GUPTA
Later Commanding Officer, INS Vikrant —1984. Giji to friends.

This quiet unassuming boxer and ace pilot, with a blue from the NDA commanded the gallant 300 Seahawk Squadron of Vikrant. Under his leadership the Hawks flew a total of 123 sorties in 14 days with devastating effect on Cox's Bazar, Chittagong and Chulna. Awarded Maha Vir Chakra. Later Rear Admiral

Late Lieutenant General J.S. AURORA
General Officer Commanding-in-Chief Eastern Command. Later Member of Parliament.

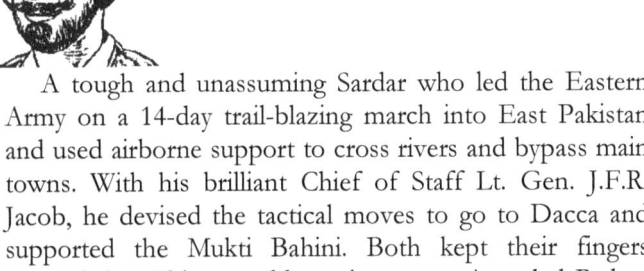

A tough and unassuming Sardar who led the Eastern Army on a 14-day trail-blazing march into East Pakistan and used airborne support to cross rivers and bypass main towns. With his brilliant Chief of Staff Lt. Gen. J.F.R. Jacob, he devised the tactical moves to go to Dacca and supported the Mukti Bahini. Both kept their fingers crossed that China would not intervene. Awarded Padma Bhushan.

Late Air Marshal H.C. DEWAN
Air Officer Commanding-in-Chief, Eastern Command. Harry to friends.

A quiet but forward-looking Air Marshal who overcame the paucity of air power at his disposal, and made the best use of sister Services and the Navy's air arm but at times took the credit for Naval actions. Awarded Padma Bhushan.

LATE RICHARD NIXON
President, USA. Tricky Dick and Foxy Nixon to friends and opponents.

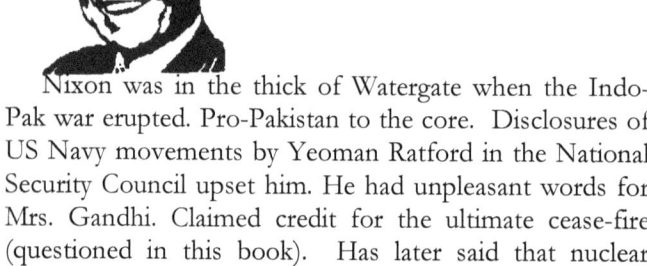

Nixon was in the thick of Watergate when the Indo-Pak war erupted. Pro-Pakistan to the core. Disclosures of US Navy movements by Yeoman Ratford in the National Security Council upset him. He had unpleasant words for Mrs. Gandhi. Claimed credit for the ultimate cease-fire (questioned in this book). Has later said that nuclear weapons may have been resorted to, if things had got out of hand.

HENRY KISSINGER
Nixon's Secretary of State. Henry to friends.

The Professor postured as the "know-it-all" for the world. This globe-trotting Secretary of State was advance man for Nixon and vacillated over feelings for India. Keen to open dialogue with China, he was bullied by Yahya Khan to choose between Mujib and himself. He is widely quoted to have said, "I am getting hell every half hour from the President (Nixon) that we are not being tough enough on India."

Late ZULFIKAR ALI BHUTTO
Prime Minister of Pakistan. Zulfi the Sindhi to friends.

He signed the Simla Agreement. Played a double game with Yahya and Mujib. An Oxford educated leader of Pakistan whose Pakistan People's Party (PPP) won only 60 per cent of the votes in West Pakistan 1970 elections, and should have bowed to Mujibur Rahman who claimed 291 out of 343 seats to form the central government. This was not palatable to Bhutto and the oligarchy in West Pakistan. He sided covertly with the military. After the war he met Mujib in Bhawalpur jail to try to work out a deal. He was done in by General Zia-ul-Haq.

Late Colonel M.A.G. OSMANY
Commander-in-Chief, Mukti Bahini.

A lesser man would have given up. A brilliant officer of the East Bengal Regiment who never married and was known as the "Father of the Regiment". Retired after a brush with Field Marshal Ayub Khan in the 1960s, but became head of Mukti Bahini. He was later Commander-in-Chief Bangla Desh and then joined politics.

Late Admiral of the Fleet SERGEI GORSHKOV
(This author thrice served as his Liaison Officer in India)

This legendary young 'sea-dog' took over the Soviet Navy in the 1950s and steered it to a size and stature to challenge the US Navy. He was a friend of the Indian Navy. He demonstrated the versatility and lethality of the Osa-class missile boats to Admiral Krishnan. He was full of praise for how they were employed in 1971. Revered in the Soviet Navy for his thesis on maritime strategy.

THE INDIAN NAVY SAILOR
In his first big test, he did admirable duty for the finest Navy.

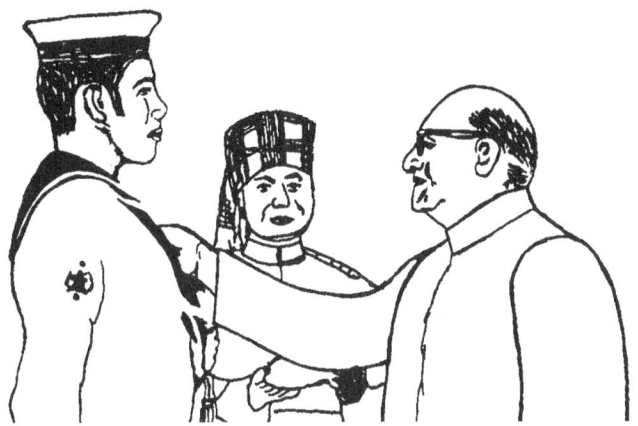

Representative of the unnamed thousands of officers and sailors who went into action on their ships, manned the hardware, did their duty with courage, and gave their all for the glory of their Service.

No salute is too big.
"Shan No Varunah"

CHAPTER 6
THE ORDER OF BATTLE
(ORBAT - 1971)

Modern warfare is an intricate business about which no one knows everything and few know very much — Frank Knox.

By 1971, India and Pakistan were separate entities for 24 years. Under Gen. Ayub Khan's military rule since 1969, Pakistan's Army became a pampered force, its might suppressing its own population in East Bengal to fulfill the dictates of its Corps Commanders. Cooperation with Pakistan Air Force was poor, says a Pakistani author, analysing causes of Pakistan's defeat. The Navy at Karachi took a back seat. The submarine arm with the long ranged mine laying PNS Ghazi was augmented with 3 Daphnes, and a surface fleet of 7 old British warships. They faced an Indian Navy with fresh Osa class missile boats, a modern lot of ships and a Naval air arm with an old aircraft carrier, INS Vikrant with Sea Hawks and Alizes. Yahya Khan accepted that the odds were in favour of the Indian Navy, but Pakistan Navy tacticians hoped their submarines would be sneakily successful. Air cover is essential in today's warfare at sea, and both navies lacked this feature in the West, since the Vikrant got assigned to the East.

The Pakistani Defence Plans

Pakistan always had good staff work with the British instilled axiom "Planning for war is a continuous process". But in 1971, it lacked a satisfactory higher defence organization, or a military aim beyond suppressing East Pakistani Bengalis. In 1970, the Military Operations Directorate defined the Armed Forces mission: defend the territorial integrity of Pakistan and destroy maximum enemy's forces; capture the most of enemy's territory by counter offensive. A 4-day war game in August 1970 showed attacks could only be met in the West. After winter 1970's Exercise TituMir, two independent armoured brigades were set up, and by August 1971, plans updated to counter-attack in the East and West. Dacca's defence was given importance and BOP (Border Outpost Posture) adopted. Pakistan conceded Indian Air and Naval superiority in the East. It assumed 6 Indian Divisions would be deployed in the East.

In the West, Gen. Hamid Khan planned to let India to occupy the untenable Bambanwala-Ravi-Bedian so a counter-offensive by his I Strike Corps would secure Jammu Tawi and Poonch: IV Corps would move from Lahore, and 18 Infantry Division was to look after the 500-mile-long Rajasthan Kutch Sector

Maritime Strategies

Maritime strategy is the total response of sea power required to achieve economic, political and military goals at sea. The Indian Navy had a 1944-vintage aircraft carrier INS Vikrant (ex-HMS Majestic), a cruiser INS Mysore (HMS Gambia), INS Delhi (HMS Achilles), 6 frigates, 8 missile boats and 4 submarines. Indian strategy was to use the Army and Air Force for the mainland thrust in the East and for the Navy to blockade Pakistan. India's indigenously built Leander INS Nilgiri (F 33, 2,080 tons), with modern fire-control system, Seacat surface-to-air missiles and an Alouette helicopter was getting sea trials but the Navy was still inadequately equipped for needed maritime reconnaissance. Indian naval tacticians were set to use the forces judiciously from India's three major Naval bases to launch offensive action.

Pakistan had a minimal navy, though with better submarines, little shipbuilding facility but an adequate ship repair yard. It had only one major naval base in Karachi, and planned deterrence to India assiduously. Its submarines could keep the Indian Navy guessing but could not expect to seek battle with the Indian Navy whose gun power and missilery was superior. It hoped to safeguard its coastline and deliver deadly probes with its submarine arm.

Manpower and Equipment

The ethnic origins of Indian and Pakistani seamen are the same and if dressed in the same uniform would be indistinguishable. The Indian Navy matched Pakistan in its workforce, with a strength of 25,000 - an edge of 10,000. The technical arms of both had adequately trained personnel though the advantage lay with India, as a number of technical sailors in the Pakistani Navy from East Bengal had been taken off sensitive posts and some had fled. Some Bengali sailors had deserted their latest Daphne Pakistan Navy submarine Mangro at Toulon on a homeward passage.

The crews of India's 8 Osa class missile boats were freshly trained in the Soviet Union. The naval pilots were superior-grade fliers and those away from flying duties were recalled to the carrier, and flew as a team irrespective of rank or seniority. This made the aging Vikrant a formidable machine but with boiler deficiency and speed restrictions she was assigned to the East. Its Seahawks and Alizes were air-worthy and able. The Indian Navy had just commissioned a squadron of Seakings from Westland Aviation but the crew had no tactical training with weapon fits still being inducted. The efficient aircraft, not yet worked up and integrated with the Fleet, were flown to Bombay post-haste when war broke out.

Naval Chief, Admiral S.M. Nanda was a charismatic tactician with superb man management. He had full knowledge of the port of Karachi, being earlier an official in the Karachi Port Trust. The later commands of INS Mysore (flagship), the Western Fleet, Western Naval

Command and his meetings with wise old sea dog, Admiral Sergei Gorshkov provided deep insight into judiciously using his Eastern and Western origin ships. The Eastern and Western Fleets, were professionally manned with the finest officer material. Most Captains had Royal Navy training and all-round experience.

In comparison, the Pakistani officers were relatively younger, had seen quick promotions without intensive work-ups, for lack of fleet support and Air Force cooperation. Pakistani authors like Gen. Fazal Muqueen Khan admit this. Their Chief, Admiral Hasan had clear tactics; be aggressive with his submarine arm, and defensive on all other fronts, till the Indian fleet was located.

In the East, Rear Admiral Sharif had a small band of officers, gunboats and patrol craft, and needed ingenuity in his tactics. His objective was to use his forces when not engaged in helping the Army to control the populace, and to patrol the coast. He never anticipated the havoc the aircraft carrier would create and trusted the Ghazi to stalk the Indian Eastern Fleet which included the Vikrant. In the West Rear Admiral MAK Lodhi (Compak) had no choice but to send his submarines afield and keep his ships closer home.

Such was the line-up of the two Navies in 1971. The order of battle with the Indian Command list is given as per the 1971 Jane's Fighting Ships. This sets the scene for what followed.

Ranjit B. Rai, Joseph P. Chacko

Naval Orbat - India -1971

President - Mr V.V. Giri
Prime Minister - Mrs Indira Gandhi
Defence Minister - Mr Jagjivan Ram
Finance Minister - Mr Y.B Chavan

Administrative

Defence Secretary - Mr K.B Lall
Home Secretary - Mr Govind Narain

Naval Command

Chief of Naval Staff- Admiral S.M Nanda, PVSM
Vice Chief of Naval Staff - Vice Admiral J. Cursetji, PVSM
Flag Officer C-IN-C Western Naval Command - Vice Admiral S.N Kohli, PVSM
Flag Officer C-IN-C Eastern Naval Command - Vice Admiral N Krishnan, PVSM, DSC
Flag Officer Southern Naval Area - Rear Admiral V.A. Kamath, PVSM

Naval Fleet

Aircraft Carrier(1) Diesel Submarine(4) Cruiser(2) Destroyer(3) Escort Destroyer(3) Frigate(19) Survey ship(3 ex frigates) Ocean Minesweeper(1) Coastal Minesweeper(4) Inshore Minesweeper(4) Torpedo Boat(6) Seward Patrol Craft(15) Support Ship & Service Craft(16)

Naval personnel

20,000 Personnel (1800 Officers, 18,200 Ratings)

Naval Bases and Establishments

Bombay (C-IN-C Western Fleet, Barracks and Main Dockyard); Visakhapatnam (C-IN-C Eastern Command and fleet, Submarine Base, Dockyard and Barracks; Cochin (Naval Air Station, barracks and Professional Schools); Lonavala & Jamnagar (professional Schools); Calcutta, Goa & Port Blair (Small Bases)

Merchant Fleet

399 Vessels of 2.5 Million Tons Gross (LLOYDS Register of Shipping)

Indian Navy Western Feet - 1971
Rear Admiral EC Kuruvilla PVSM (FOCWEF
Fleet Ops Officer Cdr GM Hiranandani NM

INS Mysore flagship West (Capt RKS Ghandhi VrC)

INS Trishul (Capt KMV Nair VrC) F-16
INS Talwar (Cdr SS Kumar VrC)

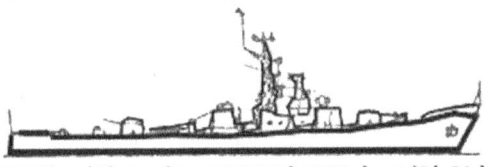

INS Kiltan (Cdr Gopal Rao MVC VSM), INS Kadmatt (Cdr S Jain NM)
INS Katchall (Cdr KN Zadu VrC)

INS Khukri (Capt MN Mulla MVC), INS Kirpan (Cdr RR Sood VrC NM),
INS Kuthar (Cdr VC Tripathi NM)

INS Ranjit (Cdr RN Singh)

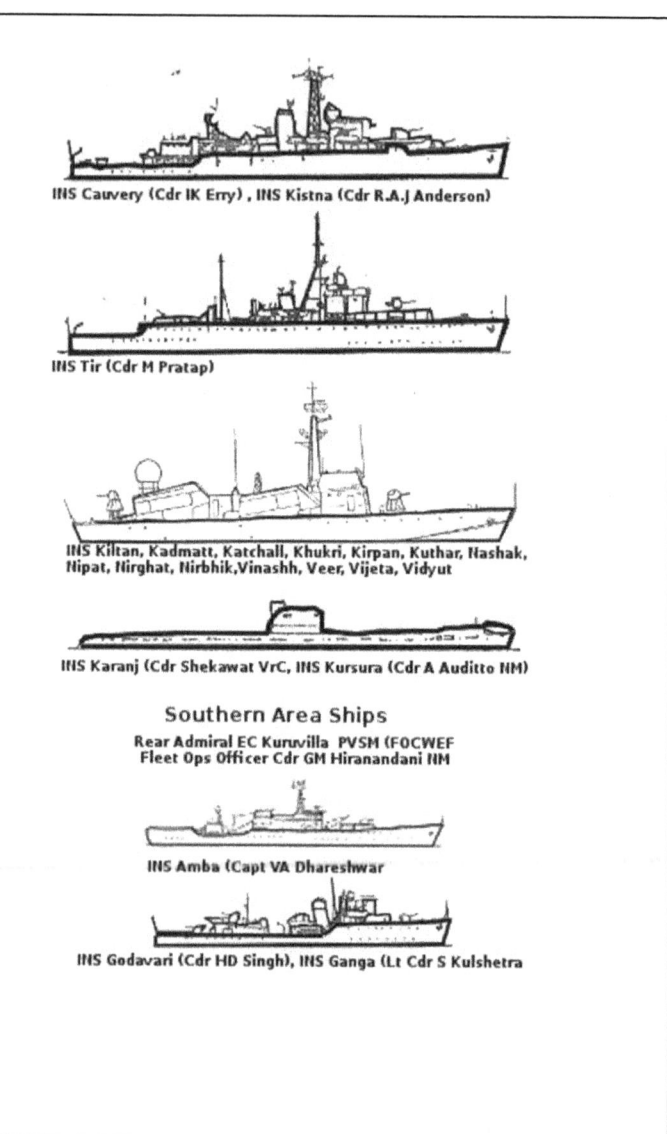

Eastern Fleet - 1971

Rear Admiral SH Sharma PVSM (FOCEF)
Fleet Operations officer Capt. SM Vyas

INS Vikrant - Flagship East (Capt S Prakash MVC)

INS Brahmaputra (Capt JC Puri VrC VSM) F16
INS Beas (Cdr L Ramdas VrC VSM)

INS Rajput (Lt Cdr Inder Singh)

INS Kamrota (Capt MP Awati VrC) P31
INS Kavaratti (S Paul VrC)

INS Khanderi (Cdr RJ Millan VrC)

Other Ships:

Landing Ship Tank - Magar, Ghariyal, Guldar
Patrol Craft - Panvel, Pulicat, Panaji, Akshay
Requisitioned Craft - Padma, Palash

Naval Orbat - Pakistan - 1971

President - Agha Yahya Khan
PSO - Lt General S.G.M.M. Peerzada
Chief of Staff - Gen. Abdul Hamid Khan
Chief of National Security – Major General Ghulam Umar
Foreign Minister - Z.A. Bhutto
Defence Secretary - Ghiasuddin Ahmed.
Chief of General Staff - Gen G.L.. Hassan
Chief Secretary (East) - Muzzaffar Hussein
Inspector General of Police – MA Chaudhary

Naval Command
C-IN-C and CNS – Vice Adm Muzaffar Hasan, HQA, SK
Chief of staff – Rear Adm Rashid Ahmad, SK, TQA
FOC PN East – Rear Adm Muhammad Sharif, SK

Naval Fleet
Cruiser(1)   Destroyer(5)   Frigate(3)   Submarine(4)   Tanker(1)
Minesweeper(8) Gun Boat(2) Salvage Tug(1)

Naval Personnel
9900 (900 Officers, 9000 Ratings)

Merchant fleet
179 Vessels of 566022 Tons Gross (Lloyds Register)

Naval Ships
Western Fleet:
Cruiser - PNS Babur
Destroyers - Badr, Khaibar, Shah Jahan, Alamgir & Jahangir
Frigates - Tipu Sultan, Tughril, Zulfiquar
Daphné class Submarines - Mangro, Hangor and Shushuk.
Gun Boats: Sadaqat, Rafaqat
Midget submarines - Chariots
Minesweepers - Muhafiz, Mujahid, Moshal, Momin, Mukhtar, Mubarak, Mahmood & Munsif
Tanker - Dacca
Salvage Tug - Madadgar
Eastern Fleet:
Gunboats - Jessore, Rajshahi, Comilla & Sylhet
1 Tench class Submarine - PNS Ghazi

Warring Navies – India and Pakistan

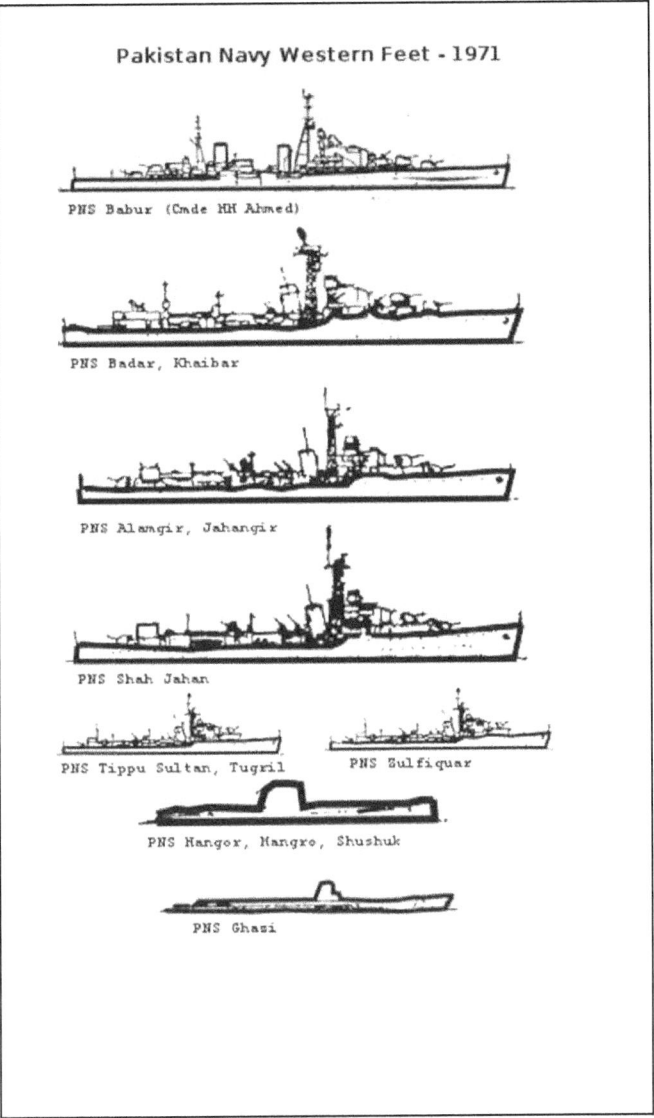

CHAPTER 7
THE MUKTI BAHINI'S

In Memoriam
The gates of our memories of Mukti Bahini will never close. How much we remember you, no one knows.
Deep in our hearts you will stay.
You will always be remembered for that your last day,
So dear God, give them the message above
Tell them we miss them
Offer them our love encore
So that we can strive for them furthermore.
Input By Col Sajjad Zahir (East Bengal Rifles & Mukti Bahni)

Ever since the reprisal of 25 March 1971 (Op Searchlight) by the Pakistani Army, there was a steady build-up of Bengali guerillas in East Pakistan. A Mukti Fauj (liberation army) was formed with its units learning the art of guerrilla war. Yahya Khan's soldiers spread death and destruction in East Bengal. They raped women (a reported 25,000 illegitimate children were born), saying cynically that they were providing better genes to the weak Hindu Bengali race. Hatred for the hoodlums in uniform increased. The activities of the Mukti Fauj, initially restricted to the country-side, engulfed East Pakistan in a civil war, and the Army of an ethnic minority attempted to quell the struggle with partial success in the first few months. The armed opposition gained momentum, and as the monsoon advanced, the Army found the guerillas becoming more audacious in destroying bridges, ambushing Army units, sinking ships and resorting to ingenious unorthodox methods.

Leaders like Abdul Haq and Mohammed Toaha objected to the mid-level Awami League cadre forming the

Mukti Fauj and left it to the East Bangla Communist Party (EBCP) led by Matin-Alauddin to lead a Maoist type of struggle (just like the one plaguing some Indian states like Jharkand, Chattisgarh, Orissa and Andhra even in 2014). In Pabna, a military leader, Tipu Biswas, became a legend by his week-long successful attack on the Army unit there. By now, arms were being distributed and the population harboured the guerrillas, who weeded out the Razakars who were collaborating with the Pakistan Army in internecine skirmishes.

The East Bengal Regiment and the East Pakistan Rifles personnel were removed from sensitive posts and put under surveillance. In the initial days, contacts were made in India, havens provided, and training facilities and funds made available across the border. The initial activities were by the Mukti Bahini, despite Pakistani allegations to the contrary. Indian Army and Navy joined later.

Mukti Bahini

Activities in East Pakistan by the Mukti Fauj now called the Mukti Bahini intensified with active Indian participation. The nucleus of the guerrilla forces consisted of the East Bengal Regiment and Rifles, now serving liberation. Many of the Sector Commanders (No.10 was Navy) were former Pakistan Army and Navy officers. There was no dearth of volunteers in the wake of the murders, rapes and subjugation of East Bengalis by West Pakistani forces. The Guardian on 3 November 1971 reported Mukti Bahini forces at 80,000, almost equal to the 93,000 Pakistan soldiers there. Refugees in India rose to over 9,000,000, many willing to be trained and armed as guerrillas. Many residing near river's, were excellent swimmers. Pakistan statements constantly referred to the guerrillas as Indian agents.

Mukti Bahini training and operations were superbly organized in India by Brig. Shahbeg Singh a Gurkha officer with experience of North East in the 1962 war (later Military Commander in the Golden Temple siege in 1984), and Oban of ITPB from Centre 22 set up in Chakrata with US agents, to train Tibetans. Young student League leaders included Serajul Alam Khan, Sheikh Fazlul Haque Mani, Kazi Arif Ahmed, Abdur Razzak, Tofael Ahmed, A. S. M. Abdur Rab, Shahjahan Siraj, Nur E Alam Siddiqi, and Abdul Quddus Makhon and the Kaderia Bahini under Kader Siddique who aided the famous Tangail air drop operation. Some groups of freedom fighters were controlled by the Leftist parties and included the NAP and Communist Parties. A strong guerrilla force led by Siraj Sikder fought several battles with the Pakistani soldiers in Payarabagan, Barisal. Three brigades (Force Z, K, S) were created by Col M.A.G.Osmany as adviser, Maj Zia-Ur-Rehman and Mohammad Mustaq. Rehman later became President and the other two rose to Army chiefs. A guerrilla group named "Crack Platoon" made courageous attacks in Dhaka city that attracted international media. East Bengal politicos had always encouraged political activity by students, who formed the Jangi Bahini (pro-Russian corps), pro-China Mukti Committee, Mukti Jot (NLF) and groups styled after Mao Zedong and Che Guevera. They were highly motivated for exploits against the Pakistan Army. A fully female Bichu (Scorpion) force was noted for suicide squads.

On 11 April 1971, the formation of the Mukti Bahini was announced by Tajudin Ahmed, Prime Minister of the proclaimed Bangladesh government operating from Calcutta, under Col M.A.G. Osmany with Chief-of-Staff Lt. Col. Abdur Robs and Capt. A.K. Khandaker as deputy. The command structure of ex-Pakistan Army Bengali officers set the scene for organized activities against the occupation army. The father of Javed Haq serving in the Bangladesh mission in 2014 fought in Sylhet under Maj Sharfullah Khan.

The Mukti Bahini sank three ships in Chittagong

harbour during the night of 15-16 August (Independence Day) and under the leadership of Lt Cdr Ashok Roy Vrc (Chapter 15). Pakistan radio on 28 September claimed their Navy killed 10 frogmen trained to lay limpet mines in Chittagong and Chalna harbours. River craft with 40/60 Bofors sporadically shelled ships going up the Chalna river to Chittagong. By 12 September, almost all culverts and small bridges between Dacca and Comilla, Jessore and Kushtia were destroyed. Cargo ships and river craft were attacked. This Mukti Bahini naval activity was with Indian Navy training and equipment, from Plassey, that was crucial to the war.

On the political front, on 8 September a consultative committee of four Awami League representatives and four from other parties was formed in Calcutta to "direct the struggle for freedom". The National Awami Party was represented by Maulana Abdul Hamid Bhashani and Professor Muzaffar Ahmed of the pro-Chinese and pro-Soviet factions. Pakistani diplomats the world over defected in support of the Bangladesh Provisional Government including Abdul Fateh, Ambassador to Iraq, and Khurram Khan Panni, Ambassador to the Philippines accusing the Pak Army of 'history's greatest genocide'. Moinuddin Ahmed Jogiondar, Political Counsellor in Lagos; Rezaul Karim, Political Counselor in London; Wali-Ur-Rahman, deputy head of the Pak Embassy in Switzerland, Humayun Rasheed Chaudhry, Minister-Counsellor and Head of the Pakistan High Commission in New Delhi who headed the unrecognized mission of Bangladesh. The communication link created between the Indian Government and the Mukti Bahini, later aided the Indian Army in December.

In September, guerrilla student groups bombed the International Hotel and in October made an unsuccessful attempt to shell Dacca airport. Guerrillas disguised as Pakistani soldiers entered the city's main power station on 3 November to destroy three main generators, shutting down industry within a 30-mile radius. Guerrilla activities in Dacca included bombing of educational institutions under the Army's control, and armed bank robberies. Curfew was imposed on 17 November with a house-to-house search for arms; 138 people were arrested and 4 killed. Two West German diplomats were killed on 14 November when their vehicle drove over a land mine.

Ex-Navy personnel /river guards helped navigate craft up tricky rivers. On 11 November, the Daily Telegraph reported that seven major regions had been declared as liberated zones by the Mukti Bahini. Pakistani troops are believed to have kept to their barracks by night.

The guerrillas kept assassinating persons collaborating with the Pakistan Government and Army. Abdul Monem Khan, a prominent Muslim League politician was shot dead at his home on 14 October. The Governor of East Pakistan, Malik, held responsible for shooting of civilians during the popular 1968 demonstrations against President Ayub Khan's regime, was a victim. A candidate returned unopposed to the Provincial Assembly was shot dead near Dacca on 7 November.

Reprisals against Hindus

The Army and the Razakars (the civilian militia) let loose a reign of terror as a reprisal for guerrillas' activities. The Times reported on 12 September: "Military terror is continuing in East Pakistan. Political suspects are still 'lifted', care taken to make their arrests unobtrusive. Army reprisals continue to be savage...17 suspects were taken from seven villages, lined up and shot. Their homes were destroyed...."

New York Times correspondent, Sydney H. Schanberg reported on 21 September: "The dozens of refugees interviewed describe the killing of civilians, rape and other acts of repression by the soldiers. Nearly all are Hindus, who said that the military regime was making the Hindu minority its target. The Army carried out massive reprisals against civilians after every guerrilla raid…. The Army leaves much of the 'dirty work' to its civilian collaborators — the Razakars, or Home Guards it has armed, and to the supporters of right wing religious political parties Muslim League and Jamaat- i-Islami".

On 12 November, Reuters correspondent, Fred Bridgland, who watched about 400 refugees cross into India in about three hours, wrote: "An elderly Hindu cultivator said the Razakars and Pakistan Army were 'taking away our women and looting and burning the villages'. He said the attacks usually followed night operations by the Mukti Bahini. Refugees from other districts also spoke of villages being burnt, women abducted and young men killed".

Dateline — 21 November 1971 Clashes with loss of life occurred between Indian and the Pakistani armed forces on the Bengal border. Kesing's Contemporary Archives notes: The fighting on the East Pakistan border was greatly intensified after 21 November, with the Mukti Bahini offensive against Jessore. The Battle of Garibpur on 20–21 November finds special mention. Pakistani statements attributed the fighting to the Indian armed forces, assisted by "Indian agents". Indian sources maintained that only the Mukti Bahini were involved. Western correspondents stated that the Indian Army's share in the fighting was exaggerated.

Clare Hollingworth, Daily Telegraph correspondent in East Pakistan, reported on 29 November that Indian troops were involved, and that she had talked with a wounded Indian sergeant in the military hospital at Jessore. "The scale of military operations has been mounted at more than battalion level, with the majority attacks made by no more than 120 infantrymen or one company".

The Times correspondent on 2 December: "Only two Indian brigades — perhaps three including reserves — were used secretly to support the front line Mukti Bahini in the Jessore area. Artillery was used, but there was no air cover, and the infantry assaults were left to the guerrillas." A Pakistani military spokesman finally admitted on 28 November that Bengali guerrillas were fighting against the Pakistan Army and that "people in East Pakistan are by and large, assisting the guerrillas". 14 Punjab Battalion supported by a squadron of 14 PT-76 tanks from 45 Cavalry crossed the border in the Jessore sector on 21 November, but withdrew after a limited defensive action. Pakistan responded with 107 Infantry Brigade, supported by 3rd Independent Armoured Squadron, with M24 Chaffee light tanks. Numerical superiority notwithstanding, 14 Punjab were unrelenting. Retaining recoilless rifles and infantry in defensive positions, the P-76 tanks pounded the Pakistani position. Unable to pinpoint the firing, the Pakistanis attacked defensive positions resulting in large casualties. 11 Pakistani tanks were destroyed, three were captured in working condition and 107 Infantry brigade was severely depleted. Indian's reported loss of 6 tanks and 40 casualties. One Indian battalion had almost destroyed the entire Pakistani brigade. Pakistanis finally called for airstrikes and pressed in three F-86 Sabres, which were promptly shot down by 4 Folland Gnats from Indian Air Force. One PAF pilot was killed and and two were taken POW. Pakistan claimed that they were on "a routine mission within Pakistani territory" and that two Indian fighters were destroyed, but this India denied.

Mitro Bahini (Allied Forces - Mukti Bahni and Indian Army), fought other battles like Battle of Hilli. With their wins, East Pakistan's North sector was virtually in their hands before the war began officially. Morale sank within the Pakistani Armed Forces in East Pakistan.

Pakistan Radio alleged on 21 November that two Indian brigades supported by a tank regiment and accompanied by "Indian agents", had attacked north-west of Jessore. Associated Press of Pakistan stated that the

Indians had stopped after losing 18 tanks and 130 men killed, against only 7 Pakistanis killed; and that Indian aircraft had strafed three villages killing 79 civilians. Lieut-Gen. A.A.K. Niazi (Pakistani Commander in East Pakistan) told journalists that Indian troops had penetrated 8 miles into Jessore. The Indian Defence Ministry denied this, stating that its troops had instructions not to cross the border; and that Pakistan, after calling the Mukti Bahini "Indian agents", had started calling them "Indian Army infiltrators". On 22 November Mrs. Gandhi addressed Parliament, "On 21 November, Pakistani infantry supported by tanks and artillery launched an offensive on the Mukti Bahini who were holding liberated areas around Boyra, five miles from our Eastern border. The Pakistani armour under heavy artillery cover, advanced to our border, threatening our defensive positions. Their shells fell in our territory, wounding a number of our men. The local Indian military commander took appropriate action to repulse the attack. 13 Pakistani Chaffee tanks were destroyed." Mrs. Gandhi did not say whether the Indian tanks had actually crossed the border. A Government spokesman said later that they had done so in order to meet the oncoming Pakistani tanks, and after advancing "a very short distance" into East Pakistan, returned within a few hours without suffering losses. Indian forces, under strict orders not to cross, now had the right to do so, following the Pakistani tank offensive. This was the only border crossing incident so far.

On 23 November, the Mukti Bahini attacked Chowgacha, an important road junction 7 miles north-west of Jessore which fell on 29 November. Burinda hamlet, 7 miles west, was then overrun by Indian troops. Colonel Osmany, Commander of the Mukti Bahini, had set up his headquarters near Jessore, and leaders of the Bangladesh movement had moved in to set up a Government in Jessore when it fell. The town held over 3,000 troops however, operating from a well-prepared system of underground tunnels and concrete bunkers.

None can deny India's case from August 1971 to assist the Mukti Bahini out of human concern for those unsung heroes who fought back against the Pakistani Army. What Pakistan writers refer to as civil war, was actually a war of liberation after Bongabondhu Sheikh Mujibur Rahman declared independence. The effort of Mukti Bahini and Mitro Bahini will be marginalized if it is referred to as civil war. This chapter is a dedication to the heroism of the Mukti Bahini.

The Indian side of the story of Bangladesh Liberation

Chief of Staff Eastern Naval Command Maj Gen J.F.R.Jacob (later Lt Gen) was 'hands on' from day one of the Bangladesh liberation. He advised Gen Manekshaw that operations in the monsoons were not feasible. "In early April, Manekshaw phoned me that government wanted Eastern Command to move immediately into East Pakistan. We had mountain divisions with no bridges or motor transport. We needed time for training. The monsoon was about to break. I said not before 15 November, by when the terrain should be reasonably firm. A meeting was held in the operations room in Delhi attended by Mrs Gandhi, the ministers of Defence Jagjivan Ram, External Affairs, Finance, Home, Defence secretary, Director Military Operations.

Manekshaw read out my brief and Mrs Gandhi accepted that we could move in after 15 November."

In his excellent book titled 1971 on the creation of Bangladesh, ex Army officer and King's College graduate Dr Srinath Raghavan, calls this a 'myth'. But this author interviewed FM Manekshaw at Coonoor in 1979, for A Nation and Its Navy At War, when commanding the Naval Academy in Cochin.

Manekshaw confirmed this, and did so later on TV too, saying the Indian Army was not ready because tanks, spares and plans and maps to wage war in the riverine terrain were deficient.

Jacob gives special tribute to the gallant resistance of the people of Bangladesh: "Let us not forget the tremendous contributions of the freedom fighters and the East Bengal battalions fighting alongside Indian armed forces. On 25 March 1971, Gen Yahya Khan ordered the Pakistan army to crack down on Dacca university and other areas."

Mujib Rehman, leader of the liberation struggle was jailed in Bhawalpur in West Pakistan for 8 months without access to news, till Bhutto met him in jail around 20 December to do a deal to remain within the Pakistani Federation. Mujib, lacking details of the liberation answered, " It is not for me to agree, but my people". He was transported back to Dacca.

Gen Jacob adds: "The East Bengal battalions moved into India, and refugees streamed into India. Mrs Gandhi ordered the army to help the freedom fighters, doing so officially on 29 April 1971. The important first defection by Hussain Ali from Pakistan's Calcutta mission led to other defections. In early April, resistance leaders began arriving at Calcutta. Prominent amongst them were Tajuddin, Nazrul Islam, Mansur Ali, Qamaruzzam, Col Osmany and Group Capt Khandeker. A government in exile was established at 8 Theatre Road, Calcutta. I suggested that they should issue a declaration, as was done by de Gaulle in World War 2. Tajuddin asked for a draft declaration. The declaration of independence was issued on 17 April at Badyanath Tala just within East Pakistan. Government of India asked us to assist the freedom fighters".

On preparations: "We initially set 8 camps up in the border areas, to train 1000 recruits each. Army HQ spelt out 3 tasks: to advise the provisional government, to equip a guerilla force of 20,000 to be expanded to 100,000 and to conduct guerilla operations in East Pakistan. We divided the area of operations for the freedom fighters into sectors. Maj Zia was responsible for the Chittagong sector. Maj Khalid Musharaf for Comilla, Maj Saifullah for Mymensingh, Wing Cdr Bashar for Rangpur, Lt Col Zaman for Rajshahi, Maj Usman for Kushtia, and Maj Jalil for Khulna. "Tiger" Siddiqui was to operate from Tangail as did Noorul Kadar and Toha. Gp Capt. Khandeker played a pivotal role in overseeing operations, as Osmany was mostly out at Sylhet with his East Bengal battalions. His contribution to the successful operations of the freedom fighters was a crucial factor in the freedom struggle. They attacked the Pakistan army and their infrastructure. They created an environment of fear throughout the Pakistan army, lowering their morale. Due credit must be given to them for their decisive contribution to the liberation of their country".

These statements fortify the author's statement that the Mukti Bahini was key to Indian Armed Forces' success in the 1971 war. On the Indian strategy, moves in the East were made after assessing that Gen Niazi would defend the towns and territory:

A. Dacca, the centre of gravity of East Pakistan, is to be the prime and final objective.

B. Fortified towns were to be by passed. Thrust lines were to be along subsidiary tracks.

C. Subsidiary objectives were to be communication and command and control centres. The Pak army was to be drawn to the border areas by operations of the Mukti Bahini.

Jacob adds that Mr Rustamjee of the BSF contributed much to the Mukti Bahini training , "Logistics was of paramount importance. The Indian Navy superbly trained Naval divers and Mukti Bahini, under Cdr M.N.Samant a submariner, for raids at Plassey and lakes. We developed the infrastructure, built up the required logistical cover.

Some 30,000 tons were moved to Tripura for a Corps. Large tonnages were moved to Tura, North Bengal and West Bengal. This we did during the monsoon before the receipt of any orders. When the war started, troops did not have to look back - everything was in place. The creating of the logistical backing was critical to our success. Regrettably the bridges were only released in mid August and were old WW-2 repairable pontoon bridges. These we were able to have repaired in time. The maps we had were 50 years old. Courtesy of the Mukti Bahini, we were able to get the latest Pakistani maps which the Survey of India reproduced. The reproduced maps were issued to our troops in November".

Gen Jacob expects that credit for the 1971 war strategy be given to him, and not Gen Manekshaw. This controversy needs tto be checked. Jacob states, "In mid-August, Gen Manekshaw and Maj Gen K.K. Singh came to Fort William with their draft operation instructions. The objectives were to be the 'entry ports' of Khulna and Chittagong. Dacca was not an objective. I pointed out that it was imperative that we take Dacca. Manekshaw was adamant that it was not necessary to capture Dacca. Gen J.S.Aurora agreed with him. Air Chief Marshal P.C.Lal in My years with the IAF, confirms that Dacca was never an objective. We had to find troops to take Dacca. In November we moved down three brigades from the Chinese border. When Gen Manekshaw found out, he ordered them back. We did not take either Khulna nor Chittagong, but won the war". Still, success or failure rested with Gen Manekshaw.

Jacob adds, "In October, we planned the air drop of a battalion group at Tangail to take part in the capture of Dacca. The drop was planned to take place on D plus 7 and the link up 24 hours later. The drop and link up took place as planned. The operation order for the drop was issued in October and was signed by SASO AVM Deveshwar, Brig Matthew Thomas (later Adviser to

Singapore Armed Forces) and Maj Gen J.F.R.Jacob. In November we sent Capt Ghosh to Tangail to mark out the dropping zone and to inform Siddiqui that he was to advance with our troops to Dacca. This Siddiqui did not do."

The Indian Armed Forces were mostly armed by the Soviet Union with payments on long term loans and barter of consumables, shoes, tea, and export of imported Western equipment, mainly by cronies of the Congress party in Rupee Rouble trade. India voted with Soviets in all UN cold war resolutions, despite professing 'Non Alignment'. Mrs Gandhi's masterstroke was signing the Indo–Soviet Treaty of Peace, Friendship and Cooperation in August 1971, that specified mutual strategic cooperation in case of threat of war. It was a significant deviation from professed foreign policy, and insurance against China, when she saw increasing Sino-American ties and blatant American support to Pakistan. The treaty was later adapted for the Indo-Bangladesh Treaty of Friendship and Cooperation in 1972, signed by Mrs Gandhi. This ensured Chinese caution when the Soviets moved 40 divisions to the Sinjiang border and 7 to the Manchurian border.

The debacles of the Sino-Indian War 1962 and Indo-Pakistani War exposed severe intelligence gaps by the Intelligence Bureau (handling internal and external intelligence). An external intelligence agency, the Research and Analysis Wing (R&AW) was formed in 1968 with founder Director and Spymaster Rameshwar Nath Kao, a former Imperial Service Police Officer. R&AW assisted the Mukti Bahini with funds but its exact role in the liberation requires access to official papers. Mrs Gandhi had a clever PMO team of Kashmiri advisors D.P. Dhar, P.N. Haksar, T.N. Kaul, and Kao, whom she listened to. While what transpired at the meetings is conjecture, Kao's own team, notably Shankaran Nair and Girish Chandra Saxena (brother of Ambassador Naresh Chandra), sized up the emerging Bangladesh scenario with precision from the larger picture down to the little nuts and bolts — contingency plans and micro details. The idea of India training and equipping the Mukti Bahini was supported meticulously.

This author is convinced through interviews with Pakistani and Bangladeshi personnel, that Mrs Gandhi sought an excuse from mid November to take offensive action into East Pakistan, but needed to egg Pakistan into conditions, so that the international community would not blame India for initiating action. Gen Jacob, adds, "On 22 November, a decision was taken to move up to some 10 miles into East Pakistan to counter Pakistani artillery fire. We used this to create jumping off areas for the coming operations. This drove Yayha Khan in desperation to order the bombing of our airfields in the West on 3 December. The war had started".

Despite PAF Sabres being shot down over East Pakistani skies by the IAF in end November, Pakistan did not act. This author re- iterates that Mrs Gandhi had warned the Chiefs that they should be ready to open fronts on 4 December 1971 and it is inferred this information was leaked to Pakistan. Jacob adds, "The thrusts into East Pakistan went as per our plans. A Para drop went off well and by 13 December our troops reached the outskirts of Dacca. On 13 December, the Soviets vetoed a US resolution and warned there would be no more vetoes. The Enterprise carrier group had entered the Bay and the Chinese were making noises". The Navy's exploits are recounted in chapters on the 1971 war.

Jacob rightly takes credit for the surrender, "There was consternation in Delhi. We were on the outskirts of Dacca. Manekshaw sent us an order to go back and capture all the towns we had bypassed but not Dacca. He copied this order to our Corps Commanders. We told our Corps Commanders to ignore this order and to proceed with the offensive as planned, recalling Horatio Nelson at the battle of Copenhagen in 1801; on being told of a flag signal to withdraw, he put his telescope to his blind eye and said 'I see no signal to withdraw, attack'. The rest is history."

On 14 December, an intercept indicated a meeting in Government house at Dacca. The Indian Air Force executed some precision bombing with tourist maps and bombed Government house. The Governor Rao Farman Ali resigned, and that evening Niazi and Farman Ali went to see the American consul General Spivack with a cease fire proposal for the US to hand to the UN, with no mention of India. On 15 December, the proposal was given to Bhutto, who rejected it and stormed out of the UN Security Council swearing to fight on.

Jacob says, "On the morning of 16 December, Manekshaw phoned saying "Jake go and get a surrender." I said, "If I can negotiate on the draft instrument of surrender" that I had earlier sent him. He said, "You know what to do, just go."

It shows the trust Manekshaw reposed in Jacob, so the ire of Jacob is misplaced. This highly respected officer converted a ceasefire into a surrender, and he later became a Governor. He is a friend of this author, and I always tell him," Sir, in the Armed Forces, the Commander takes the credit for success and the punishment for failure." In the Navy, it's called Command Accountability.

A Nuremberg type of trial is in progress in Bangladesh for war crimes committed against Bengalis. Even a former Minister, Syed Md Qaisar of the Jana Party who led the Razakars, has been indicted.

CHAPTER 8
PROLOGUE TO VICTORY IN THE WAR OF 1971

The British were adept at the rules of the colonial game, for survive they did, by the theory of divide and rule and quit; time and again. Britannia created two Pakistan's, East and West, but separated by a thousand leagues of Indian terrain. Never could East and West meet – the reality of 1971. – Author

Extracted from the writings of Hasan Zaheer, Brig. Salik and Col. Jafri:

Relations between India and Pakistan have been and still remain strained, marked by a blow-hot blow-cold approach and mutual distrust. The erstwhile British rulers created Pakistan in two segments in 1947 over 1000 miles apart. The people of West Pakistan comprising Sindhi, Baluchi and Punjabi Muslims had only one feature in common with the people of East Pakistan — religion. In their cultural heritage, language, physical environment, economic resources, temperament and history, no two people could be more unlike each other. There was no place for mutual empathy between them, no sense of common caring and sharing. These differences were accentuated by the fact that the seat of political power in Pakistan lay in the West as a matter of right. The people of East Pakistan appeared to be taken for granted. When democracy yielded place to dictatorship, the alienation between the two became more permanent. Even though the Awami League was formed in 1949, East Pakistan also failed to produce any leader of stature save Maulana Bhashani, and later Sheikh Mujibur Rahman, a protégé of Suhrawardy. The rapid succession of leaders in Pakistan following the death of Mohammed Ali Jinnah is noteworthy: Nawabzada Liaquat Ali Khan assassinated in

1951; Khwaja Nazimkuddin Khan (1951-53) dismissed; two Mohammed Alis, Suhrawardy (1956) and then came Chundrigar in 1957 for 55 days. The last in the line of civilian leaders was Malik Feroze Khan Noon (1957 to Oct 1958) a quiet, polished, well read, and accomplished gentleman. In what was to become a new breed of military rulers, he was thrown out of office in 1958 by Mohammed Ayub Khan, a general with good tastes in wine and women, and links with the infamous Christine Keeler. Nepotism and corruption took roots in the polity of Pakistan till one day, on 29 March 1969, the General abdicated in favour of General Yahya Khan. It was during this leader's tenure that the scene for "Bangladesh" was set.

Ever since the day in 1948, when Jinnah visited the Dacca University to impose Urdu as the lingua franca of Pakistan and was heckled, it was clear that in East Pakistan, resentment to the superior attitude and chauvinism of the military rulers of West Pakistan was building. Yet despite pestilence, floods and a series of Governors who adroitly ruled East Pakistan, the people there weathered the storms. Intrigues by rulers were supported by the famous anti-Indian American, John Foster Dulles, who acclaimed Pakistan as the bulwark of freedom in Asia. The feelings of East Pakistanis were well summed up by a right-wing leader in the Constituent Assembly when he said: "The attitude of the Muslim League was of contempt towards East Bengal, towards its culture, its language, its literature and everything concerning East Bengal. In fact, far from considering East Bengal as an equal partner, the leaders of the Muslim League thought that we were a subject race and they belonged to a race of conquerors." (Quoted in Keith Callard, Pakistan — A Political Study, London).

The 78 million Bengalis are different in language, culture and even diets from the 58 million West Pakistanis. The westerners are all light skinned, rugged and generally healthy and hardened, inhabiting a large expanse of arid land, while the easterners are small, dark skinned, soft natured people with a lush tropical and richer land. Yet more resources were allocated to the West than to the East, and here lay the chasm designed by the British, and accepted by the people of the subcontinent in their quest for freedom. It had to come to a divide one day.

The elections of 7 December 1970 though peaceful, brought about a sea-change in East Pakistan. Dacca's Pakistan Observer commented: "We made it, we did it. The era of people's rule has begun. We are entering from darkness into light." It appeared as if the Bengalis despite their chasm had reached their goal. For having a fair election, the hatred against the West subsided. However, this happy and hopeful atmosphere soon faded. President Yahya Khan, on the horns of a dilemma, twice delayed convening the National Assembly, and it ended as a mere meeting in March 1971.

By coincidence, on 30 January 1971, two young Kashmiris hijacked an Indian Airlines Fokker Friendship plane from Srinagar to Lahore and blew it up there. India remonstrated against Pakistan's complicity and stopped all Pakistani overflights. Thus at a time when free movement was essential to the two Pakistans, a sense of isolation was created, which was termed an Indian plot.

The situation in East Pakistan was deteriorating fast. Rear Admiral S.M. Ahsan (who became CNS after the 1971 war), the Governor Rao Farman Ali, and Lt Gen Sahabzada M. Yaqub Khan recommended a political solution, but Gen Yahya Khan, impelled by Zulfikar Ali Bhutto, clamped down reprisals on 25 March 1971, with murder and rape in Op Searchlight.

Mujibur Rahman under trial in 1968 in West Pakistan, for his role in the famous Agartala conspiracy case, had returned to East Pakistan as a hero. Now, the most popular champion of the people's aspirations was being denied his right to be the leader of Pakistan, and was jailed.

The Press Notes issued by the Martial Law Administrator on 19 August and on 28 September 1971 on Sheikh Mujibur Rahman's trial are telling, and Kevin Rafferty's report in the Financial Times, London, dated 12 October 1971 summed up the situation Excerpt from The Dawn, Karachi 29 September 1971: "A Special Military Court was convened by the Chief Martial Law Administrator to try Sheikh Mujibur Rahman in camera for waging war against Pakistan and other charges. The trial commenced on August 11, 1971. The prosecution has so far examined 20 witnesses in support of the charges. The trial is in progress with Mr A.K. Brohi as the defence counsel. The public will be informed of further progress of the case in due course of time. Meanwhile people should in their own interest refrain from saying or doing anything which may constitute a contempt of court or a breach of secrecy of the trial proceedings, or which may tend to prejudice the case of either the defence or the prosecution."

Mrs Gandhi appealed to heads of state throughout the world, asking them to solve the problem of millions of refugees to India and the turbulence in East Bengal, essentially of Pakistan's making. She asked the USA to stop arms aid to Pakistan. Failing to elicit an appropriate response, and on learning that Henry Kissinger secretly visited Peking via Rawalpindi in early July to arrange Nixon's visit to China, Mrs Gandhi suspected that a Washington-Islamabad- Peking alliance was in the offing. She lost no time in signing on 9 August 1971, the 20-year treaty with Moscow which proposed steps for co-operation, peace and collaboration. Clause 9 reads as follows and is a far cry from the non-alignment India professed: "In the event of an attack or a threat thereof, the two (India and USSR) would immediately enter into mutual consultations in order to remove such threat and to take appropriate effective measures to ensure the peace and security of their countries."

Mrs Gandhi's Diplomatic Campaign

After Mrs. Gandhi's talks with President Nixon in Washington on 4 November, the White House stated that the President supported the withdrawal of troops from the frontiers by both sides. At dinner Mrs. Gandhi graphically depicted the magnitude of the refugee problem thus: "Imagine the entire population of Michigan State suddenly converging on New York State, and imagine the strain it would cause on the Administration and on services such as health and communications and on resources like food and money — this not in conditions of affluence, but in a country already battling with problems of poverty and huge population ... From those who value democratic principles, we expect understanding and a certain measure of support ... Our people cannot understand how those who are victims and who are bearing a burden and have restrained themselves with such fortitude, should be equated with those whose actions has caused the tragedy."

Mrs. Gandhi paid a visit to Paris between 7-10 November, during which she had talks with President Pompidou and the French Premier, M. Chaban-Delmas. She also received M. Andre Malraux, the distinguished novelist and former Minister of Cultural Affairs, who offered to serve with the Mukti Bahini. M. Malraux served with the Republican Air Force in the Spanish Civil War and commanded the Resistance in Alsace-Lorraine during the Second World War.

In a television interview abroad on 8 November, Mrs. Gandhi said that she was prepared to meet President Yahya Khan to discuss all the problems, but that East Bengal was "not a problem between India and Pakistan but between West Pakistan and the Bengalis. It is perhaps inevitable today that Bangladesh should become independent," she added, "but I do not think that East Bengal would wish to be associated with West Bengal, as the latter is industrialized and would be the dominant partner."

Mrs. Gandhi visited Bonn between 10-13 November for talks with Herr Brandt, the West German Chancellor, who was convinced that "a political solution of the problem of East Pakistan must be found that will eliminate the existing situation of strife and ultimately enable the refugees to return home." The Federal Government would contribute DM 50 million towards the relief of the refugees.

Mrs. Gandhi on 12 November said that the Indian Government had to give the Mukti Bahini a "minimum of aid" because the Indian people, especially in West Bengal, demanded this, and because it could not prevent them from using Indian territory for recruitment and training, as the frontier was too long for effective control.

Mrs. Gandhi told Parliament on 15 November that international opinion had shifted from a "tragic indifference" to a growing sense of urgency in seeking a political solution to the Bangladesh issue. She had been told of the U.S. decision to stop all further arms shipments to Pakistan but learnt that arms were not being supplied from British, French or West German sources.

Outwardly in Dacca, Bhutto had referred to Mujib as the future Prime Minister of Pakistan, but when autonomy was demanded by the East Pakistanis, Bhutto sided with the generals to suppress the East and buy time for a West Pakistani coalition government. He played a double-dealing game with his generals, siding one and befriending the other for which later he paid with his life.

Bhutto also visited Peking from 5 to 8 November for with a delegation, including Mr. S.M. Khan (Foreign Secretary), Air Marshal A. Rahim Khan (C-in-C of the Air Force), Lieut-General Gul Hassan (Army Chief of Staff) and Rear Admiral Rashid Ahmed, for talks with Chou En-Lai. Much importance is attached to this visit in the final escalation of attack by the Pakistan Air Force on Indian airfields. There appears to have been an understanding that

China would give diplomatic support in the United Nations to the quelling of the uprising in East Bengal, and to supply arms and even intervene in the event of war. This has now been revealed by Henry Kissinger. The non-compliance of the Chinese, when the crunch came, is attributed to a misunderstanding, fear of USSR, and doubt on the part of the Chinese. It could also have been that Bhutto misrepresented the facts to his military leaders.

India could not rule out an attack from the north. Gen Manekshaw and Gen Aurora were prepared for it. They had recommended to the Defence Minister that December would be the time for any action in Bangladesh, as at the height of winter, snow would begin to fall, preventing the Chinese from any large- scale activity. A Press Trust of India story datelined 13 August 1985 is reproduced, "At a banquet in honour of the Pakistan delegation, the Chinese acting Foreign Minister, Mr. Chi Peng-fei, said, 'The Indian Government has crudely interfered in Pakistan's internal affairs and carried out subversive activities and military threats against Pakistan by continuing to exploit the East Pakistan question, which is the internal affair of Pakistani people themselves. It is absolutely unpermissible for any foreign country to carry out interference and subversion under any pretexts'."

On 2 December, Yahya Khan in a letter to Nixon, formally invoked Article 1 of the Pakistan–US bilateral Agreement of 5 March 1959 for direct military assistance from the US against Indian aggression. He also requested for a strong statement condemning Indian aggression, calling an immediate end to hostilities, and withdrawal of forces from the border; and another statement, urging the Soviet Union to stop military support to India.

At 1.20 p.m. on 3 December in Rawalpindi, the COS informed the Commander Eastern command: 'Total war imminent. Redeploy force in accordance operational tasks. Consider areas of tactical strategic and political importance.' The President dictated a brief statement and directed it to be broadcast immediately.

Pakistan's Defence Adviser and Foreign Secretary heard the news on the radio, and frantically tried to confirm it from each other and staff, and then called a meeting of the emergency committee. They obtained the Presidential orders to enforce the war stage plans, and decided on a blackout throughout West Pakistan. Yahya Khan asked the Foreign Secretary to bring the Chinese and US Ambassadors separately to the President's House for a briefing by him.

The Pakistan Air Force commenced attacks on Indian airbases at 5.20 p.m. The pre-emptive strike assumed that the Indian planes were on the forward bases and parked in the open. Zaheer called this 'a drastic breakdown of Pakistan intelligence' and the attempts were so clumsy that not one Indian plane was lost on the ground, depicting India's preparedness for war. The PAF did not make any claims and the strike was termed simply a defensive move aimed at preventing the IAF using forward bases The course of the war showed that it did not achieve even this modest aim.

During the night of 3 and 4 December, Pakistan army formations launched limited offensive operations; some ground was gained. The primary aim of these formations was to draw the Indian reserves into the open. Yahya Khan sent an urgent message to the Shah of Iran requesting 'gracious consideration' of the urgent need for gunboats and missile carrying helicopters.

Late Brigadier Siddiq Salik, an officer in the Pakistan army's public relations directorate at the time, wrote an excellent account of events in Dacca after the 1970 elections, titled 'Witness to Surrender'. In that book, he cites a comment that sums up the attitude of the army in East Pakistan. According to Salik, the General Officer Commanding, Major General Khadim, within the hearing of fellow officers said: "I will muster all I can – tanks, artillery and machine guns - to kill all the traitors and, if necessary, raze Dacca to the ground. There will be no one to rule; there will be nothing to rule."

The military cracked down on the politicians and the people they led. Operation Searchlight began on the night of 25 March 1971, and its basis for planning clearly stated: "AL (Awami League) action and reactions to be treated as rebellion, and those who support (the League) or defy ML (Martial Law) action be dealt with as hostile elements. AL has widespread support even amongst EP (East Pakistan) elements in the Army." Troops moved with full force against Awami League support.

It has come to light that on 13 December, then Sqn Ldr Vinod Nebb (VrC and Bar) took off from Hashimara in a MiG-21 escorting Hunters when he saw a blackish Otter flying to Dhaka. The PAF had been decimated, so he wondered if it was a UN or foreign or friendly plane that was cleared. Any attack that he could have easily carried out would have killed all in the Otter. He inquired of traffic from Hashimara control but no one seem to know, except that Wing Cdr Chandan Singh used to fly an Otter with the Mukti Bahini, flying low. Nebb let the Otter alone. Only when he landed did he learn that Gen AAK Niazi used to fly low in an Otter and land on roads cleared by the troops on visits. Nebb claims if he had got Niazi, the war may have ended earlier. In love and war, all is fair and luck plays a part.

It was not Niazi's only lucky day. Gen Niazi received Gen JS Arora GOC-in-C Eastern Army Command for the surrender on 16 December and both drove to the Race Course for the ceremony.

En route people were trying to get at Niazi. Gen Arora says he shouted,"Jai Bangla", and people went delirious, and so he kept Niazi safe and flew him to Calcutta and debriefed him there. Niazi has commented on how his last week was miserable.

Ranjit B. Rai, Joseph P. Chacko

The Reality of the Pakistani Navy in 1971 from 'Bubbles of Water'

1971 started off pleasantly enough, but as the year rolled on it started having the makings of a grand tragedy that finally descended on the country at the end of the year. It turned out to be the most traumatic period for the whole nation. The eastern half of the country was lost and in the Navy, ships and lives were lost at sea and elsewhere. The Pakistan Navy had been left unprepared for the war of the missile age. That was the reality. What unfolded was a major loss of morale at the national level and within the Navy as well.

But even in this grim period, there have been incidents of human drama, of personal valour, even of humor, that have shone through the darkness at that time. A lovely human interest story relates how Lt Cdr SQ Raza was on duty in the Maritime HQ at Karachi in the thick of the 1965 war. He asked Cmde Rauf for four hours leave in the afternoon. When he came back he was a married man, and spent his honeymoon night on duty in MHQ. On the Indian side in 1971, Lt Cdrs Gigi Gupta and Mike Bhide, a fine criketer who had safely ditched a plane too, flew off the INS Vikrant to Bangalore, got married overnight – to two sisters, and hastened back the next day!

Col. Riaz Jafri (Retd) wrote in 2007: "In early July 1970 I was posted to East Pakistan as the Principal Staff Officer (GSO-1) to late Major General Rao Farman Ali Khan – in charge Martial Law (Civil Affairs) and saw events unfold from the vantage point of the Governor House, Dacca – epicenter of the entire activity in East Pakistan. With events of the past too, buried in files which popped up at random in my official work, all these presented me with a clear picture of all that was happening there and why ... They had spread the troops in a thin line all along the border, weakening themselves all over. There was no depth, no reserves, nor second lines. There was enemy

(Indians) in the front, and enemy at the back (Muktis).They never realised that it was not the territory, but the capital of the country that mattered. It had to be the Warsaw, the Paris, the Moscow, the Berlin and in our case Dacca, without which, unless captured by the enemy, the country would not fall. If only they had concentrated all the troops in Dacca, made a fortress out of it and fought there for months, which they could do, the East Pakistan story would have been different. We still wouldn't have been able to avert the creation of Bangladesh, but it would have come into being by the intervention of the world powers, and probably the UNO itself. Pakistan would not have had to suffer the ignominy of a defeat."

More recently, Pakistan has released parts of the Hamoodur Rehman report. UNI reported: Former chief of army staff, General Tikka Khan, has stated that the reason why he withheld the publication of the Hamoodur Rehman Commission Report on the disintegration of East Pakistan was because it contained a top secret plan of the Pakistan Army. However, after certain modifications had been made in the report, he gave clearance for its publication. Even today there is controversy over Mr. Bhutto's role during the 1970 elections, when it is believed he had opposed transfer of power to Sheikh Mujibur Rehman after Mujib's party emerged as the majority party in the erstwhile East Pakistan, for which the military hanged Bhutto.

The Ominous Signs of an Unavoidable War

Operations in the Eastern Indian theatre were closely guarded. The personnel involved were tight-lipped. Army moves towards the east, induction of Bengali naval officers and sailors into Calcutta, planned by DNI Cmde M.K.Roy (later Vice Admiral) and put under Cdr M.N. Samant for covert operations, and Capt R.P.Khanna NOIC Calcutta for administration, are legend. Reports of naval divers cohorting with Mukti Bahini forces did appear sporadically in the Press, but details were never divulged. The stories of Lt Cdrs J.K. Choudhry and Ashok Roy (in another chapter) are illustrative. A number of naval divers from Command Clearance Diving Teams were transferred to Calcutta. Lt Cdr Sajjan Kumar, a pious clearance diver must have served many a daring mission along with his UK- trained colleagues, Lt Cdr G.C. Martis, B.C. Mahapatra, MCPO-II and Leading C. Singh, MVC, who were decorated for heroic action. There will be a number of others whose praises can only be sung when the official records are released, if any were kept.

War fever in Pakistan

Arnold Zeatling, Lahore A.P. Correspondent, on 15 October 1971 reported, "With war fever mounting along the West Pakistan border with India, businessmen of Lahore are sending away their families or making plans to do so. Bank officials say many people are withdrawing their money or transferring their accounts to other cities. Peasant families are leaving their homes near the border. Motorists are decorating their cars with signs saying 'Crush India'."

Sydney Schanberg, New York Times, reported, "The armies of India and Pakistan are now confronting each other along their borders. Most Western diplomats here in New Delhi are inclined to believe that West Pakistani troops moved up first and that the Indians moved in response. According to high Indian sources, the build-up in West Pakistan began last month, and by last Thursday virtually all Infantry and Armoured Divisions in West Pakistan were at, or within, striking distance of the border. Some border area canals have been flooded as barriers, and Pakistani civilians have evacuated several border areas, some on orders from the army and others on their own, out of panic, sources say. Some of the heaviest troop concentrations are reported to be at points where the Pakistanis crossed the Indian border in the three-week war over Kashmir in 1965. The border areas in East Pakistan, where it is believed there are four or five Divisions, have also reportedly been strengthened. The Indians are also said to have four or five Divisions along their side of the border. President Agha Mohammed Yahya Khan of Pakistan has charged that the Indians have eight Divisions there."

At a news conference, Prime Minister Indira Gandhi was asked about urgings of the Great Powers for restraint. "It seems very simple and plausible to say Pakistani troops will withdraw," she said. "But Pakistan has been escalating the situation by putting troops all along the border, by their hate-India campaign, and by their call for Jihad (holy war). This is not a one-sided matter. You cannot shake hands with a clenched fist. As you know, everybody admires our restraint. We get verbal praise and the others who are not restrained — get arms support."

This alluded to the continuation of arms shipment to Pakistan by the US under Nixon's direction (see Tilt and Blood Telegram).

Prelude to a War

The Indian armed forces were certainly worked up. The Navy assessed threats to shipping, opened a dialogue with ship-owners, beefed up intelligence. The Fleets - the Western and the newly formed Eastern Fleet - spent more time on sea maneuvers and worked up the newly acquired missile boats in Practice Missile Firings (PMFs). One missile boat was allocated to the Western fleet to ensure it could attack Karachi if ordered, foraying the Saurashtra coast and calling at Okha whenever feasible. These were also the fateful days when the fleet practiced anti-submarine warfare, the biggest challenge that faces any fleet. Lt V.K. Jain, a bright electrical officer was permitted to research and experiment on INS Khukri's sonars, to enhance sonar detection. Surely the Indian Navy respected the strength in under-sea warfare of the Pakistan Navy through their newly acquired Daphnes and the PNS Ghazi (Defender of the Faith). The Pakistan Navy was equally aware of the Indian Navy's fire and missile power and the range of the 'F' class ex-USSR submarines. It depended a lot on its own submarines to foray forward, whilst its ships planned holding a defensive posture nearer home. Attention was paid to command and control aspects. Tactics were accordingly evolved. (The author used the Pakistan Navy's strategy in Exercise Brasstacks).

The arguments, professional in nature which crop up between a Fleet Commander (Chandy Kuruvilla) and his boss ashore (Kohli) is a common feature in all naval engagements before final plans are made. It centered round the control of missile boats and got resolved. Interestingly, even in the Falklands war, the arguments between Admiral Fieldhouse (Commander-in-Chief Fleet) and Admiral Sir Leach (First Sea Lord) as far as control of the Fleet was concerned, had to be resolved at Margaret Thatcher's level. The First Sea Lord was thereafter kept out of the day-to-day operations. Such is the nature of war's nitty-gritty. Many false alarms were raised. Ships at sea reported submarine contacts, and false starts to skirmishes kept everyone in operations rooms on tenterhooks. Submarine crews loaded and unloaded torpedoes and carried out war patrols, when not offering anti-submarine warfare practice to ships of the Fleet.

On the Eastern sea-board, the newly formed Fleet on 16 October 1971 was also getting into gear for any eventuality. The aircraft carrier Vikrant (sold in April 2014 as scrap for Rs 60 crores) was handed over to the East. The reasons for doing so will ever be debated. With boiler trouble, her speed was restricted. Since nothing succeeds like success and the only enemy submarine in the East, the Ghazi, sank too early to cause any damage, the decision has always, in retrospect, been deemed as correct. The Vikrant embarked pilots from all over and worked up the Tigers (300 Seahawk squadron) and the Cobras (310 Alize squadron). As Vizag harbour could not accept the Vikrant, the ship perforce had to operate between Madras and deep-water ports off the Andaman Islands. Her movements were classified but she was seen in Madras in August/ September, since every year during the monsoons, Madras was her habitat. That year was no different but the swords on board were sharper. The ports of Port Blair and Port Cornwallis which offer excellent and deep water for a big ship like the Vikrant saw the ship take respite between flying operations. A letter from Lt Cdr Ashok Sinha, a Seahawk pilot indicated how he was rushed from the Andamans to the carrier for operational duty. He was finding his tour of duty in the Andamans a trifle boring. In a lighter vein, he confides, "It was Yahya Khan who got me transferred out of Port Blair and on to the flat-top and I can't thank him enough."

The Times of India had the following headline on 11 November 1971: "Border Situation Still Grave — Pindi Provocation Continues" and another sideline on the front page: "Vital Steps After PM's Return". The newspaper reported: "With Pakistani troops attempting to intrude into Jammu and Kashmir and their guns continuing to shell posts of Tripura and West Bengal, the situation on Indian borders continues to be grave. Indian troops had instructions not to cross the border and have not done so. For long, Pakistan has been describing the Mukti Bahini as Indian agents. Now they have gone a step further. They are describing the forces of the Mukti Bahini as Indian battalions. The report that a submarine had been sighted near Kanyakumari was without basis, he said. (Surprisingly though in retrospect, this could have been the PNS Ghazi in transit.) On the subject of vital steps, the first question to be decided by the Political Affairs Committee of the Cabinet on Mrs Gandhi's return from abroad is whether a state of emergency should be declared in view of the grave situation on the Eastern border and the increasing intrusions into Jammu and Kashmir. The Defence Minister Mr Jagjivan Ram also toured the Rajasthan border. Emergency was declared in Pakistan on 23 November 1971.

Was this pre-war period an undeclared war? The editorial in the Nepal Times on 30 November 1971 sums up the situation: "Aerial shooting of Sabres and tank battles fought by the armies of India and Pakistan have confirmed widespread fears that war is now imminent in the Indian sub-continent. The world now realizes how close the two countries are to war. The military rulers of Pakistan have even said that "undeclared war" is going on between the two countries and accordingly proclaimed a state of emergency throughout that country." As Gen Reinhard Gehlen of the German Intelligence, by gleaning media reports intelligently, could predict the happenings of World War II to Hitler, a discerning professional could do likewise by reading the samples quoted above and below:

President Yahya Khan's BBC interview: "If fighting continues along the border between East Pakistan and India, it may lead to war. I cannot just tell my Army to stop it and take it. For the defence of the country, I will not turn the other cheek. I will hit back." Pakistan Times, Lahore, 2 August 1971.

Z.A. Bhutto, Chairman PPP: "PPP would extend whole hearted co-operation to crush the Indian aggression". —Pakistan Times, Lahore, 24 September 1971.

Lt. Gen. Bakhtiar Rana:"India, in spite of her military superiority, can never defeat Pakistan. If we remain united, India will get another crushing defeat."—Imroze, Lahore, 24 September 1971 President Yahya Khan: "I have no reason to tell you war is not imminent because it is ...If the Indians escalate with a view to capturing territory and installing a puppet Bangladesh regime, that will be war." - Newsweek magazine, 8 November 1971. In his talk to troops in Sialkot: "If a war is thrust on us, in spite of our best efforts to avoid it, the valiant armed forces of Pakistan, who repose their trust in the strength of their faith and the help of Allah more than anything else, will defend every inch of their sacred soil and crush the aggressor." Morning News, Karachi, 13 November 1971, President Yahya Khan: "In ten days, I might not be here in Rawalpindi. I will be fighting a war." —AP, 25 November 1971.

The Indian Armed Forces could clearly read war in all these utterances and got prepared without much goading from higher quarters. Naval Headquarters also did their homework earnestly. Understanding between the Service Chiefs, General S.H.F. Manekshaw (later Field Marshal), the late Air Chief Marshal P.C. Lal and the late Admiral S.M. Nanda improved (though Lal did resent Manekshaw's overbearing ways and denied him becoming CDS). Their co-operation was to witness heights of glory. The Defence Ministry also shed some of its bureaucratic ways, and financial powers were delegated to the Services, as a one-time measure. All these measures were to pay rich dividends in December. This was the time to sharpen one's sword, oil the barrel, warm the bell, sponge out the gun and be ready for war.

CHAPTER 9
THE WAR DIARY 1971

Slowly but surely came the call: The sudden war surprised us all; Hard was the trial, but why complain We trust to do it, if called again, Many gallant lives came to an end
They died, as they lived, as everyone's friend; But for the dead parting came suddenly
One was never able to say good bye.
—Dedicated to those who gave up their lives on both sides.

Indian and Pakistani forces clashed on the East Pakistan border since 21 November. Mrs Gandhi let the Armed Forces be aggressive, hoping Pakistan would open the war. She issued orders to be ready for war on 4 December, which were possibly leaked by her Security Adviser RN Kao to Pakistan. War began on 3 December, when the Pakistan Air Force made surprise attacks on Indian targets. This chapter is a brief description of the 14-day war which ended with the Pakistani forces surrendering in the East on 16 December with historical and geographical repercussions. The unilateral cease-fire by India and its acceptance by Pakistan's Yahya Khan and the reasons for India's success are discussed in later chapters.

On the Pakistani side, the Hamoodur Rahman Report, ordered by the government of Pakistan after the war, which analysed the Pakistani defeat has this to say, 'Due to corruption... lust for wine and women and greed for land and houses, a large number of senior army officers, particularly those occupying the highest positions, had not only lost the will to fight but also the professional competence necessary for taking the vital and critical decisions demanded of them for the successful conduct of the war.'

Much bloodshed could have been avoided if Pakistan had made genuine efforts to arrive at a political solution in its Eastern wing.

The war is a pointer for India and Pakistan to seek closer ties to avoid another 1971; as the next time it could be nuclear.

The Build-up

October 15-21 – Pakistani troops intermittently shelled Indian villages in Hilli and Radhikpur with Border Security Force (BSF) returning fire. Mines planted by Pakistani saboteurs were uncovered near Agartala. One Sub Inspector killed in mine explosion. Pakistani troops open fire in Shikarpur in Nadia district, Barman-Para border in Garo Hill. Four killed at Kamalpur. Two bogies of train derailed between Karimganj and Dharmnagar. Pakistani saboteurs damage a bridge south-east of Belonia.

October 23-26 - Pakistani saboteurs destroyed a bridge on the Agartala-Simla road, a vital link to the northern part of the state with 5 killed and 25 injured in heavy Pakistani shelling on Agartala and Kamalpur and some villages in Karimganj and Talai Bazaar. Two PAF Sabre-jets violated Indian air-space over Agartala.

October 29 – November 8 - Kamalpur shelled by Pak troops causing casualties and destroying buildings. Dalgaon border village looted by 100 Razakars. Pak saboteurs burn to death 4 refugees in a refugee camp near Shillong and damage bridges in Tripura, Meghalaya and Cachar. BSF recovered 6 kg explosives in Srinagar.

Indian troops returned provocative Pak firing, and only 'hot chased' the Pakistan Army back. A briefing: "Indian artillery based in defensive emplacements within the Indian territory knocked out Pakistani guns. Our Army has strict orders not to cross the border."

November 12-23 - Pakistan fired 60 mm mortar bombs

near Agartala and a battalion overran the Shikarpur Nadia border outpost but was repulsed by BSF and Indian troops. Provocative acts by Pakistani troops in Tripura, Meghalaya, Assam and West Bengal with shelling of Bakshinagar in Tripura, killing or wounding 75 refugees. Eight Indians killed in unprovoked shelling of Karimganj.

November 22 - 4 IAF Gnats shot down 3 Sabres trying to strafe army units in Boyra, north-east of Calcutta over the Boyra area. Flying Officer Khalil Ahmed, brother of Aziz Ahmed Khan, ejected. The other pilot, shot down by Donald Lazarus, was Flt Lt Parveez Mehdi Qureshi, later Chief of Air Staff Pakistan. Major H. S.Panag rescued them from being thrashed by men of 4 Sikh.

November 23 to 30 - First tank battle. Pakistan mounted a heavy artillery and tank attack on a liberated Boyra area. Indian troops threw back the attack destroying 13 Pakistani Chaffee tanks. A battle for Hilli.

December 2 - Pakistani Air Force Sabres strafed Agartala and shelled the town.

3 December (Friday) — The First Day

Dawn broke on 3 December with high tension in the air. That evening Pakistani Air Force (PAF) fighters struck at seven major air fields—Srinagar, Avantipur (Kashmir), Amritsar, Pathankot, Ambala (Punjab) Barmer and Jodhpur (Rajasthan)—between 1740 and 1810, hoping to cripple the Indian Air Force. The Indian aircraft had been dispersed, and only a little damage was caused. At 1830 hours the Pakistani armoured forces and infantry crossed the cease- fire line in Kashmir in the Poonch sector and heavily shelled 11 border posts in Kashmir and Punjab. As Keesing's Archives puts it, Pakistan had four aims: (1) to reduce the pressure on the forces in East Pakistan by creating a diversion in the West; (2) to occupy territories in Kashmir and Rajasthan; (3) to bargain terms of settlement in the East; and (4) to secure intervention of the great powers or the UN.

The timing of the attack is attributed to the following factors:

— Bombing operations on 3 December would be facilitated by a full moon, and surprise India.
—Attack by Muslims on Friday, their holy rest day, would surprise India.
—If operations in Kashmir were delayed, snow would cause hindrance.

Pakistan sought to convince the world that the Indian Army had launched an offensive between 3.30 and 4 pm, but could not prove it. As the Prime Minister, Defence Minister and Finance Minister were out of Delhi at the time, the response to the Pakistani attack took time. At 11 pm President Giri signed the proclamation of Emergency. A war telegram of sorts was released from Delhi indicating the Emergency and the three Services went into action, for the very contingency they had got ready for.

Lady Luck smiled on the Indian Navy because the majority of Eastern and Western Fleet ships were out at sea on manoeuvres on that day. Naval bases were put on alert, the war room at Naval Headquarters and Maritime Operation rooms at Bombay (where the author kept night watches), Cochin, Visakhapatnam, Okha, Madras and Calcutta were activated with Commanders and their staffs in attendance. Defensive measures against pre-emptive underwater attacks, control of merchant shipping, and dowsing of navigational lights were promptly ordered.

The nation was glued to the radio sets for the announcement that Mrs Gandhi made just after midnight:

"I speak to you at a moment of grave peril to our country and to our people. Some hours ago, after 5.30 p.m. on December 3, Pakistan launched a full-scale war against us. The Pakistan Air Force suddenly struck at our airfields in Amritsar, Pathankot, Srinagar, Uttarlai, Jodhpur, Ambala and Agra. Their ground forces are shelling our defence positions in Sulaimanki, Khem Karan, Poonch and other sectors.

Since last March, we have borne the heaviest burden and withstood the greatest pressure, in a tremendous effort to urge the world to help in bringing about a peaceful solution and preventing the annihilation of an entire people, whose only crime was to vote for democracy. But the world ignored the basic causes and concerned itself only with certain repercussions.

The situation was bound to deteriorate and the courageous band of freedom-fighters have been staking their all in defence of the values for which we also have struggled, and which are basic to our way of life. Today, the war in Bangladesh has become a war on India. This has imposed upon me, my Government and the people of India a great responsibility. We have no other option but to put our country on a war footing. Our brave officers and Jawans are at their post mobilized for the defence of the country. An Emergency has been declared for the whole of India. Every necessary step is being taken, and we are prepared for all eventualities.

I have no doubt that it is the united will of our people that the wanton and unprovoked aggression should be decisively and finally repelled. In this resolve, the Government is assured of the full and unflinching support of all political parties and every Indian citizen. We must be prepared for a long period of hardship and sacrifice. We are a peace-loving people. But we know that peace cannot last if we do not guard our democracy and our way of life. So today, we fight not merely for territorial integrity, but for the basic ideals which have given strength to this country, and on which alone we can progress to a better future. Aggression must be met, and the people of India will meet it with fortitude and determination and with discipline and utmost unity. Jai Hind!"

The Prime Minister spoke in a voice charged with little emotion and more grit. It made men at sea want to do their best for their country. It was reminiscent of Sir Winston Churchill's famous speech at the outbreak of World War II, when he warned the nation of ups and downs but predicted ultimate victory.

A message from Chief of Naval Staff Admiral S M Nanda at the outbreak of hostilities was clear:

"Pakistan has committed an unprovoked aggression against us and our defence services have been ordered to meet this challenge with full courage and determination. My objective is to seek and destroy Pakistani lines of communication and along with the sister services, inflict the maximum damage on the enemy war machine.
I expect all officers, sailors and civilians in the Navy to do their duty and act according to the best traditions of our great Service. No sacrifice should be too much for us. Let us write a new and glorious chapter in the history of our Service."

Civil defence measures of blackout and regulation of night traffic came into effect and India was at war with Pakistan on the Bangladesh issue, though open declaration of war was absent.
The Western Seaboard - Flag Officer Western Naval Command Vice Admiral S N Kohli. Chief of Staff Cmde PN Thapar.
The aims of the Western Fleet were clearly to deliver a blow to enemy ships and installations; to defend our own coast and shipping. The Western Fleet with the more powerful missile-fitted units saw most of its units at sea on 3 December, out for a sortie. They had exercised regularly and returned to harbour on 30 November. The line-up for

the task at sea lay on Mysore (Flag R Adm E.C. Kuruvilla, Flag Capt R.K.S. Ghandhi, Fleet Ops Officer Cdr G. Hiranandani), Trishul (F 15 Capt K.M.V. Nair), Talwar (Cdr S.S. Kumar), Khukri (F 14 Capt M.N. Mulla), Kuthar (Cdr U.C. Tripathi), Kirpan (Cdr R.R. Sood), Kiltan (Capt Gopal Rao) Katchall (Cdr K.N. Zadu) Kadmatt (Cdr S. Jain) and 8 Osa missile boats (K 25 Cdr B.B. Yadav) recently acquired from the USSR and manned by the Indian Navy with not a Russian on board. One missile boat was attached to the Fleet, and the fleet support tanker Deepak (Capt. P.C. Andrews) had to replenish the Fleet. The submarines Karanj (Cdr V.S. Shekhawat, later CNS), and Kursura (Cdr A. Auditto), were to patrol marked areas, and Karanj was at sea waiting to kill off Karachi, but with strict orders of positive identification of Pakistani warships before attacking - which hampers a submarine Commander's initiative in otherwise unrestricted warfare. Other ships and mine-sweepers in the order of battle were ready to go wherever ordered.

The Eastern Bay of Bengal Seaboard - Flag Offcier Commanding Eastern Naval Command Vice Admiral N Krishnan and Chief of Staff Cmde M.S.Grewal.

The Eastern Fleet in the Bay consisted of the Vikrant (Flag R Adm S.H. Sarma, Flag Captain S. Prakash Fleet Ops Cdr Vyas), Brahmaputra (Capt J.C. Puri), Beas (Cdr L.Ramdas), Kamorta (Capt M.P. Awati, P31), and Kavaratti (Cdr Subir Paul), nominated as the 'Strike task' group. The submarine Khanderi (Cdr R.J. Millan) formed the subsurface force and Landing Ship Tank Craft Magar (Cdr T.N. Singhal), Gharial (Lt. Cdr A.K. Sharma, and Guldar (Lt. Cdr U. Dabir) were nominated for transportation and amphibious role. The Rajput (Lt Cdr Inder Singh), Panvel (Lt Cdr J.P.A. Noronha), Pulicat (Lt S. Krishnan) and Akshay (Lt. S.D. More) were the local Defence group with Desh Deep, the light vessel for afloat support. They all received the famous flash signal from their Commander-in-Chief: "Commence Hostilities

Against Pakistan."

Commanding Officers opened sealed orders, rehearsed battle drills, briefed their command teams and gave that ultimate in Command - Float, Move and Fight your ship to near death, deliver deadly blows and retire with victory, unscathed. The arming policy was upgraded and ships companies were busy fuzing shells in magazines. This oft-taught drill, occasional in peacetime, was now conducted on the full war ammunition outfit. Many a young heart must have beat harder, as accidents can take place.

Near midnight, INS Rajput on patrol off Visakhapatnam attacked a suspect underwater disturbance with depth charges. Little later, a loud under-water explosion with a flash was reported by the Coastal Battery. Her depth-charge attack could have led to the destruction of PNS Ghazi (CO Cdr Zafar Md Khan, Lt Cdr Pervez Hameed, Lt Cdr Samshad Ahmed, 8 officers and 80 sailors), which was a demoralizing blow to Pakistan. Admiral N Krishnan used information warfare to indicate that the big carrier Vikrant was off Visakhapatnam enroute to Madras. The Ghazi, waiting for the prized carrier, fell prey to a watery grave herself (chapter 13). Was she mining the Vizag channel, did she go over a mine, or blow up by herself? Cmde Sydney Sarathy and diver Lt Cdr Sajjan Kumar confirmed it was an internal (hydrogen?) explosionas the hull burst outwards. No mines were found. On 14 August 2013, INS Sindhurakshak exploded in Mumbai Naval Dockyard. Reports are that it was a missile / torpedo explosion caused by mishandling. The Southern Seaboard - Flag Officer Southern Naval Area Rear Admiral V A Kamath, Cochin.

The Southern flotilla comprised of the Amba (Cdr V.A. Dhareshwar), Ganga (Lt Cdr S.K. Kulshrestha) and Godawari (Cdr H.D. Singh) sailed with orders to intercept Pakistani merchant ships. They patrolled off choke points. As there was no Fleet Commander at sea, the operations were independent and monitored by Rear Admiral V.A. Kamath, a strict disciplinarian who was jokingly said to open his mouth only to take a swig at his pipe.

4 December 1971 — the Second Day

The fear of outside intervention was high. India invoked the Indo-Soviet Treaty of Peace, Friendship and Co-operation which provided for consultation in the event of threatened attack. This was also good insurance against China.

The second day should have been chaotic, but India's defence forces retaliated in unison. Four IAF Hunters of the OCU under Wing Cdr Don Conquest set the Kemari oil tanks afire at Karachi. The IAF downed 33 PAF planes, attacked enemy tanks and forward positions. The Army moved east into Bangladesh. The Defence of India Bill gave wide powers to the Defence Ministry and subordinate commanders. In the Ferozepore sector, one Pak enemy brigade of IV Corps (Lt Gen Bahadur Sher) supported by air, armour and artillery attacked the Indian position near Hussainiwala but was repulsed. An attack on Chhamb by I Corps of Pakistan (Lt Gen Irshad Khan) was contained. Pakistan officially declared war and called up all servicemen and persons under 60 years. President Yahya Khan exhorted his nation to "give the hardest blow of Allah Ho Akbar to the enemy. God is with us. We are at war with a cunning cruel enemy. Our brave ones tore the enemy to pieces in the 1965 war. This time God willing, we shall strike the enemy harder than before."

In the Bay: The ferocious and rare White Tiger, painted across each flying machine, gives its name to the British Seahawk Jet Fighter Squadron INAS 300. The Cobras are the French built Alize Squadron INAS 310 flying off the Vikrant for ground and anti-submarine missions. Both were commissioned in 1960; the former by then Cdr Acharya and now led by Lt Cdr S. Gupta, and the Alizes by Cdr (O) M.K. Roy and led by late Lt Cdr Ravi Dhir. The Tigers were waiting to kill and the Cobras to bite. The early hours of 4 December saw the Vikrant scouring the seas off Cox's Bazar. The first sortie of 8 Seahawks catapulted and screamed off the deck at about 1100—destination Cox's Bazar airfield. Pilots commissioned in the UK under Tahiliani were led by Gigi Gupta, Gulab Israni, Ash Sinha, Fido Sharma and A.K. Mehra as section leaders and Mike Bhada and others. The anti-aircraft gunfire was braved and much damage done to the airfield. A hero's welcome awaited the return of the flight when the fighter controller reported all eight contacts on the radar screen. A proud C-in-C East messaged his commanders: "Cox's Bazar attacked by eight aircraft. All airfield installations destroyed. Air Traffic Control on fire. Power house and wireless station severely damaged. Fuel dump ablaze."

The Seahawks went screaming away again to wreck the well- fortified Chittagong airfield. Facing medium-to heavy anti-aircraft gun-fire, their results boasted of one harbour and control tower damaged, fuel dump set ablaze, two gunboats immobilized, six Pakistani merchant ships attacked in outer anchorage, and two damaged heavily. Vikrant's birds returned to mother unhurt, Ramsagar's Alize hit by anti-aircraft fire was repaired quickly. The enemy made this signal: Chittagong harbour and base under heavy air attack.

With the Tigers digesting their kill, the Cobras gave no respite at night. 4 December (now Navy Day) saw the Vikrant's finest hours, the pilots and 1200 ship's crew writing history with bravery. Cdr H.M.L.Saxena (later DNO) pepped up the men. Cdr Biloo Choudhry (later ONGC Member), the tough-talking engineer, kept the engines full steam ahead, despite problems in boilers. The restricted speed later kept her away from the Western Seabord.

The escorts Brahmputra (Capt J.C.Puri) and Beas (Cdr

L.Ramdas) in company of the Vikrant (Capt S. Prakash) had their share of excitement when they attacked what they thought was a submarine. Lt. D'Silva and Sub-Lt R.K.Hukku on Brahmputra saw a periscope and 4.5" guns opened up on the contact but this was a false contact (similar to incidents in the Falklands). This submarine 'kill' was declared much later, and got mixed up in media with that of PNS Ghazi which was sunk earlier. It boosted Eastern Naval Command morale with the fliers having created havoc ashore. Eastern Naval News, January 1972, dramatised the supposed submarine action.

Vikrant picked up a submarine contact at about 1330 hrs and carried out prompt attacks with mortars. Escorts joined the deliberate attacks compelling the submarine to come up fast at a steep angle, the bow and part of the fin breaking surface in a flurry of frothy spray. She fired a couple of torpedoes which went wide. A few 4.5" shells caught on her casing. Alizes joined the fray and the sub got their depth charge with a loud flash. The submarine was seen diving—or was she dying?—never to be heard of again.

A PTI report on 4 December said, "Chittagong harbour was seen ablaze as ships and aircraft of the Eastern Naval Fleet bombed and rocketed it today. Not a single vessel could hereafter be put to sea and several direct hits were made on its headquarters complex as well as transit camps and enemy fuel tanks. The enemy was caught in a pincer movement with Cox's Bazar port also hit.

In the West: CNS Nanda hoped the Western Fleet would open the War Orders for a missile attack off Karachi. The Pakistani Fleet failed to come out, which confused Commander Chandy Kuruvilla. A civil Cessna flew some distance from the Western Fleet, which was 150 nm from Karachi. The Fleet Operations Officer felt the Fleet's position was compromised and failed to head for Karachi 3/4 night. The C-in-C West (Vice Adm S.N.

Kohli) too opened orders, anticipating his fleet being on its way to Karachi, with a missile boat, but the Fleet got sidetracked into intercepting merchant ships and began a hunt for the Pakistani Fleet. Hence Kohli set in motion the attack on Karachi by K25. The Kiltan (Cdr Gopal Rao) for Command and Control and Katchall (Cdr K.N. Zadu) were to accompany Nipat (K25 Cdr Babru Yadav, CO Lt Cdr B.N. Kavina). Nirghat (Lt Cdr I.J. Sharma) and Veer (Lt Cdr O.P. Mehta) were put on their way. Kohli kept asking whereabouts of the Fleet with Nanda anxious to hear good news, but got wireless silence. The C-in-C in the Maritime Operations Room (MOR), had fingers crossed, having let his killer dogs loose with no air cover.

These small Soviet 80-ton craft were not for attack but for close-range defence from home ports. Restrictions of range, fuel, speed and sea states were overcome by the 'Necklace' (related elsewhere) and crafty planning. The IAF Hunters on 4 December attacked Kemari oil tanks. The missile attack at night by K 25 sank PNS Khaibar (D-163) with 222 brave Pakistani shaheeds, PNS Muhafiz (M-163) with 33 shaheeds and a merchant ship. C-in-C Kohli told the press the Navy had sunk ships off Karachi and set Kemari oil tanks on fire. IAF did not report the Karachi attack by Hunters as Wing Cdr Conquest on landing was rushed to Jaisalmer to stop a tank offensive.

5/6 December — The Third Day

The battle was now fully in East Pakistan. Mukti Bahini forces moved in complete concert with the Indian Army in liberated areas and entered Balmonirghat. The Soviet Union vetoed the Security Council resolution for a cease-fire on the ground that Pakistan was the aggressor. In the West, Pakistan's major infantry attack, supported by armour at Longewala, was repulsed with IAF support. At night, 2 brigades of Pakistani troops, supported by armour, attacked Indian positions twice in the Chhamb sector, a scene of fierce fighting and tank battles. The Army advanced into the Sialkot sector, engaged in a tank battle in the Khem Karan sector and captured Chadbet in the Kutch in a pre-dawn attack.

In the Bay: The Vikrant was now mounting sortie after sortie to the west of Khulna, Mongla and Chalna. Only a white flag would save lives on ships and shore bases. The Chief of the Naval Staff made the famous signal: "Good shooting, well done. Hit hard and keep on hitting." FoC-in-C East, not to be outdone, sent a brief message to his Command, "Motto for Eastern Fleet is 'Attack, Attack, Attack'."

As the carrier pilots gained combat experience, they chose targets to keep the balance in their favour. At Mongla, they faced heavy anti-aircraft fire from guns on river banks and mounted on Pak gun-boats, two boats getting silenced. At Khulna, anti-aircraft fire spat forth from batteries and from merchant ships. On Pussur river, the port wireless station, the lifeline for Pakistan naval communications was put out of action. When the merchant ship Ondarda spat anti-aircraft fire, the Seahawks sent her down with rocket attacks. Ships making a ring at sea and precise air strikes with no loss, completed the blockade of the East. Mrs Gandhi had the confidence to recognize "Ganga Praja Tantri Bangladesh" in the Lok Sabha, adding "Our thoughts at this moment are with the father of this State (Mujibur Rahman).

On 6 December the pilots focused on Chittagong at IAF's request. The Seahawks pounded the strong bastion to send barracks and workshops up in flames. The Patenga battery of 12 to 15 anti- aircraft guns was silenced, and an armed merchant ship struck. The 'Cobras' navigated by the light of a steel mill towards the blacked-out city airport which was bombed and cratered, thus adhering to C-in-C Krishnan's "Attack, Attack, Attack."

The coordination between the three C-in-Cs had been excellent. A signal from AOC-in-C East Air Marshal

Dewan testifies to this: "Extremely happy to hear good work done by your boys. Request you search for grass landing strips in your area and render them unusable. Suggest you neutralize runways in Chittagong and Cox's Bazar area, both by bombardment and airstrikes."

In the West and South: Merchant ships were re-routed. In the South, Godavari intercepted MV Pasni. Submarine Karanj was in wait off the Pakistani coast, but no Pakistan Navy ships came out to seek battle.

How the Media Saw It: Ceylon Broadcasting: "All Pakistani international flights operating through Colombo have been suspended." PIA's commercial flights between the two wings of Pakistan via Colombo were suspended, and other flights like the Canton halt at Colombo, allowed only for refueling. Ceylon affirmed that no military hardware or personnel will be allowed to be carried by Pakistani planes touching Ceylon for refueling.

The Times of India reported on 5 December: "Pakistani aircraft intruded into Bhuj at 4.55 a.m. and dropped two bombs without causing damage. Five enemy planes dropped two bombs on Okha port at 7.30 p.m". The Okha oil tank caught fire and NOIC Cdr Khambatta's men heroically fought the oil fire.

6/7 December — The Fifth Day

Lt Col Baig commanding 25 Frontier Force surrendered at Comilla with 8 JCO's and 235 men. This was a day of political activity and a lull in naval operations. Harold Wilson, former British PM said in an interview to the Times of India that America supporting Pakistan was 'stupid and ill considered". A news item hinted that Nixon might visit Pakistan enroute to China. Thirty MPs protested outside the US Embassy in Delhi.

The Chief of Staff of the Pakistan Army told General Niazi, heading the forces in East Pakistan, that there was every hope of Chinese activity soon. A Pakistani author

Gen Fazal Muqueen Khan, writes there was no basis for this, but General Niazi in a forlorn position, kept pestering the high command. On 7 December, Jessore cantonment was occupied by the Indians as 107 Brigade withdrew towards Khulna. The rout of the Pakistan Army had begun.

Gen Khan, the Pakistani author, adds, "Lt General Niazi, who had lost the war in his mind by December 6, had by December 10 given up all hope of any help. Later when General Farman Ali had sounded Soviet, British, French and U.S. representatives in Dacca to take control of East Pakistan, General Niazi and Admiral Shariff had agreed. When Farman Ali's statement was countermanded by Yahya Khan, he requested that he be allowed to face a court martial to vindicate his honour."

East Pakistan was in collapse even with only four days of war. An interesting incident from Keesing's Archives: A UN aircraft was proceeding to Bangladesh to evacuate casualties but near the coast it came within a few miles of the Vikrant. Since this neutral flight was not made known, the Vikrant showed its anti-aircraft wrath and the aircraft flew back. The Vikrant was on the ball, but not our lines of communication with the UN. The next day the UN markings were clearly identified.

How the Media Saw It: PTI on 7 December reported the Eastern Command's Maj. Gen. J.F.R. Jacob as saying, "The Indian Army today entered Jessore airfield to clear Jessore cantonment and town. Troops made a big thrust from Bongaon Road and liberated Sirsa. Fighting was around Dinapur in the north. Operations were in progress to clear Jamalpur town to Mymensingh Sector. In the Sylhet Sector, Sunamganj town has been taken. Comilla cantonment and town has been surrounded."

A naval citation read, "Cox's Bazar was the main target on December 7. There was perfect division of labour, with White Tigers concentrating on the airfield and the Cobras preferring fuel dumps. Our pilots then headed for

Chittagong; Seahawks carried out rocketing raids at the Patenga point. Silence from the battery indicated earlier raids had done their work. That evening our fliers saw the first sign of impending Pakistani surrender. Pakistani craft off Chittagong and in Cox's Bazar were flying large white flags from their masts".

The fleet was now ideally placed for a strike on Barisal where Mukti Bahini was facing enemy troop concentration. Alizes carried out a moonlight attack though no ship movements were observed in the Tetulia, Bighai and Bishakali rivers in the Barisal area. But the Seahawks in the next wave destroyed 3 barges with troops, arms and equipment.

In the West, a UNI correspondent on 8 December wrote, "Dera Baba Nanak proved the dead-end for the Pakistanis. Retreating, they left their dead behind. In the 4-hour lightning action on 7 December, our troops drove out the enemy and now hold 60 square km of Pakistani territory. The captured arms include Chinese anti- tank guns, rifles and recoilless guns with American markings."

8/9 December — The Seventh Day

The political news of the day was disturbing. The UN General Assembly voted upon an earlier resolution for Indian and Pakistan to cease-fire immediately, and withdraw armed forces. India's stand was unambiguous, that no cease-fire could come about without a free Bangladesh to enable return of the refugees. Surprisingly, Sadat's Egypt and Bandaranaike's Ceylon voted with USA and China. Britain and France displayed some conscience by abstaining. Ceylon voted pro-Pak on the plea that the Tamil minority could pose a similar danger to Sri Lanka's territorial integrity; their premonitions came about with Indian involvement (see Op Pawan).

The Army's advance at high tempo ensured the liberation of Comilla, Bramanbaria, Chandpur and

Dandkandi. A bridge-head on Meghna river was established with heli borne crossing (see map on back flap). In the western Chhamb sector, Pakistanis mounted a fierce attack with an additional brigade, supported by armour and air cover. Indian troops just about held their ground. The western bank of Munawar Tawi was occupied, the Sialkot front advanced, Naushera raided, an attack in Dera Baba Nanak repulsed, and 5 posts in Kargil captured. Flight Lt Wazir Ali Khan piloting a MIG-19 was shot down and Lt Gulam Mohamed of 19th Punjab taken prisoner.

In the Bay: Air strikes showed results. The Eastern Fleet was in full command of the seas and air spaces. The PAF in the East was written off. AOC-in-C Eastern Command commented "The remains of PAF in Bangladesh are operating from Cox's Bazar and Chittagong. Army position was engaged by Sabre jets in Agartala area twice. You make runways unfit by heavy bombardment /air effort." Yet C-in-C Eastern Naval Command did co-operate with air-strikes on Chittagong and Cox's Bazar, even though better poised for a strike on Barisal's enemy troop concentrations. Such decisions underline the need for a theatre Commander. Mountbatten, a young Rear Admiral when appointed to Burma in 1943 insisted on being Supreme Allied Commander: "In an efficient planning organization on high level, there should be no doubt who is in Command of the whole show." The Combined Allied Chiefs of Staff at Quebec did agree to the designation, allowing him to inject his own ideas into all plans. In this case, the request was from Dewan, and was complied with by Krishnan. India has no CDS or even thoughts of moving to Theatre Commanders, except in Andaman & Nicobar Islands. Indian Armed Forces have 15 -commands, separately located.

Alizes went into Barisal area at moonlight but no ships were observed in Tetuha, Bighai and Bisukali rivers. A second wave of six 'Tiger' Seahawks in the Barisal, Bakarganj and Patuawali areas destroyed 3 barges laden with troops and arms, and hit Pakistani troop concentrations and gun positions. This proved Krishnan's view to decimate troop concentrations in preference to airfields.

The Defence Minister, Jagjivan Ram, with ocular proof, announced Ghazi's sinking (of 5 days earlier) on 9 December to great ovation in Parliament.

Hard-pressed Pakistani troops used riverine craft and merchant ships, disguised in neutral colours, to escape. These were the targets for the IAF and Naval Aerial Forces. The Eastern Fleet intercepted enemy merchant ships including 4 tugs and the merchant ship Baquir which tried flying a UN flag with a caption "UN Supplies for Humanitarian Relief" on her sides but carried contraband and 4 Pakistani officers and 18 soldiers. Some tugs tried to escape but 4.5" gun fired across their bows was enough to line them up towards Indian ports.

The interception of Azul Hasan Maru (actually Anwar Baksh) near the Pusur river proved most dramatic. The 7,235-ton Pakistan merchant ship carried hundreds of tall Pathan soldiers posing as labourers. Lt Cdr Raz Bazaz of INS Beas, discovering the ship's actual crew, knew his boarding party of 18 could not contain such a large number. A sentry had to shoot a Pakistani jawan who tried to attack him. Raz Bazaz went forward with a light machine gun, warning the frenzied mob to behave. But seeing their leader lead an assault, he opened up fire and the leader fell in a pool of blood just two feet from him. Courage brought Anwar Baksh to Sandheads and all crew taken prisoner: Raz Bazaz was an unsung hero who, depressed by the incident kept a low profile, not even mentioned in dispatches. Seniors felt he should have avoided the killings. Raz Bazaz left the Navy.

In the West: The second raid on Karachi was let loose. INS Trishul (F 15 Captain K.M.V. Nair) and INS Talwar

(Cdr S.S. Kumar) rendezvoused with missile boat INS Vinash (Lt Cdr Vijay Jerath) to proceed for a strike on Karachi. A UN General Assembly resolution (104 for, 11 against) called for a halt to the war, but not for simultaneous settlement of political issues. The Soviets voted No. Britain and France abstained. Indian Ambassador Samar Sen said Bangladesh had come to stay and no power on earth could undo it. Meanwhile the Times of India (9 December) wrote that the gates of Dacca had opened with the capture of Ashugang, Daudhkhandi and Chandpur on the Meghna's eastern bank. An amazing crossing in IAF helicopters. Air Marshal M.M. Engineer AOC-in-C Western Air Command noted: "Chittagong airfield and Cox's Bazar were bombed damaging airfield hangars and rail tracks. Fishing craft and small boats on the Karnapuli were seen flying white flags." The Pakistani Army counter-attacked Prigunj in the Rangpur-Dinajpur sector but was beaten back. Jessore sector was in the hands of the Indian Army.

How the Media Saw It: A PTI report from Jaipur: "Some 2,000 sq. km of Pakistani territories are in Indian hands in Barmer sector. Indian troops advanced from Gadra and Khokahrapar and now face enemy positions in Nayachor, across the border". The Indian Express, with a "And Now to Dacca" headline: "With the capture of evacuated Comilla, the biggest cantonment in Pakistani-occupied part of Bangladesh, and Brahamanbaria, an important junction north of Akhaura, the ring is closing round Dacca. Indian troops fighting with the East Bengal Battalion found Comilla evacuated. The Pakistani troops' bid is to make for Barisal and Narayanganj to effect a get-away." Fierce fighting raged in the Chhamb Sector where Pakistani troops and tanks launched a massive attack, "The Indian Air Force, active during the day in contrast to the nocturnal preference of the PAF, damaged 12 aircraft of the enemy. Indian gunners went for the PAF planes while the IAF helped blunt the tank attack in the Chhamb

Sector. Six tanks were destroyed in today's operation".

10/11 December — The Ninth Day

With Indian armed forces and Mukti Bahini in full concert, Noakhali was liberated. Jamalpur fell and 581 Pak soldiers surrendered. Hilli and Mymensingh were liberated. The Padma (Lt Cdr Roy Chaudhry), Palash (Lt Mitra) and Panvel (Lt Cdr J.P.A. Noronha) softened up Khulna for the Army advance. On the Western front fighting for Kargil and Poonch was in full swing with a counter-attack in Chhamb. The battles for Nayachor in the Barmer sector and capture of Chat Bhet were on. 18 Pak Division had fallen back in Rajasthan by 10 December. The Indian Army regained the initiative, capturing the salient at Islamgarh and three posts.

In the West: The second attack on Karachi succeeded, with the missile boat INS Vinash ably assisted by Trishul and Talwar. The Fleet was engaged in capturing Madhumati to the south when the sad news came of INS Khukri going down with 18 officers and 176 sailors off Diu.

In the Bay: US Naval Task Group 74 Force consisting of the USS Enterprise, Decateur, Parsons and LPD Tripoli was sent into the Bay of Bengal with Admiral Zumwalt unaware of this (see chapter on America's Tilt). Earlier a Royal Navy Task Force had turned away to Sri Lanka.

How the Media saw it: UPI reported Senator Frank Church remarking that Nixon was seriously considering giving arms to Pindi. Reuter ruled out diversionary Chinese moves or more concrete backing to Pakistan but it would show up "Soviet backed Indian aggression" in the UN. India's air losses were heavier than Pakistan's for the first time. Three IAF planes were lost and Lt Cdr Ashok Roy's Alize failed to return (see separate chapter). Banner headline of the Indian Express: "Enemy Thrust in West Halted". It was the fifth major attack in a row. The Times of India confirmed "Pak Troops Beaten Back in Chhamb". The capture of two gunboats put 15 Pakistani vessels totally out of action. Merchant ship Baquir was captured. Swaminathan S. Aiyar of the Times of India summed up the action of 10 December: "Indian troops put themselves in a position to launch a final assault on Dacca by crossing the Meghna river at Ashuganj. Indian troops occupied the river ports of Mongla, and Chalna in Khulna district was freed by the Mukti Bahini. In the Jessore sector, Indian troops are fighting at Lalmonihar Ghat on the Madhumati river, that guards the route to Faridpur and Goalundo Ghat. Phulpur, 22 km west of Mymensingh has been freed". The Meghna crossing by 11 helicopters was a path-breaking feat.

The tally of losses by the Indian Express: Pakistan aircraft 75, tanks 129, warships 3, gunboats 12; India aircraft 33, tanks 49.

Hilli, on West Bengal's border, was liberated after a week's ding-dong battle. Mymensingh and Jamalpur fell to Indian soldiers marching from the northeast, paving the way for a thrust south towards Dacca. The retreating Pakistani army blew up the famed Hardinge rail bridge over the Padma close to Rajshahi.

12/13 December — The Eleventh Day

In Comilla, 1000 Pak troops surrendered some attempting escape into Burma. The noose tightened on the Pak troops. On 12 December, Indian paratroopers mounted an assault on Dacca. POW camps mushroomed as over 3,000 surrendered.

Amphibious Op Beaver was a fiasco

Op Beaver in East Pakistan was to enable landing of one company 1/3 Gurkha Rifles, two companies 11 Bihar, 881 Light Battery with ASC and medical platoons under Brig SS Rai, south of Cox's Bazar to prevent escape of Pakistani stragglers. The Army Chief, as Chairman Chiefs of Staff, suggested the operation which NHQ planned for 12 December. Chief of Staff Eastern Army Command Maj Gen Jacob took charge and nominated the beach which had a bar. The Navy's biggest Landing Ship Tank (LST) INS Magar was a make-shift tanker for INS Vikrant, so 2 smaller LSTs INS Gharial (Lt Cdr Sharma) and Guldar (Lt Cdr U Daber) were nominated. A merchant ship MV Vishwa Vijay, with no toilets or cooking for 1500 jawans, transferred them to the LSTs at sea. Maj Mastana AMC slipped and drowned. With dates of landing changing, the ships arrived late on 15th. Untrained Gurkhas first landed into the deep bar, carrying heavy 85 lbs weights on their shoulders. In the rising tide, 3 drowned and 2 were saved and operations stopped till a rope was passed ashore. INS Gharial got stuck. A half hearted landing of some 170 personnel followed, luckily with no opposition, to be welcomed by the East Bengalis.

On 13 December Gen. Manekshaw's third message to Gen. Farman Ali re-emphasized the need to surrender to avoid bloodshed. President Nixon had discussions in the National Security Council to end the war. Mrs Gandhi at the Ramlila grounds hinted at USA's anti-communist desire to stand for liberty, pointing to its contrary overtures to China, and siding with Pakistan in military pacts, even as East Pakistan's voice of independence was subjugated. Gen. Farman Ali asked UN Secretary-General U Thant's help in repatriating his troops, which Gen. Yahya Khan asked to be disregarded. There was news of 5 Pak planes landing in Akyab, Burma to evacuate personnel. The Western sector saw comparative stalemate with aerial activity off Baroda and Jamnagar. Recapture of 3 posts in Kargil restored communications to Leh. Dera Baba Nanak and Poonch sectors saw sporadic firing. An attack was planned in the Pathankot-Samba sector. Indian troops had scored a victory in the Chhamb. In Jaipur, Indian troops were mopping- up after the battle for Nayachor.

In the Bay: The period 11 to 14 December was most crucial to ensure a total Eastern blockade by the Indian Navy leading to an early surrender. Intelligence of Pakistan's last-ditch stance: "Two coasters ready at Gupta crossing. A/A defences strengthened. Runway repaired. Foreign ships cleared off the harbour. Own [Pak] five merchant ships disguised. Naval personnel deployed in defensive position and integrated with fortress defence. Further mining of approaches will be carried out". Pakistan Navy, with British and Chinese mines, was being readied for defensive mining to disrupt the port of Chittagong. The C-in-C East, Krishnan informed the Fleet that senior enemy officers were planning escape to Burma by air or by hugging the coast and approaches to harbour were likely to be mined. His instructions were to put Chittagong airport out of commission; and attack ships both by air and surface units in harbour if they break out. "The enemy must be destroyed."

In response, aircraft from Vikrant pounded Chittagong, Barisal and Rajapur through 11 and 12 December. Cherinpa airfield 32 km north of Cox's Bazar was attacked. The fleet exercise of closing in for bombardment called Naval Gunfire Support (NGFS), practiced on islands like Pigeon near Karwar and Batti Malv off the Andamans, became a reality. One ship reported, "The most conspicuous landmark, the twin casuarinas, was visible. Barely five miles off the town of Cox's Bazar, in broad daylight, this was a most daring attack. The water turned a muddy brown as ships crossed the 10 fathom line. The course altered to port to bombardment course 340 degrees. The flag atop the air-traffic control tower was now visible. 'All Positions, this is GDP—we will carry out a direct bombardment', flashed the orders. A young sailor caressed every shell ready to settle an old score, when his parents had to abandon home in Dacca due to atrocities. But his ears, like everybody, were trained for the order,

"Four- five, engage." The guns belched flame, the first salvos leaving the barrels found their mark and the control tower was hit. The Mukti Bahini a few days later informed the Captain of Beas that when the tower was bombarded, a PAF officer named Miya Qasim was holding a conference and all were killed. This officer had perpetrated the most inhuman atrocities and was one of the most notorious Pakistani military tyrants in Bangladesh. Seeing warships so close with troop landings imminent, the enemy ran for dear life. A garrison left for Burma in a convoy of trucks; and the liberated town fell into the hands of freedom fighters. The following ships in Chittagong, Khulna, Chalna, Mongla and Pussur river were identified as wrecks: Pakistani naval ships—Town Class, 6 patrol boats; 3 Rajshahi class gunboats - PNS Jessore, Comilla, Sylhet; and 6 other gunboats surrendered. Pakistani merchant ships damaged included Karnaphuli (6876 GRT); Surma (5890 GRT); Al Abbas (9142 GRT); Anis Baksh (6273 GRT); Only PNS Rajshhai, with all its personnel under the creditable command of Lt Sikandar Hayat, escaped.

As the Media Saw It: The Indian Express: "The 'Operation Bangladesh' reached its climax when the battle for Dacca began. An 'adequate force' was air-dropped in and around Dacca, and foreigners evacuated. Indian troops have also launched an attack on Daulatpur cantonment in Khulna. The troops and navy are also closing in on the port of Chittagong. People were cheering as the IAF bombed the military targets and air-dropped troops. The Mukti Bahini was engaged in fierce fighting with 2,000 guerrillas operating in the city. While POWs were taken in mopping-up operations in Laksham and Chandpur, enemy troops began to get into their naval craft to escape. The Indian Navy sent many of these down to the bottom of the Bay of Bengal. Pheramara, Khaksha and Kumarkhali were liberated. The Kuthi-bari post of Rabindranath Tagore at Silaidaha and the ancestral house of revolutionary Jatindra Nath Mookerjee, are situated in the liberated areas. The Eastern Fleet continued airstrikes against Chittagong, with bombing raids at Rajapur and near Barisal, damaging military installations. Cheringa air strip, 32 km north of Cox's Bazar, was also attacked.

A PTI report on 13 December said, "Naval aircraft from INS Vikrant are creating havoc with every sortie in the coastal Bangladesh where the Pakistani military machine is still holding out. The Indian Navy holds sway over the Arabian Sea and the Bay of Bengal. Pakistan has confirmed that the Indian Navy rules the waves off its coast. It has warned all merchant ships to approach Karachi at their own risk."

15 December — The Thirteenth Day

The end was near. Lt Gen. Raina of 2 Corps was mopping up the Jessore Sector. Lt Gen. Sagat Singh of 4 Corps ruled over the Sylhet upto Meghna. Maj Gen. Dalbir Singh 9 Division had approached Khulna in strength. Brig Hardev Singh Kher with 95 Brigade had paradropped 500 troops at Tangail 61 miles north of Dacca and was to capture Lt Col Sultan Ahmed of the 31 Baluch. This was possible because the Mukti Bahini provided full support. In the Western sector, Lt Gen Tikka Khan was being restrained in the Chhamb sector and Lt Gen K.P. Candeth in Sialkot sector had gained ground. In the Rajastahn and Barmer Sector ably commanded by Lt Gen G.C. Bewoor, the Army occupied 3000 sq. miles of Pakistani territory.

In the Bay: It was Indian Navy Day - 15 December- and as ENC News puts it: The landing force was sailed from Calcutta on 12 December. The LSTs arrived at their destination late in the night of 15 December. One of the LSTs was beached and the first wave landed. More platoons in successive waves followed. Cox's Bazar was seized and the southern route was firmly and finally cut off. Pakistan's trapped soldiers had to surrender.

In the West: The Western Fleet was intact, the

blockade complete and MV Madhumati, a Pakistani merchant ship, captured. Its Captain gave intelligence that the Pakistani Naval Fleet was ailing and had remained in the vicinity of Karachi. So the Indian Fleet did not come to battle. The next day, the 14th day of the war, was the day of the surrender.

As the Media Saw It: "Dacca Army Chief Seeks Truce" was the headline of the Times of India story on 15 December: "As a token of good faith, Gen Manekshaw directed the cessation of air action over Dacca, where Gen Niazi and his forces were holding out". Voice of America said that President Yahya Khan had advised Gen Niazi to stop fighting if necessary. "Pak Troops Give up in Bangladesh" headlined the Times of India the next day: "Bangladesh was freed from the colonialist yoke of West Pakistan when its occupation forces under the command of Gen A.A.K.Niazi surrendered to the combined forces of the Mukti Bahini and the Indian Army."

The instrument of surrender was signed by Lt Gen A.A.K. Niazi, Chief of the Pakistani Army in Bangladesh, at 4.31 p.m. IST on 16 December and was accepted by Lt Gen Jagjit Singh Aurora, GO C-in-C, Eastern Command. Radio Pakistan, while making no mention of the surrender by the Pakistani forces, told its listeners that the fighting in the Eastern theatre had ended, "following an agreement between the local commanders of India and Pakistan."

Postscript: Lt. Gen. A.A.K.Niazi as a POW confessed: "I and my people have had no rest during the day and night, thanks to your Air Force. We have changed our quarters ever so often, trying to find a safe place for a little rest and sleep, so that we could carry on the fight but we have not been able to."

CHAPTER 10
AMERICA'S ANTI-INDIA PRO-PAKISTAN TILT

True friendship is a plant of slow growth and must undergo and withstand the shocks of adversity before it is entitled to the appellation. – George Washington 1783

One aspect of the Indo-Pak wars of 1965 and 1971, which will always be debated is the USA's partiality towards Pakistan - commonly termed as the 'tilt'. This is because the West treated Pakistan as an ally in CENTO and SEATO and later made Pakistan a non-NATO ally, using its strategic geography to its advantage. Ambassador Husain Haqqani in his book Magnificent Delusions (BBS Public Affairs 2013) has explained how Pakistan was aided with funds and arms, and used by America to support its war on terror in Afghanistan (2001-2013). But the leaders of Pakistan and its military played a double game hunting with the hounds (USA and ISAF) and running with the hares (Taliban and Lashkar-e- Taiba LET). The world cannot ignore Pakistan's strategic geography and its nuclear arsenal, and Pakistan army takes untoward advantage of that even today.

Discussion on what led to the 1971 war must include various aspects of the 'tilt', and the USA's role needs a full expose in this book. President Nixon, in his memoirs, writes that amidst the Watergate scandal, the most explosive event of 1971 occurred at the year-end halfway around the world from America, on the Indian subcontinent. Nixon's involvement was high but he clouds the matter by taking credit for the cease-fire. His conviction was that Mrs. Gandhi may have had designs on West Pakistan as well as on East Pakistan. He thought the arrival of TG 74 (USS Enterprise, Decatur, Parsons and

Tripoli with Marines and 25 Helicopters) in the Bay of Bengal would cause India to think twice, because it was his personal order. Of his meeting with Mrs. Gandhi on 4 November 1971 Nixon wrote: "I later learned that even as we spoke, Mrs. Gandhi knew that her generals and advisers were planning to intervene." He also called her by expletives in the recorded Nixon tapes. More recently, it transpires that Nixon indicated that the nuclear threat was suggested through the USSR.

It seems clear that Mrs. Gandhi's decision to call for a cease-fire in the West, soon after the surrender in the East by General Niazi, was in no way dictated by US Naval TG 74's arrival in the Bay, or the USA's nuclear threat if there was one. Admiral S.M. Nanda had assured Mrs. Gandhi he had issued Rules of Engagement (ROEs) and his Captain would not take on US ships but ask their Captains on board for drinks (which the US forbids on American merchant and naval ships). Russia informed India that it could no longer stall a UN Security Council resolution.

Indian naval commanders had requested for the rules of engagement if an Indian Navy submarine came up with the American task force during the war. The clear guideline was positive identification of enemy before attack, which in fact hampered the actions of Indian Navy submarines. One could not, in the 'fog of war' put it past a naval submarine captain to unleash a salvo of torpedoes, if he felt his own safety was being threatened. That is the ultimate in any rules of engagement — to attack in self-defence. Whilst Nixon had his reasons for ordering Admiral Tom Morrer, Chairman Joint Chiefs of Staff to secretly sail the US task force into the Bay of Bengal through the Singapore Straits by night, Admiral Elmo Zumwalt Jr, then Chief of Naval Operations, who was not consulted, was most unhappy. He claimed Nixon had sent the ships in 'harm's way', a term coined after Pearl Harbour. Zumwalt has elaborated on this in his book 'On Watch' in a chapter entitled "The Tilt".

Kissinger was denied an Indian visa in 1956

Henry Kissinger was Secretary of State during this turbulent period and has given his version of the 1971 war. He opened the USA's connections with China through the good offices of Pakistan. An incident in the 1950s may have caused deep personal pique to Kissinger and created a feeling of animus against Indians, which only changed much later. Late N.K. Bhojwani was Secretary of the Department of Parliamentary Affairs in 1955 when he came to know Kissinger at the Harvard Seminars, and has narrated this incident in an Indian Express March 1972 article entitled "The Tragedy of Henry Kissinger: From Image Maker to Image Breaker". Excerpts:

"Henry Kissinger was the brain, heart and soul of an annual event which he organized for several years running at Harvard University. This was the International Seminar to which he invited intellectuals from several countries in Asia and Europe. The seminar aimed at fostering understanding... of the American way of life. Kissinger organized the seminar programme with great competence and imagination. At the Harvard seminar in 1955 he suggested that I organize a seminar in India as a reunion of selected participants of previous seminars. He was of the view that India was a very important country in international affairs and needed to be understood. As the arrangements for the seminar reached an advanced stage, it became known that Asia Foundation in US had a hand in financing the seminar. This Foundation was then suspect in India as a CIA channel. The organizing committee decided to abandon the project. It was my unpleasant task to inform Kissinger that for unforeseen reasons we felt compelled to cancel the reunion. The reason for this was not mentioned (visa difficulty).

Thus we missed an opportunity of educating Kissinger in Indian affairs. He had every reason to resent this abrupt unexplained abandonment of a pet project. It is bound to have struck him as a clumsy recompense for the hospitality and cordiality extended to us by him and several other individuals and organizations in the US. The incident may not be significant in terms of political or international relations, but may have left personal resentment simmering in Kissinger and probably was the root cause of his anti-India stance".

The American Pulitzer Prize winner columnist Jack Anderson, who was to embarrass the US Administration on its foreign policy, often trained his guns on Kissinger. Admiral Zumwalt in his memoir On Watch (NYT 1976) writes that when Anderson was on a visit to India, the US Navy Yeoman Chief Petty Officer Charles Radford, stationed in Delhi at the American Embassy was his Liaison Officer. The duo struck an interesting friendship over meetings with many Indians. Anderson had grown fond of the people and the country. He assiduously followed the events of 1971 and to his luck, Yeoman Radford was then on the innermost secretarial staff of the National Security Council (NSC) in Washington, with access to the confidential discussions. Charles Radford was pro-India and unhappy with the anti-India deliberations in the Council. He leaked these and the movement of TG-74 to Anderson. Admiral Zumwalt further states that when he tried to book this errant yeoman, he was prevented from any disciplinary action for fear of disclosure. All he was allowed to do was transfer Radford to a Naval station far from Washington.

The Tilt - as Kissinger saw it

The world's largest democracies, India and USA, were at war ideologically on the future of East Pakistan in 1971. In Nixon's Memoirs (Simon and Schuster 1978), an illuminating chapter is 'The Tilt: The U.S. and the South

Asian Crisis of 1971'. A first- hand account from three of the main characters, Kissinger, Zumwalt and Patrick Moynihan, has a unique questioning flavour. This author cites these to endorse an opinion that the USA (after procrastination) starting with warm responses to Pakistan, finally fuelled and abetted Pakistan to act as it did in East Pakistan.

The White House political denizens, Nixon and Kissinger, were "marooned in homeland". The people of America seemed opposed to the Administration's "tilt". When the foreign policy of a President is questioned by the majority of his own people, it gives reason for others to doubt the honourable nature of his intentions. It was difficult to believe that the statements Kissinger makes in his book are his, so shorn are they of diplomacy.

For instance: "The gulf in perception between the White House and the rest of the government became apparent in an option paper, prepared for the July 23, Senior Review Group Meeting. It recommended that, if China intervened in an India-Pakistan war, USA should extend military assistance to India, and should co-ordinate its resources with the Soviet Union and Great Britain. Nothing more contrary to the President's foreign policy, could ever be imagined. He repeatedly stated that we should lean towards Pakistan, but every prop that was made went contrary to his instructions". This depicts the power of a US President. In later years, President George Bush Jr was to send US troops to Iraq and Afghanistan despite opposition and public opinion, which President Obama is correcting.

India identified with the misery of brutal killings and rape due to actions of the Pakistan military in East Pakistan.

Indian hearts and minds were shocked. India rose to the humanitarian cause, to redeem their brethren from the shackles of repression. Moreover, it had disastrous effects on India's economic and political structure. The refugee influx of millions of Bengalis into West Bengal was alarming. In such circumstances, to take the stand that it did, absolved India of the guilt of war, but Kissinger had a contrary opinion. He insistently interpreted the Indian strategy "as a stand for pre-eminence on the subcontinent".

USA could have enlightened Pakistan on the implications of war and restrained it by withdrawing all support, but this did not happen. Kissinger justified it thus: "The victim of attack was an ally to which we had made many explicit promises concerning precisely this contingency. Clear treaty commitments, reinforced by other undertakings, dated back to 1959... we could not ignore them."

Elsewhere: "The fact was that over the decades of our relationship with Pakistan, there had grown a complex body of communications — some verbal, some in writing, whose plain import was that USA would come to Pakistan's assistance if attacked by India."

About Indo-US relations Kissinger writes: "By 1971, our relations with India had achieved a state of exasperatedly strained cordiality, like a couple that can neither separate nor get along..." India was a nation of huge potential which USA needed to befriend, but he writes "We moreover had every incentive to maintain Pakistan's goodwill. It was our crucial link to Peking, and Pakistan was one of China's closest allies." He elaborates: "The US could not condone a brutal military repression in which thousands of civilians were killed. There was no doubt about the strong arm tactics of the Pakistan's military, but Pakistan was our sole channel to Peking." The USA was slowly but surely driving a wedge into its poor relationship with India. But the final straw was the report that in spite of contrary assurance, a Pakistani freighter sailed from New York to Karachi with military equipment. The New York Times charged the Government with breach of faith and the Washington Post on 5 July could barely contain its outrage. It lashed out at "the astonishing and shameful record... We have classic example of how the system really works: hidden from public scrutiny, administrative officials have been supplying arms to Pakistan, while plainly and persistently telling the public that such supplies were cut off." The USA can never be exonerated for such duplicity.

Democratic leaders often claim a view free from partisanship. But mortals, rarely if ever, can transcend petty prejudices. If personal opinion is to colour a decision of larger dimensions, it must stand the test of reason. Nixon had a profound distrust of Indian motives, and this stemmed from his apparent dislike for its leader. To quote Kissinger, "Nixon had no time for Mrs. Gandhi's condescending manner. Privately he scoffed at her moral pretensions... and suspected that, in the pursuit of her purposes, she had fewer scruples than he." Nixon had labeled her "a cold blooded practitioner of power politics." Bhutto on the other hand was lauded for his doings, and was thought to be "elegant, eloquent, and subtle. Bhutto was at least a representative who would compete with Indian leaders for attention." Nixon later realized, but never admitted, that he had laid his bet upon a wrong horse.

Admiral Zumwalt sees the Tilt through Naval Eyes

Some excerpts on the "tilt" from Zumwalt's book 'On Watch' throw light on the US Naval view.

"The war provided a vivid illustration of the thesis I had presented to the President in August. The United States tilted towards Pakistan, but tilt as we would, we could not affect the war's outcome. We had no 'relevant power' in that part of the world, even after we had sent Task Force 74, consisting of the nuclear carrier Enterprise and supporting ships, into the Indian Ocean as a token of our concern".

On the subject of Soviet entry and US response in the Indian Ocean he writes: "The pattern of Soviet expansion in the Indian Ocean was already clear when Henry Kissinger and I held our 6 November 1970 meeting, and we discussed its implications in some detail. On 9 November 1970 Kissinger promulgated National Security Study Memorandum 104, which called for "an assessment of possible Soviet naval threats to US interests in the Indian Ocean area and the development of friendly naval force and basing alternatives consistent with varying judgments about possible threats and interests over the 1971-1975 period." These were the beginnings of Diego Garcia.

On Pakistan specifically, Zumwalt reveals: "A little later came NSSM 118 ordering a Contingency Study on Pakistan's secession. Finally NSSM 133 required contingency planning on South Asia. This piling of study upon study resulted in a verbal mudslide. The first response of the United States to these events was to stop military assistance to Pakistan — India had not received any since the India-Pakistan war of 1965 — as one way of persuading Pakistan to make concessions in East Bengal. However, the Pakistanis were stubborn and slow to respond and India was fast getting hotter. Then, in July, Henry Kissinger astounded the world by showing up in Peking. That event was partly made possible by the good offices of Pakistan in helping review communication channels between the United States and China that two decades of disuse had all but atrophied. Indeed, Pakistan was the starting point for the last leg of Henry's secret journey."

Alluding to the actual activity in the Pentagon and White House, Zumwalt lists dates and meetings to show how unclear USA's intentions were: "The Washington Special Action Group met on India-Pakistan on 17 August, 8 September, 7 October, 22 and 23 November and 1, 3, 4, 6 and 8 December, a schedule that reflects accurately the administration's cycle of concern. As I re-read descriptions of those events, I am struck most by the mood of bafflement they convey. All the principal members of WSAG were officials close to the top of the government, men presumably adept at influencing events; Henry Kissinger in the chair, John Irwin or Alexis Johnson, both great professionals from State, Dave Packard from Defense, Richard Helms or his deputy from CIA, Tom Moorer or other chiefs from the Joint Chiefs, one of several top officials from AID. Yet the minutes show them groping for and never finding a line of action that might make America a factor in the ever more turbulent situation on the subcontinent".

On Jack Anderson's revelations, Zumwalt notes: "A second notable feature of those minutes is their depiction of Henry Kissinger's increasing irritability, not to say fury, in his persistent inability to divert India by as much as hair from the course it had chosen. Doubtless a statesman shouldn't take his failures personally, but Henry is not the only statesman who does. It was with this aspect of the WSAG meetings that Jack Anderson, in his celebrated revelations of the WSAG minutes, had the most fun."

On the entry of the US Task Force into the Indian Ocean: "On 10 December, a Presidential order that was not discussed with the Navy in advance, created Task Group 74, consisting of the nuclear carrier Enterprise and appropriate escorts and supply ships, and sent it steaming from the gulf of Tonkin to Singapore. The order did not specify what TG 74's mission was, nor could anyone, including the Chairman on the Joint Chiefs, tell me. In talking with Mel Laird and Tom Moorer, I sought to be sure that these ships either had a mission or were not sent in harm's way. Yet in harm's way they did go".

The superpower game in the Indian Ocean in the 1971 war is well summed up by Lieut. Commander W. Hickman, US Navy in the United States Naval Institute proceedings 1979:"Likewise, in the Indian Ocean the

Soviet presence has raised the stakes in the game of naval diplomacy. During the Indo-Pakistani War of 1971, both the United States and the Soviet Union deployed significant naval forces to the Indian Ocean. At the outbreak of the war on 3 December, both superpowers had only a nominal naval presence. The Soviets moved first by deploying two surface-to-surface cruise missile (SSM) equipped ships (a "Kynda-class" cruiser and a conventional submarine) from Vladivostok on 6-7 December to support the non-SSM-equipped ships already in the Indian Ocean. On 10 December, the United States formed Task Force 74, consisting of the attack carrier Enterprise (CVN-65), the amphibious assault ship Tripoli (LPH-10), three guided missile escorts, four destroyers, and a nuclear attack submarine, ordering them into the Andaman Sea shortly thereafter. In apparent response to the US Task Force, the Soviets deployed another task group consisting of a "Kresta" class cruiser, a "Kashin" class destroyer, and two submarines on 12-13 December. The deployments on both sides can be seen as an attempt to convince both allies and adversaries of the strength of the respective commitment to the area. Although the Soviet presence in all likelihood could not have prevented the US force from intervening militarily had that been its mission, it could have made such intervention very costly, both in military and political terms. The Soviet actions in this crisis are examples of how the Soviets can represent themselves as the adversaries of the "imperialist aggressors" and protectors of beleaguered nations. Thus can they reap huge propaganda benefits in the Third World."

Interestingly, another view of the tilt is provided by Daniel Patrick Moynihan's In A Dangerous Place (Berkley Publishing Group 1980). He explains the dilemma between the United Nation's legal stance and USA's interests: "The second large event of the 26th General Assembly was the third Indo-Pakistan war. The quintessential conflict of the age: racial, religious, linguistic. Nathaniel Glazier and I had organized a seminar at the American Academy of Arts and Sciences on ethnicity. We argued that the single largest theoretical failure of Marxism was its inability to predict or to account for the ever more salient role of ethnic conflict —racial, religious, linguistic— in the modern age. This was something not unoriginal. Yet more and more I was persuaded of the need to fight ethnic issues on ideological lines".

He continues: "The Indo-Pakistan war offered an occasion. Pakistan, the autocracy, behaved with irredeemable brutality toward its own people in East Bengal. India, the democracy, had intervened.

The United Nations sided with Pakistan, and legality, one supposed, was also on that side. But the United States was supporting Pakistan for far more complex reasons. They had done Kissinger the favour of getting him to China in 1971. For Nixon, there was the large concern of demonstrating to the Chinese — in the first test of a new relationship — that the United States was a reliable ally. Neither argument entirely persuaded me. I could only repeat to the President that India was a democracy. At the end of the General Assembly I appeared on 'Meet The Press' and went over the argument in public. The President was wrong, I said, and the United States should be ashamed. The following summer, as I sat out the presidential campaign in a farm in New York, it came to me that Nixon would now begin to see India as the one large power he had not really dealt with in his first term, and that he would ask me to go there as Ambassador in his second. This he did, and I did— neither of us knowing he would not really have a second term".

The Blood Telegram

Archer Blood who had served in East Pakistan in 1962 as a junior diplomat, had got fond of Bengalis, and was the

US Consul in Dacca since 1970. His reporting from April 1971 of the genocide by the Pakistani Army irritated President Nixon, who did not want to hear anything against his friend President Yahya Khan. Gary J. Bass, a journalist, decided to re-look at the 1971 Indo-Pak war and carried out long research, poring over the recently released official records of US history, meeting many Indians in India, including Lt Gen Jacob, the hero of the 1971 war, and reproducing Nixon's transcripts in his book on the 1971 war, with analyses.

Archer Blood's wife Meg Blood too contributes to Bass' Blood Telegram and describes the genocide in East Pakistan, which was ignored in Washington. Blood was transferred out on 4 April 1972, exactly a year after he made his first dispatch. The career to which he was devoted ended with non-descript postings. Bass writes, "Nixon and Henry Kissinger, the brilliant White House National Security Adviser, were driven not by Cold War calculations, but a starkly personal and emotional dislike of Indians and India... Nixon enjoyed his friendship with Pakistan's military dictator, Gen Agha Mohamed Yayha Khan, who was helping to set up the top secret opening to China. The White House did not want to be seen as doing anything that might hint at the break up of Pakistan - no matter what was happening to the civilians in the east wing of Pakistan."

Trying to trace duplicity in how and when India appears to have decided on war, Gary Bass, in Blood Telegram (page 82), calls Mrs Gandhi's actions a Shadow War. He later quotes K C Pant, the young Minister of State for Home Affairs, who, with his wife, was close to Mrs Gandhi. Pant has this to say, "There was, as far as I know, no intention to provoke a war, or create a situation where war became inevitable. That was not the intention at all." Bass adds, "But in fact, Mrs Gandhi's government was planning for war from the start, and escalated it roughly as the crisis wore on." He quotes Mrs Gandhi, "I KNEW

THAT THE WAR (his capitals) had to come in Bangladesh". Finally Gary Bass clearly concludes that the real decisions, which ended in a bloodbath, were taken in private by Nixon and Kissinger. Nixon once told his Cabinet,"Down in the Government are a bunch of sons of bitches we have checked and funded and 96% are against us." Scott Butcher, Blood's junior political officer who had drafted the Blood Telegram in Dacca, rode out Nixon's and Kissinger's wave of reprisals, but Archer Blood was hounded to the end, as his wife Meg relates. Archer Blood and the Blood Telegram substantiate much that is written in this book.

In his analysis, Gary Bass in Blood Telegram admits,"The West Pakistani elite scorned the 'Bengos' as weak and un-martial. It would have been hard to make a united Pakistan function even if it had the best government in the world, which it did not. Democracy was always going to be a terrible challenge for a country that was literally split into two."

How honest Kissinger has been in his memoirs has been questioned and while Kissinger claims to have wanted peaceful settlement, he was all for appeasing Yahya Khan — Pakistan's drunken dictator. The Bangladesh problem should have been the test for the US, as she always boasted of being the propagator of peace, protector of the oppressed, the champion of liberty and custodian of fundamental rights. Yet the United States' attitude to the Bangla problem was guided more by her friendship with Pakistan and gratitude to that nation's leaders for having opened up a US dialogue with China, rather than objectivity and adherence to proclaimed principles. This tilt of 1971 could well have marked another turning point in India's quest to seek Soviet friendship and aid, especially on the arms front, which the Soviets welcomed. If USA is to understand India, the tilt towards Pakistan has to cease.

The above, when viewed in toto, makes it evident that the Indian Ocean has been looking for a local master. In

1971 the Indian Navy lifted its head as a potent tool for India's role in the Indian Ocean, and as of writing, the Indian Navy has scripted a Maritime Military Strategy and Doctrine based on Mahanian theory of power play, to safeguard the Sea Lines of Communications (SLOCs) and choke points in the IOR even for China and Japan. This encouraged the Defence Minister AK Antony to dub the Indian Navy as the 'net security provider' in the IOR The 58,000 strong Indian Navy is in expansion with aircraft carriers, ships, submarines and planes under acquisition to fulfill its expected role, and seeks to check China in the Indian Ocean. The author suggests a course correction with a more suited Portuguese 'Albuquerquian' maritime strategy. The Arthshastra states, "Friends make power – not just ships."

Chapter 11
Osa Missile Boats' Nylon Necklace

L'audace, L'audace, Toujours de L'audace.
(Boldness, Boldness, Always Boldness) - Napoleon

India started acquiring Soviet ships and submarines in 1965 when Britain stopped its line of credit and refused funding to build Oberon class subs. Mountbatten observed "I managed more favourable terms for the construction of a British submarine but it all took so long that this transaction fell through". Pakistan had acquired USS Diablo (PNS Ghazi sunk in 1971 off Visakhapatnam), and the Indian Navy was concerned. In September 1965, an Indian delegation in Moscow agreed to acquire 4 Foxtrot submarines (Kalvari class), 5 Petya anti submarine vessels (Kamorta Class), a depot ship (Amba).

Defence Minister Y B Chavan had seen the Osa class missile boats offered by Admiral Gorshkov operating in the Black Seas for port protection. Their short range and seaworthiness were a dissuading factor, though China, Indonesia and Egypt had acquired them. The submarine support ship Amba was acquired for the vital security of Andaman & Nicobar, just 60 miles from Indonesia. President Soekarno loaned Pakistan two W class Soviet submarines Nagarangsang and Bramaastra in the 1965 war. Lt Basuki and Lt Sultan Ahmed, with small crews, sailed them to Karachi from Jakarta on surface. Admiral Y.H.Malik, CNS of Pakistan Navy 1988,then a junior officer on Bramaastra, said no Indian warship was ever sighted.

Revival of Interest in the Osa Class missile boats

On 21 October 1967 in the six day war the Egyptian Navy Osa missile boats sank the Israeli destroyer Eilat (ex

Z Class Royal Navy) with 47 dead. The P-15 missiles were fired from boats in port, when the Eliat was operating near the Sinai coast. The low silhouette and stealth characteristics gave them the advantage of surprise. The Indian Navy, yearning to enter the missile age, recommended their acquisition to deter 'hit and run raids" on the Saurashtra coast, the kind the Pakistan Navy conducted off Dwarka by their Destroyer squadron of 5 ships led by PNS Babur in the 1965 war. They falsely claimed to media that a ship was sunk, when only one cow died!

In his book Admiral Kohli states: "Intelligence had suggested that the Pakistan Navy was considering acquisition of missile fitted frigates. To forestall the dangers of a missile attack by Pakistan on Bombay, I had enquired from Admiral Gorshkov whether they had a mobile missile battery which could be deployed for the defence of Bombay. He replied in the negative. He later persuaded the Indian Navy that for defence of Bombay and major ports, the small Osa class missile boats would be ideal." Project Alpha Kilo for Rs 20 crores for 8 boats and 11 months training in Vladivostok was signed.

The Osa Boats And The Towing Necklace

It was a stroke of luck for eight 240 ton Osa Class missile boats to arrive aboard heavy lift ships at Calcutta's Kidderpore docks, in early 1971 just before the war. Russian agency Chinoy Chablani who serviced Bhilai steel plant machinery, used Calcutta Port Trust's heavy lift cranes to unload, for training ship INS Cauvery and INS Tir to tow the first lot. Calcutta was chosen because Bombay Port only had a Shrayan 80 ton crane.

Each missile boat was armed with 4 SS-N-2 Styx anti-ship missiles (instead of the normal two), fitted with 3 Russian 4000 hp M-503G diesel engines for 35 knots at full power for short ranges, and the boats' Rangout radar

(NATO Square Tie) with bursts of directed power could detect surface targets over 40 miles in anomalous weather well beyond the Styx maximum missile range of 30 miles.

It is interesting how the bold attacks on Karachi by the short range Osa missile boats germinated. Innovative constructor officers of the Naval Dockyard at Vishakapatnam used Garware nylon ropes sent from Pune for trials as berthing hawsers, converting them into a towing 'Necklace'. The author as First Lt under Cdr I.K. Erry on INS Cauvery had towed 2 boats from Calcutta in rough monsoon seas. Two towing hawsers on passage to Vishakapatnam had parted and splicing them at sea was a challenge, which I mentioned to Chief of Staff Commodore M.S.Grewal while requesting spare towing hawsers. He called ND(V) whose constructors, after consulting Soviet guarantee specialists, inserted light nylon hawsers all-round the Missile boats in clamps fixed on the boats for lifting by cranes, like a necklace. They welded more clamps in a system to connect a tow and easily release it. This generated an idea to enhance the range of Osas (literally 'wasps') from home base under tow, then let them loose for attack, an operational ploy the Russians had never thought of. Vice Admiral N Krishnan used this in his draft plan for the 1971 war, which he gave Nanda.

The 8 Osa boats fortunately enabled Admiral Surendra Nath Kohli the Flag Officer Commanding Western Naval Command to set up facilities and commission the "25th Missile Boat Squadron" at Bombay under Russian trained Cdr Babru Yadav at INS Angre with access to berths in Naval Dockyard. The Technical Position (TP) for missile testing and stowage was set up under Russian trained Cmde B.G.Madholar at Mankhurd in suburban Bombay. The missiles were sent to Lion Gate dockyard after preparation by Vladivostok-trained electrical officers Lt's Promod Bhasin (later awarded VSM) and B.V.M.Rao. Western Command simulated attacks on Karachi and one Osa was attached with the Western Fleet in tow. Necklaces were used.

Admiral Nanda's ingenious War Plans

Napoleon believed in lucky generals and he attributed decisive victories to 'luck and timing'. So did CNS Admiral S.M.Nanda, the 'Bomber of Karachi', citing 'boldness and secrecy' as important attributes in the 'Indian Principles of War'. Few know that Nanda did not dictate the key Operational Orders for the daring attacks on Karachi to his HQ staff but to a young relation sworn to secrecy. These were sent to Western Naval Command as charge documents. He took Vice Admiral S.N.Kohli, Flag Officer Commanding-in-Chief Western Command into confidence, to exercise the Osa boats for the intended operations. He informed PM Mrs. Indira Gandhi of his plans to attack Karachi. In a closed door Chiefs of Staff meeting chaired by Gen Sam Manekshaw, he asked Air Chief Marshal P.C.Lal for an air strike on Karachi at dawn on the first day of the war.

When Manekshaw found Lal considering this suicidal, Sam said in Punjabi, "Chotta brah ek strike mang raha hai. De de," (small brother is asking for just one strike, give it) and added "Marenge to marenge, asi ladayi karan ja rahi hai, mohabaat nahi." (Die if we must, we are going to war, not to make love). Thus would flamboyant Manekshaw confront operational issues head on. He spoke to Mrs. Indira Gandhi in a tone of confidence and acted like a Chief of Defence Staff which irked Air Chief Lal. When Manekshaw was promoted to Field Marshal as Army Chief after the war, and was being considered for CDS, ACM Lal objected. Nanda, on tour in Bombay, when sounded by Secretary Govind Narian, smiled, "You can promote any one with as many stars as you like - as long as you do not take away any of mine." The IAF has objected to a CDS since then till 2012, a seminal loss to the nation, which was brought out in the Kargil war, by strategist

K.Subrahmanyam.

Nanda employed the RN Staff College tri-appreciation technique, and asked for three independent operational war plans from his DNO Commodore O.S.Dawson, NA Capt. V.P.Duggal and Vice Admiral Nilkanth Krishnan (appointed as Flag Officer Commanding- in-Chief Eastern Naval Command). He allotted one missile boat to be in tow to Rear Admiral Chandy Kuruvilla the Western Fleet commander to lead the strike on Karachi. The Fleet Operations Officer feared the fleet was spotted on 3 December by a civilian Pakistani plane and though close to the Makran coast, steered away and failed to strike, belying Nanda's expectation. Nanda had made the war signal and Mrs. Gandhi had broadcast that war had broken. A disappointed Nanda reviewed plans and spoke to Kohli to execute Op Trident.

The high point of the 1971 'war at sea' was the Navy's landmark missile attack on Karachi by the Osa class missile boats on the night of 4th December in Op Trident and 8th December in Op Python. That same day, 4 IAF Type 56-A Hunters of the Operational Conversion Unit (OCU) under Wing Cdr Don Conquest from Jamnagar attacked the Kemari oil tanks in the opening bell' of the war.

The necklace was the starting point to plan the missile attack on Karachi in 1971. It was luck, and the ingenuity of the young naval constructors' creativity. Since then naval architects and young officers have made many innovations to modernise a rising Navy.

The Weapons Engineering and Electronics Systems Establishment (WEESE) at Delhi, the Naval Science and Technology Laboratory (NSTL) at Vishakapatnam, Naval Physical Oceanographic La (NPOL of Cdr Paulraj fame) at Cochin and Nuclear School at Vishakapatnam have contributed much. The Indian Navy has talent in innovating ship designs too.

Chapter 12
The IAF - Indian Navy Attacks on Karachi

"Pakistan initiated the 1971 war on 3 December. On the 4th morning, a chance IAF Hunter attack set Kemari oil tanks on fire, across the harbour from the Pakistan Naval Academy PNS Rahbar, where the Naval Band played on at the Passing Out Parade. The young officers were enthused to join the war and serve Pakistan, the 'Land of the Pure'." - Author.

The Song of the Missile Boats, 1971:

"Now take courage my lads, 'tis to Karachi we steer
To add something more to this wonderful 1971 year,
'Tis to honour I call you, as free Indians, not slaves For who are so free as the sons of Bharat's waves. Come, cheer up my lads, 'tis to Karachi we steer

The prize clearer than all, to the Indian's dear, To honour your country, and your Navy,

Be always ready sailorman, and stand steady. Come load up my lads, 'tis to targets we steer

Missiles we'll fire, build on the crest of none we fear, Again and again let's repair to Karachi my hands, And yet retire to Mother India, our beloved land".

The Indian Navy's stars of the 1971 war were the recently acquired Osa missile boats which offered minimum radar targets, had speeds over 30 knots with 4 SS-N-2 (P-15) Styx missiles with 40km range flying at 9 mach, nd fitted with ingenious towing necklaces. With months of arduous work-ups and practice missile firings in Vladivostok's harsh climate, the crews exhibited professionalism and camaraderie to the Soviet Navy. Captains and ships' companies from the 25th Missile Squadron and technical personnel prepared the volatile liquid fuel Styx oxidizer rocket engines meticulously to sink Pakistani targets off Karachi over 30 km away by November. The boats powerful I band Rangout radars in high power mode performed brilliantly to track targets for the kill in Op Trident and in Op Python on 4 and 8 December nights respectively.

IAF Hunters' serependitious attack on Karachi

By sheer happenstance and luck which favours the brave, four IAF Hunter aircraft of the IAF's Operational Conversion Unit (OCU) carried out a daring mission early on 4 December 1971 and set Karachi's Kemari oil tanks ablaze, though credit was inadvertently claimed by the Indian Navy for many years. At dusk on 3 December, the Pakistan Air Force struck seven IAF airfields. The IAF could respond only next morning, not having night fighting capabilities.

At midnight Mrs. Indira Gandhi broadcasted, "The war on Bangladesh has become war on India. We have no option but to put our country on war footing." Military commanders immediately opened and executed their operational orders. During the planning, CNS Nanda had asked Air Chief Lal for a strike on Karachi, but Air HQ staff, unaware how crucial it was for the Navy fighting its first war, opined that a mission to Karachi was not feasible. Karachi was out of range for the Hunters, and safe only after the Badin (Pakistan had set up dummy radars too) and Drig Road American supplied radars were neutralized by the MiG-21s from Jamnagar. The Navy received low priority.

Yet, in the late hours of 3 December, when the Jamnagar air base was pitch dark and wives re-located to the city, the OCU head, Wing Commander Don Conquest learnt they, the 'Top Guns', had no assigned role for the morning. Conquest approached his OC, the legendary Air Commodore Pete Wilson, and told him that his boys were now capable of a strike on Karachi, as they had recently inducted Hunters Type 56A and 235 gallon drop tanks, "What will our wives and children who were shunted from the base's Bhangi Barracks to Jamnagar town say? That we stayed on the ground?"

Pete Wilson, busy readying MiG-21s to hit Badin and Drig Road at first light, let Conquest plan his mission. Air HQ Ops Room cleared it with, " Do what you want. We are too busy here". Early on the 4 December morning, four OCU "Top Guns" took off for "target Karachi" with road maps in a formation take off. The Hunters could not carry rockets. Two 235 gallon drop tanks were slung on the pods, to enable a high-low-high sortie with five minutes over target, with 20mm cannons. Strike leader Conquest (now in Australia), Sqn Ldr (later Gp Capt) S.N. Medhekar his winger, Flt Lt (later AVM) P.K.Mukherjee and Flt Lt (later Wing Cdr) S.K.Gupta recall that mission.

Don Conquest recounts, "As per SOP (standard operating procedure) we dipped our noses off Karachi and fired a few rounds into the sea to test our guns. Mukherjee's guns had jammed, so three pressed on at 500 ft along the coast. As we neared the city, the large oil tanks loomed out of the skyline, their silver paint shining in the rising sun. We made two runs without difficulty and after the first, there were huge balls of fire and volumes of smoke coming out of the storage. The smoke haze made flying dangerous; we aborted the other runs and flew back. Some ships opened ack ack fire." Before Conquest could file reports on landing at Jamnagar, he was ordered to fly his OCU to Jaisalmer. Indian Army tanks were under siege at Longewala by Pakistani Pattons. Air HQ was not made aware of the damage caused at Karachi till much later. This is common in the "fog of war", so well described by Churchill in his Nobel Prize volumes on the Second World War.

The sight of balls of fire seen from the Naval Academy Karachi close by is still etched in the memory of the

Pakistani, UAE and Saudi officers who took part in a parade on that fateful morning. RADM Khalid Wasay recalls, "I was a lieutenant at the Navac. On 4 December, we were to hold a Passing out Parade and at about 0830 (PST) three aircraft appeared overhead and the next thing we heard was explosions. Later smoke billowed from the oil tanks. Four days later, when we had doused the fires the tanks were hit again." Baluch Engineer Cdr (late) Iftikar Ahmed, known to the author, recalled how the IAF planes flew over the Naval Dockyard at Karachi. He knelt and thanked 'Allah' that they did not attack the Daphne submarine he was supervising to send to sea.

In Rear Admiral Zahir Shah's book, Rear Admiral K.M. Alam, Captain of the Pakistan Naval Academy, says: "When the war with India spread to West Pakistan on 4 December, an air attack on Karachi was expected. But that was the very morning the Passing out Parade was scheduled in PNS Rahbar. Commander Riaz, my XO and I, both had our fingers crossed. The sirens started wailing and an air raid followed. The ack ack guns opened up, including those around the Academy. During the attack one of the oil tanks in nearby Kemari was hit and burst into flames with a big whoosh! The Academy shook, some windowpanes were smashed. Everyone wondered how there could be a parade. Rear Admiral Rashid Ahmad, called to say he would take the salute. I assembled the cadets and ordered that even if Manora came under attack, they were to carry out the drill. There were Saudi and Gulf naval cadets. Avoiding the conflagration at Kemari — and the ceremonial boat ride — Admiral Rashid took the circuitous road to Manora. The air raid warning was on, when he arrived. With a look at the empty sky, and prayers in our hearts, the parade began. The country was in the midst of a war; oil tanks across the harbour were burning fiercely, but the band played on."

Why did the IAF not make much of this amazing achievement right then? The simple answer is that by 5

December Navy's C-in-C at Mumbai, Vice Admiral S.N. Kohli received the code word "Angar," signifying success of the killer boats in Op Trident, and BBC radio reported oil tanks at Karachi were on fire, nothing more. Kohli announced to the media that the "Osa Killers" had sunk three ships later identified as the PNS Khaibar, PNS Muhafiz and MV Venus Challenger (which disappeared for 2 days). The strike on the oil tanks, was claimed as one last missile was fired towards the shore. Commodore Vijay Jerath's book '25 Missile Squadron', clarifies that the last missile fired landwards by Nipat did not have a clear line of sight, and run towards the tanks, and would have had to fly over the city. The Styx missile radar gate opens and locks on and dives on to the first strong radar echo, and a land echo is strong. The newer missiles in the Indian Navy like the Klub and BrahMos are more discerning, with better radars and GPS homing and finger-printing for land targets with terrain mapping.

Describing the fate of the land bound missile, the Officer in Tactical Command (OTC) of Op Trident, Captain Gopal Rao in INS Kiltan, saw it ditching on to the beach. He wrote so in USNIPs and is quoted in Triumph to Transition. When the Hunter attack was brought to the notice of late Air Chief P.C. Lal by P.K. Mukherjee, Lal magnanimously said, "Let the Navy take the credit. War is on." Don Conquest is content that he was awarded the Vir Chakra for his bravery in the Battle of Longewala. The land battle was dramatised in a controversial film, Border by J.P. Datta, with the Hunters given a reduced role.

This revelation does not detract from the brilliant and bold planning by CNS, Admiral S.M. Nanda's staff, and the superb execution by his missile Captains at sea. The lesson for Indian leaders is that synergy of operations among the Armed Forces, when exercised, is their biggest force multiplier, and Indian strategic planners must strive for it.

Op Trident 4 December and Op Python 8 December

On 4 December evening INS Kiltan (OTC Cdr Gopal Rao) and INS Katchall (Cdr K.N. Zadu) were ordered to R/V with INS Nipat (CO Lt. Cdr B.N. Kavina Cdr Babru Yadav, K-25 embarked), INS Nirghat (Lt. Cdr I.J. Sharma), and INS Veer (Lt. Cdr O.P. Mehta). They fueled at Porbunder from Poshak to execute Op Trident, under shore control. The Fleet, to Nanda's disappointment, had failed to hit Karachi with INS Vinash. Electrical officer Lt. Promod Bhasin (later Vice Admiral as Chief of Material and builder of India's first nuclear submarine INS Arihant) was USSR trained. He prepared the missiles, which performed superbly. He was the youngest officer to be awarded a VSM.

The missile force on 4 December was under C-in-C West Kohli's control. He visited the Maritime Operations Room often that evening (the author kept night duties in MOR with Lt Cdr Madhvendra Singh, later CNS). Like 'Killer Dogs' let loose, the three boats approached Karachi in darkness, and launched their Styx missiles on ships off Karachi. Pakistani officers in the control room did not realize it was a seaborne attack. Assuming it was an air attack, like that fateful morning, the confused Pak defences were in disarray to arrange seaward defence. Searchlights got turned on, and star shells fired. The missile boats attacked without retaliation, and retired with 5 of 12 missiles still intact. CNS Muzaffar Hassan at NHQ in Karachi asked Air HQ at Rawalpindi for a strike on the retiring boats. "Cannot spare a sortie!" was the answer. The Indian Commanders were decorated for their heroic foray, with 2 MVCs (Rao and Yadav) and 3 VrCs.

Keesing's Archives says: "In the biggest naval battle since the Second World War, an Indian Task Force sank the Pakistani destroyers PNS Khaibar (formerly HMS Cadiz) and Shah Jahan (formerly HMS Charity) and two mine sweepers off Karachi in the early hours of 5

December and subsequently shelled naval installations in the port". In fact, PNS Khaibar D-163 under Capt Nasseem Mallik/ Lt Cdr Fazal Ahmed sank with 8 officers and 213 sailors and minesweeper PNS Muhafiz M-163 sank under Lt Arshad Aleem with 32 sailors at 2235, and MV Venus Challenger floundered in minutes. The credit of rescue work goes to German built patrol boat PNS Sadaquat, gifted by the Saudi Arabian Navy.

The Times of India of 6 December wrote, "An Indian Naval Task Force inflicted a crippling blow on the Pakistani Navy, sinking two destroyers and damaging another in a surprise attack on Karachi. Units of the task force then went as close as 25 kilometers off Karachi harbour and shelled several strategic installations". The 'fog of war' was evident in reporting. What was unreported: Veer suffered an engine problem and limped back when Cdr BB Yadav K25 asked the missile boats to retire. INS Kiltan did not receive the message and pelted towards Karachi. Veer nearly fired a missile on seeing her so close to Karachi. Engineer officer Lt. Puri on Veer, heroically put boothas (cloth pieces) on a hot leaking oil pipe to stop the leak, searing his bare hands, but allowing Veer to get away from Karachi.

On 8 December at 2230, Lt Cdr Vijay Jerath, a shipmate of the author on training ship Tir, known as 'Jerry', was let loose off Karachi in INS Vinash in Op Python by Capt Curly Nair (F15) on INS Trishul (Nair having taken over a worked up ship from Capt Ram Tahiliani) with INS Talwar (Cdr S.S. Kumar, who was Jerath and the author's XO on Tir). Jerath executed a magnificent attack and fired all four missiles in succession at four different targets at Manora anchorage.

In the words of the Pakistan Navy, "The first missile flew over the ships at anchorage, crossed Manora island and crashed into the Kemari oil farm… The missile was reported to COMKAR who passed it on to Air Defence Korangi. There was a huge explosion and flames shot up high. The fire caused by the air attack on 4 December had been put out only a day earlier after concerted efforts... The British owned MV Harmattan sank immediately and SS Gulf Star flying a Panama flag and tanker PNS Dacca (Capt S.Q.Raza Sitarra-I Jurrat) were damaged, as they took one missile each around 2245".

Dacca was hit in no. 7 port fuel tank, luckily just above the water line and the motor boat and fuel hoses caught fire. "Abandon Ship" was piped and many jumped, but eight officers and 37 senior sailors stayed on board. "Abandon Ship" was cancelled and the fire was fought heroically. Jerath in his book clears many doubts that confirm the missile fired landward on 4 December could not have hit the oil tanks, as the line of fire was not clear. Jerath had a clear line of sight to the Kemari oil tanks on 8 December and asked Trishul and Talwar to keep westward off Karachi, as he did not want to lock on them by mistake. The IAF claimed it hit the tanks on 8 December but there is no evidence. There were reports of bombs falling in Taj Agra and Bihar colonies near Mauripur. On 9 December at about 2130, IAF Canberras hit the 'warping in' jetty at the Pakistan Naval Dockyard Karachi with two 1000 lb bombs, when Lt Miandad and Lt M.Qutubuddin and 20 sailors died. The confusion was caused by an unverified claim in a chapter by Gp Capt. Badhwar of the Canberras, in ACM P.C.Lal's autobiography, 'My Years in the IAF' (completed by his wife after his death). The fact is that on 4 December, the IAF Hunters hit the Kemari tanks, and the Navy did so on the 8 December.

CNS Vice Admiral Muzaffar Hassan again asked Air Chief Air Marshal Abdul Rahim Khan for an air strike on 4 December to attack the retreating ships, but PAF could not spare the effort and only later an airstrike group was formed. Karachi's fuel and ammunition depots, and more than 50 percent of the total fuel requirement of the Karachi zone was reported to have been blown up in the raids. The result was a crippling economic blow to

Pakistan and the PAF was hard hit. On 9 December, a false alarm of another missile attack was reported and PAF Sabres went for PNS Zulfiqar but were called off.

The Times of India wrote. "Today calls for a salute to the Navy. Vice Admiral Kohli, who heads the Western Fleet, is perfectly entitled to make the claim that the second raid mounted by his men on Karachi harbour is one of the most daring in naval history. The task force did not confine its attention to Karachi alone. It went as far as Gwadar harbour 448 km west of Karachi, and to Jiwani, another 48 km away to give them a pounding. The objective was probably to show that these faraway places cannot provide sanctuary to the enemy's hard-pressed fleet".

What largely contributed to the big victory was the 'daring and perfectly timed action' of the units. Independent observers have compared the operations of 4/5 December with the sinking of British warships, Prince of Wales and Repulse by the Japanese off Singapore in 1941. The Indian Navy sank more than two warships, but the kill is not as important as the element of surprise involved in the operations and the shock caused to the enemy, heralding missile warfare at sea. Indian Express reported, "Karachi in the west was the obvious target for isolation because it was the home of the bulk of the surface ships of the Pakistan Navy. Therefore, taking the Pakistani pre-emptive strike of 3 December as the signal the Western Naval Command got ready to tackle the enemy at its strongest point."

A Pakistani Civilian's Perspective

"I was there in the middle of it all. There is a row of tanks all along the oil pier at Kemari, on the north of the Coast Road. I was working as Sales Development Engineer and received a call to come to the office at Dawood Centre. All the managers and engineers were told that PAF had attacked IAF bases and an attack by IAF was expected any time. We were asked to volunteer to keep duty. In 6 groups on shift basis we were posted to Kemari. I was posted at Kerosene terminal and I was told that my job was to control any fires that broke out, and it was to be my decision to order evacuation, if the fire got out of hand.

As I was approaching the terminal gates early next morning (4 December) I saw two aircraft approaching from the sea, I took them to be Sabres, but when the Hunters dived, I realized that we were under attack. Aircraft strafed with incendiary bullets. First target was DPL tanks and then ESSO terminal where I crouched behind a wall. Three fuel tanks at DPL terminal caught fire and one light diesel tank in Esso terminal.

We spent the next few days to try to put out the fire and cool other tanks. Smoke covered the whole skyline. This saved us from further hits, as IAF were attacking at evening and dawn. The fires were coming under control, when again, early morning while approaching the terminal, I came across a river of fire. A Styx missile had hit a tank full of crude (8 December). The crude was flowing on to the road and going into the sea while on fire. It took most of the morning to contain the fire. This time even the flames could be seen from afar.

A total of five tanks (out of nearly a hundred along the coast road) were attacked. Three belonged to DPL with fuel oil, one to Esso with LDO and one of PRL crude; approximately 10 to 15 thousand tons. All the jet fuel (actually a high quality kerosene), gasoline and diesel was safe; the war effort was not affected. The damage was very light, all things considered, but it gave the appearance that the whole coast line was burning.

While people like myself were able to phone home, labourers' families were in panic and rickshaw after rickshaw was coming all day with crying women trying to check on their husbands, sons or fathers. I felt deeply about the misery caused by war to the families of the poor who were only trying to eke out a living. Loss of the bread earner makes the family destitute. I did this not out of bravery but because it was a duty. There were nearly 200 employees of all the oil companies assigned to their respective terminals. I will do it again if left with no choice, but I will try to avoid war if at all possible. Thankfully there was only one loss of life at the PRL terminal".

This Pakistani engineer's tale displays the anguish caused to common people because India and Pakistan's militaries are at loggerheads leading to war. Both militaries need to meet to garner trust and hopefully sign a 'No War Pact' (that Pakistan had once proposed, with Pandit Nehru responding "War against whom?").

Inder Malhotra wrote a leader article in the Times of India on "The Indian Navy's Finest Hour—The Triumph and After", "As far as free India's own sea power is concerned, it is the first time that Indian warships have gone into action since Admiral Kanoji Angre of the Marathas and the Zamorin of Calicut unsuccessfully challenged the naval might of the British, who were able to conquer this country at least partly because of the sad neglect of the sea by the Moghuls. A frontal attack on Karachi, the pride and the main base of the enemy navy, would by itself have been a remarkable achievement. To bag three enemy warships in a single engagement, barely 20 miles from the Pakistani shore, without any loss to our naval task force, makes the achievement sensational. But what makes it altogether unique in maritime history is that the performance was repeated within 72 hours with such audacity as to send the Indian fleet within eight miles of the shore batteries at Karachi and to attack the entire 300-mile Pakistan coast from there to Gwadar to Jiwani.

The Eastern Fleet has, in the meantime, established its supremacy in the Bay of Bengal. It has not only blockaded the West Pakistani-occupied Bangladesh ports completely but also relieved the Air Force of the task of bombing enemy targets in the riverine delta in Bangladesh to enable it to attend to more urgent tasks elsewhere.

This has been the result of the wise decisions of the Naval Headquarters to assign the aircraft-carrier, Vikrant, to the Eastern Fleet, although the Western Fleet which had it for years was naturally sorry to let it go. Our admirals had rightly calculated that, as in the air, so on the sea, the Pakistanis would attempt a pre-emptive strike. Nothing could confirm this assessment more clearly than the presence of Pakistan's submarine, the American-built Ghazi, off Visakhapatnam at exactly the same time when the PAF planes were attacking Indian air bases on the evening of 3 December. But the Indian warships not only sent the Ghazi to the bottom of the sea but also took other counter-measures. Having thus foiled Pakistani designs, the Indian Navy put into operation the second part of its strategy of attacking the enemy in its citadel, with results which are already well known. This is not all. Since the beginning of the Indian naval attacks, Pakistan's foreign trade was been almost completely immobilized. On the other hand, the Indian merchant ships, temporarily confined to the ports at the start of hostilities, were once again on the high seas. But this does not mean that the Pakistani Navy was in no position to act at all. No war can be wholly one-sided as is shown by the loss of an old frigate (Khukri) through Pakistani submarine action. However, when all is said and done, there can be no doubt about the supremacy of the Indian Navy in both East and West.

An intriguing feature of Pakistan's pathetic performance on the sea has been the utter failure of its Air Force to come to the aid of its Navy even at Karachi. One reason for this has been the almost perfect co-ordination between the Indian Navy and the Indian Air Force. In directing the co-ordinated war effort of the three sister Services, the Indian High Command is not unaware of recent history. It knows that the almost complete victory of the Chinese and North Korean forces during the Korean war was undone by the Inchon landings of the US troops. Sooner or later — sooner rather than later — the liberation of Bangladesh will be complete, and in this the Indian Navy will have played its part with distinction."

The author, as a young Flag Lt to Rear Admiral S.G.Karmarkar, first met Inder-ji in 1964 at his Malabar Hill flat, talking as he thumped out a Times of India editorial on his typewriter, and was impressed by the eminent journalist's prescience. Indeed, what Inder Malhotra predicted above, did come to pass.

Chapter 13
PNS Ghazi goes to a watery grave

It is not easy to follow the track of a submarine. Or tell where the sea swallows the dolphin. Where Leviathan taketh his pastime?
What the ocean calleth her home?
– Acknowledgement to John Hopwood
"Ghazi lies at Vizag's doorstep as a dead monument and a reminder that aggression by Pakistan will not pay".

In comparison to the Indian Navy the Pakistani Naval officers were relatively younger, had seen quick promotions and not had the benefit of intensive work-ups, for lack of fleet support and poor Pakistan Air Force cooperation. This has been admitted by many Pakistani authors including Gen. Fazel Muqueen Khan. Their Chief, Admiral Muzzafar Hassan was aware of all these lacunae, which possibly gave him the clear line of tactics; to be aggressive with his submarine arm of Daphne PNS Hangor and PNS Ghazi, and defensive on all other fronts, till the Indian Naval Fleet was located. CNS Pakistan's objective was to use his forces when not engaged, in helping the Army to control the populace in East Pakistan, and surface ships to patrol the coast. He anticipated the havoc the aircraft carrier INS Vikrant would create in the East and trusted PNS Ghazi to stalk the Indian Eastern Fleet. In the West, Rear Admiral M.A.K.Lodhi (Compak) was left with no choice but to send his submarines afield and keep his ships closer home.

The Indian Navy respected the strength in under-sea warfare of the Pakistan Navy, with their newly acquired Daphne and the PNS Ghazi (ex USS Diablo Tench class Submarine - Defender of the Faith) built by Portsmouth Naval Shipyard, US and transferred to Pakistan Navy:

2410 tons submerged, speed 20 knots on surface and 10 knots submerged, carrying ten 21 inch torpedoes, 6 in the bows and 4 in the stern, radius of action 14,000 miles at 10 knots, with a complement of 90 officers and sailors, and able to lay mines.

It would be equally true that the Pakistan Navy were aware about the Indian Navy's fire and missile power and the range of the 'F' class ex-USSR submarines and that it would depend a lot on its own submarines to foray forward, whilst its ships planned holding a defensive posture nearer home.

On the Eastern sea-board the newly formed Indian Fleet on 16 October 1971 was also getting into gear for any eventuality. The aircraft carrier Vikrant was handed over to the East, as she had problems in boiler A1 which restricted her speed. The reasons for transferring the aircraft carrier to the East will ever be debated, but Vikrant did a stellar operational task of blockade and destruction of Chittagong, Cox's Bazaar, Mongla, Khuna and Chalna. Since nothing succeeds like success, and the only enemy submarine in the East, Ghazi sank too early to cause any damage, the decision has always, in retrospect, been deemed as correct. The Indian Navy generated tactical communications to show the INS Vikrant was operating off Vishakapatnam when actually she was working up with all recalled experienced pilots and a few new pilots off the Andaman's. Later this enabled the Navy to set up an Information Warfare (IW) cell. This author contributed at NHQ.

Luck favours the brave. Service leaders often quote this saying in their war briefing. In war, as in love, an element of chance always exists and so discussion will go on, whether it was Pakistan's ill-luck or a deliberate attack that sent PNS Ghazi (Cdr Zafer Mohammed Khan) to a watery grave a few miles off Visakhapatnam on the night of 3-4 December 1971, with no survivors at all. Was it that INS Rajput and another patrol craft Akshay, which were both on patrol off Visakhapatnam, scared them with a depth-charge attack to panic and dive deep and hit the bottom of the sea? Did a mine explode in the submarine's vulnerable hull when attempting to lay mines? Did the submarine suffer some mechanical problem and lose buoyancy and dive into Davy Jones Locker? (This apellatation is an anglicization of 'Divya Loka', the Hindu God of the Sea). All these are moot questions, and can never be answered with certainly for not one of those 90 on board is left to tell the true tale. Yet it is true that the Indian Navy's luck was very much the contributive cause for the Ghazi's demise, just when the war had begun.

PNS Ghazi was formerly USS Diablo, a Tench-class submarine built at the US naval shipyard at Portsmouth. It was given on lease for training of Pakistan Navy personnel as part of the US military aid programme. The Pakistan Navy entered the submarine era earlier than the Indian Navy by acquiring this submarine on 1 June 1964. Till then only a handful of Indian officers and sailors had been trained in the UK at HMS Dolphin in Portsmouth under the UK Military Training Assistance Programme (UKMTAS) and were to form the nucleus of the Indian Navy's submarine arm when eventually four F class submarines (Kalvari, Khanderi, Karanj and Kursura) were acquired progressively from the Soviet Union in 1968-70.

The Ghazi was a comparatively old boat in 1971 but had long- range capability and had thus been deployed on patrol 1,500 miles away from Karachi presumably to attack the Vikrant which, Admiral Krishnan, by a ruse, had put word out that it would be off Visakhapatnam. The submarine must have been stealthily waiting for its prey. Even though a clause existed in the US-Pakistan loan deal that the Ghazi would be used only for training purposes, such an agreement goes overboard in a real-time threat situation.

A news report states that Chintapalli Satyalu and Chintapalli Achayya of Kotha Jalaripeta found a life jacket floating near Visakhapatnam on 4 December and alerted the Navy, being paid Rs 400 . Next day, Naval personnel went and found the wreck at the same spot. The events leading to the announcement of the sinking of the Ghazi, as reported in a leading newspaper, makes interesting reading. It must be noted the submarine sank on the midnight of 3 – 4 December, but when Admiral S.M. Nanda was informed, he wanted ocular proof, which was provided by divers on 7 December, and log books and a life raft and remnants were sent to NHQ. Defence Minister Jagjivan Ram announced the news to the thumping of tables in Parliament on 8 December.

Sinking of Ghazi

The Express New Service of 10 December reports: The Pakistani attempt to sink the biggest prize of all — INS Vikrant, India's aircraft carrier — was nullified by the Eastern Naval Command on 3 December by sinking its submarine Ghazi. The fact that the submarine was so close to Visakhapatnam within seven hours of Pakistan's treacherous air attack on India on the evening of 3

December tells its own tale. This is positive proof of the pre-planned aggression by Pakistan against India, says Vice-Admiral N. Krishnan, Flag Officer C-in-C of Eastern Naval Command.

The Times of India (7 December) added a footnote: During the 1965 Indo-Pakistan conflict, Ghazi, meaning 'Defender of the Faith', was damaged by an Indian destroyer. It was sent to Iran for months of repairs and refitting earlier.

The interesting point to note from the Press cuttings is that though Ghazi sank on the night of 3-4 December, the announcement was made to the nation only on 9 December. The Nistar, the Indian Navy's diving tender and submarine rescue vessel, acquired in the late 1960s from USSR with diving-bell facilities, was ordered to get ready to search and go on top of the likely position of Ghazi for salvage. Thereafter, an approximate position of the submarine was established, and three floating bodies of Pakistan Navy sailors, brown skinned like Indians, but circumcised, were also located along with some papers, signals, a notice to mariners signed by Pakistan Navy's Chief Hydrographer H. Sawarkhan and a seaman's knife. All confirmed that Ghazi lay dead. Lt. Cdr. Nagrani, a submariner himself, proceeded to Delhi to display items found to Delhi. These items are housed in the Maritime Museum at Mumbai.

The exploits of Pakistan submarines are discussed in this book in various chapters. PNS Hangor was responsible for sinking INS Khukri. The strength of the Pakistan Navy submarine arm in 1971 comprised a total of four submarines, the three 700-ton 'Daphnes', Hangor, Shushak and Mangro, all commissioned in 1970, and Ghazi, which was replaced by a new Ghazi in 1975 when the Pakistan Navy purchased the Portuguese Daphne class Cachalote. This means a Ghazi still serves the Pakistan Navy and is a memory to those officers and men who went down on the first day of the war. What was to be the trump card of the Pakistan Navy to stalk the Vikrant and the Eastern Fleet ships, and possibly merchant ships, entering Visakhapatnam, was foiled. The loss of a submarine must have been realized by the Pakistan Naval Headquarters on 4 December, when the IAF and Navy attacked Karachi. One can imagine the the demoralization of that Navy?

The loss of Ghazi and sinking of Khukri set this proud arm of the Pakistan Navy thinking soon after the war. The future acquisitions of Agusta submarines from DCNS (France) and construction at the Karachi Shipyard Ltd were well planned and a separate logistics department was set up. To meet the challenge of nuclear submarines of the Indian navy, Pakistan's navy has fitted the MESMA (Module d'Energie Sous-Marine Autonome) self-breathing steam system to ensure submarines like the nuclear boats do not have to surface to charge batteries. This is the future and the Indian navy too has been hunting for a Air Independent Breathing System (AIS), and DRDO with Larsen & Toubro Ltd has made one at the Ambarnath laboratory. A Maruti car was driven to Cochin from Mumbai with a hydrogen based fuel cell. Even today the submarine arm of the Pakistan Navy is elite, and has produced two Chiefs of Naval Staff. It has 5 Agostas.

THE GHAZI LIVES ON

Had the Ghazi lived, it would have had a tale to tell Of hardship, endurance, courage and the tumultuous swell

That would have stirred many a seaman's heart. But alas, she fell prey to lack of underwater art.

The remains are rough notes and many a dead body Found first by Chintapalli of Vizag in a 'todi.'

For surely and certainly Fourth December Seventy one

Was a fateful day when the sea battle began. The Ghazi instead of stalking the Vikrant Exploded not far from Vizag's sea front.

For the Indian Navy, it was a lucky shot

On what was the very first day of the victory trot. The proud countrymen of Pakistan did learn Of the sad loss on the very same morn That they bore the wrath of missiles on Karachi Fort.

Set forth by the brave killers who went for that very port. Now only a memory of those ninety lives And many who depended on them, and their wives, Lives by the meaning of what was the Ghazi. For defender of that faith is the new PNS Ghazi.

The Loss of PNS Ghazi from The History Of The Pakistan Navy, abridged by the author. Within East Pakistan, riverine traffic, on which the supply lines of many widely dispersed army units largely depended, was being subjected to increasing attacks by Mukti Bahini. Their naval elements had embarked upon a well planned campaign aimed at disrupting shipping activity in East Pakistani ports. After the reorganisation of the Indian Navy into the Eastern and Western Fleets, the four gun boats stationed at Chittagong were no match for the massive Indian Naval deployment there. When the aircraft carrier Vikrant was transferred to the Eastern theatre, the existing naval imbalance in that area was grossly aggravated.

Several measures, including the despatch of a destroyer and two minesweepers to the Eastern theatre, were under consideration at Pakistan Naval Headquarters towards the end of the year. None of the measures were feasible. The Pakistan Navy was in no position to respond to the naval challenge in the East, when its capacity to undertake even limited operations in the West was far from adequate. The Indian Navy, on the other hand, could maintain overwhelming strength in both theatres. It was in this desperate situation that the decision to deploy Ghazi on India's eastern coast emerged.

Ghazi's deployment to the Bay of Bengal must be regarded as a measure taken to rectify a strategic posture that was getting out of step with military realities. Our response to Indian military deployments around East Pakistan was a series of ad hoc measures, taken from time to time, as a reaction to the Indian build-up. Despatch of Ghazi to India's Eastern seaboard, not part of the original plans, was one such step taken at the insistence of our Military High Command to reinforce Eastern Command. Pressure on the Pakistan Navy to extend the sphere of its operations into the Bay of Bengal increased with the growth of Indian and Indian- inspired naval activities around East Pakistan.

The strategic soundness of the decision has never been questioned. Ghazi was the only ship which had the range and capability to undertake operations in the distant waters under control of the enemy. The presence of a valuable target in the shape of the aircraft carrier Vikrant, the pride of the Indian Fleet, in that area was known. The plan had all the ingredients of daring and surprise which are essential for success in a situation tilted heavily in favour of the enemy. Indeed, had the Ghazi been able to sink or even damage the Indian aircraft carrier the shock effect alone would have been sufficient to upset Indian naval plans. The naval situation in the Bay of Bengal would have undergone a drastic transformation, and carrier-supported military operations in the coastal areas would have been affected. So tempting were the prospects of a possible success, that the mission was approved, despite several factors which militated against it.

Against it was the consideration of Ghazi's aging machinery, overdue for a re-fit. It was difficult to sustain prolonged operations in a distant area, in the total absence of repair, logistic and recreational facilities in the vicinity. At this time, submarine repair facilities were totally absent at Chittagong - the only port in the east. It was on these grounds that the proposal to deploy Ghazi in the Bay of Bengal was opposed by Captain Submarines and many others. The objections were later reluctantly dropped or overruled due to the pressures mentioned earlier.

On 14 November 1971, PNS Ghazi, under the command of Cdr. Zafar Mohammad Khan, sailed out of harbour with war orders issued to the Commanding Officer. A report expected from the submarine on 26 November was not received. Anxiety grew with every day that passed, after frantic efforts to establish communications with the submarine failed to produce results. Before hostilities broke out in the West on 3

December, doubts about the fate of the submarine had already begun to agitate the minds of submariners and many others at Naval Headquarters. Several reasons could, however, be attributed to the failure of the submarine to communicate.

The first indication of Ghazi's tragic fate came when a message by NHQ, India, claiming sinking of Ghazi on the night of 3 December, but issued, strangely enough, on 9 December, was intercepted. Both the manner of its release and the text, quoted below, clarified very little: "I am pleased to announce that Pakistan Navy submarine Ghazi was sunk off Visakhapatnam by our ships on 3/4 December. Dead bodies and other conclusive evidence floated to surface yesterday - 091101 EF." Their mysterious silence for 6 days, between 3 December, when the submarine was claimed to have been sunk, and 9 December, when the message was released, could not be easily explained. It gave rise to speculations that the submarine may well have been sunk earlier, at a time when the Indians were not ready to accept their involvement in the war. Failure of Ghazi to communicate after 26 November strongly supported such a possibility. As it happened, the release of the message on 9 December also served to divert attention of their public from the sinking of Khukri on this very date, even though the claim of sinking Ghazi was apparently made a few hours before the loss of Khukri.

The claim that Ghazi was sunk by an Indian ship has been contradicted by responsible Indian authors in accounts of the incident published after the war. The official version of the account given by Vice Admiral Krishnan, as quoted by Commodore Ranjit Rai in "A Nation and its Navy at War" is quoted here:

"On the night of the third, after the treacherous attack by Pakistan, it was appreciated that a pre-emptive underwater attack against the Naval Base at Visakhapatnam might be imminent and local naval defences were immediately put in readiness. In addition to all precautions within the harbour, two ships sailed out just before midnight on a mission. On obtaining a contact, an urgent attack was carried out with depth charges. The sound was, however, lost after the attack and the ship proceeded on her mission to join other units out at sea. Shortly after midnight and just before the Prime Minister's broadcast to the nation, a very loud explosion was heard rattling several window panes in buildings near the beach. This was reported to me by our coast battery which was awaiting any likely surface attack on Visakhapatnam.

We assumed that the explosion heard was probably the result of our attack and commenced our searches. The Eastern Naval Command Headquarters, as part of defence preparedness, had enlisted the support of all local fisherfolk and they had been briefed on what to do in events such as these. Two fishermen, on picking up a life jacket and other debris, lost no time in bringing these across to the Command Headquarters. Further searches could not be very extensive due to bad weather. Yesterday, however, we found three bodies and a lot of flotsam and jetsam. There is ample evidence available from these, that the submarine destroyed was none other than the Pakistani ship Ghazi." The bodies found were given a sailor's burial at sea, in accordance with Service custom and with appropriate ceremony.

Another version of the incident, substantially at variance with that given by Vice Admiral Krishnan was published in the 1972 edition of Indian Defence Journal "Chanakya". Numerous contradictions in the published Indian versions of the incident, viewed with suspicion and doubt in Pakistan, have led to the conclusion that the Indians do not know how Ghazi sank.

The only information on the subject from an independent source comes from an Egyptian naval officer, serving at that time on an Egyptian submarine under refit in Visakhapatnam harbour. He has confirmed the occurrence of a "big explosion" in the vicinity of the harbour "around late night". So powerful was the explosion that rocked the harbor that some of the shores supporting the submarine in the graving dock, where she was docked, fell off. There were no naval ships, as reported by this officer, outside the harbour, and it was not until about an hour after the explosion, that two Indian naval ships were observed leaving harbour.

Since all 82 members of her crew lost their lives, it is unlikely that the mystery of the circumstances in which Ghazi sank will ever be unveiled. Commodore Ranjit Rai concludes: "... at that time how the Ghazi was sunk remained unclear, as it does today."

It was not until 10 February that the loss of Ghazi was officially acknowledged with a terse announcement by a Pakistani Defence Ministry spokesman that the submarine Ghazi was lost on passage from Karachi to Chittagong where she was to report on 26 November. The intervening period between the Indian announcement on 9 December and the official acknowledgment of the submarine's loss by Pakistan was one of anguish and agony for the family members of the crew. Even after the official announcement, many of them kept hoping that their dear ones would one day return home. Rumours that some members of the crew had survived, and were taken prisoners of war, prolonged their agony.

There can and should be no doubt about the courage and dedication of her Commanding Officer and crew. An ironic feature of war is that courage and valour in an unsuccessful campaign are rarely rewarded in the same manner as similar, or even lesser acts, in a successful operation of war. And so it was with Ghazi. A naval establishment, PNS Zafar named after the Commanding Officer, was commissioned at Islamabad on shifting of Naval Headquarters to the capital after the war. Soon afterwards, the road crossing that gives access to the Naval Residential Sector in Islamabad, where the establishment is located, acquired the name of 'Zafar Chowk', and turned into a notable city landmark. Enshrined here, far removed from where the submarine lies in the watery depths, is the memory of those brave officers and men who, in the relentless pursuit of the enemy, sacrificed their lives for their country, and the true story of their courageous deeds remains untold.

The obituary for the Ghazi is a plaque of an Urdu couplet found on one of the bodies: "We are far from home, when will we see our loved ones again." R.I.P. Ghazi.

Chapter 14
INS Khukri falls prey to PNS Hangor

At sea, especially in war, the Captain and his team must act unhesitatingly without orders, in emergencies which are not infrequent, in the spirit and manner their superior would desire.

The war at sea was going well for India, and with the first five days bringing their measures of triumph — namely the attacks on Karachi, the sinking of Ghazi and the exploits of Vikrant - all these had created a tremendous sense of confidence in this small sea- going arm. The first major blow to the Indian Navy came on the fateful night of 9 December. It rocked the Navy when the reality of actual war hit the sea-going community at large.

The 1,200-tonne Khukri formed part of the Western Fleet Task Force which was hunting enemy submarines in the Arabian Sea. Whilst the officers and men were tuned in to listen to the All India Radio news at 8.50 pm on the ship's SRE (Sound Reproduction Equipment), Khukri was hit by more than one E-5 French torpedo, fired from one of Pakistan Navy's three newly acquired Daphne- class submarines, Hangor (Cdr. A. Tasneem) about 40 miles off Diu Head. In command was Captain Mahendra Nath Mulla a 45- year old tall, strapping Royal Navy-trained anti-submarine warfare specialist with earlier command experience of destroyer INS Rana and Second-in-Command of INS Krishna (the Kistna). One can picture him on the bridge of his ship, after helplessly realizing that hope was lost, and forced to give the order "Abandon Ship'. Then he directed his second-in-command to cast life-boats and buoys into the sea. In carrying out this vital task, 33-year-old Lt Commander Joginder Kumar Suri also went down with the ship. The file report from the Times of India of that day is reproduced:

Captain Mulla goes down after saving his shipmates

Eighteen officers and 176 sailors went down with the anti- submarine frigate, INS Khukri, as she sank in minutes in the Arabian Sea, torpedoed by PNS Hangor on the night of December 9. Capt. Mahendra Nath Mulla stood by his ill-fated shipmates to the last and shared their destiny, despite having an opportunity to save himself. The story of the gallant commanding officer's efforts to rescue as many as he could, was told by eye-witnesses among the survivors. It was dramatized on radio by Melville de Mello.

Many of the younger, inexperienced sailors preferred the false security of the sturdy steel deck of the frigate below their feet to the unknown dangers lurking in the bosom of the sea. The 183- cm-tall Captain Mulla himself pushed them into the sea, directing them to swim away. When one of them offered him a life-jacket he said, "Go on, save yourselves: do not worry about me." There was no confusion, no panic because the Captain's calm had transmitted itself to his men.

As the survivors were swimming away to avoid being sucked in by the sinking ship, some of them looked back. The ship was sinking fast and the sea was closing over the bridge, the highest part of the ship's super structure, from where the Captain assumes command. Captain Mulla was sitting in his chair on the bridge. He had faithfully to the very last, to the best of his ability, served those who had served him so well. Six officers and 61 sailors who have survived will ever remember Captain Mulla's stoic demeanour and calm in the face of adversity. The whole nation cherishes the memory of this hero.

Captain Mulla's actions are in the highest traditions. The Captain of a ship is the last man to abandon ship when the ship sinks fast, as could happen in war. Many would be still endeavouring to save the ship, as it happened in the case of the Khukri. "While the highest traditions of a Captain going down with his ship are fully appreciated, the Royal Navy cannot afford to lose experienced commanding officers. They are therefore, to endeavour to save themselves, so that they may live to fight another day ..." This was the British Admiralty Order during World War II. It might well be so, but Captain Mulla followed the traditions set for captains of going down with the ship when all endeavours to save it proved futile. Captain Mulla was awarded MVrC posthumously.

The sinking has evinced very keen discussion on the issues that such large casualties, resulting in loss of life of this nature, throw up. Was Indian Navy's damage control ability in doubt? Can two or three torpedoes sink a ship like the Khukri specially built for anti-submarine warfare with British 170/174 sonar sets and Mortar MK 10? What speed was the ship doing? What after- accident search and rescue measures were taken to reduce loss of life? The discussion still goes on, but some factors are touched upon in this chapter along with some facets of human life.

The Khukri was well manned, worked up, and the Second-in- Command of the ship Lt. Cdr. J.K. Suri, 33, a bachelor, was in fact, a specialist communications officer. An excellent Navy squash player, unfortunately he was a poor swimmer. He was on the bridge when the torpedoes hit. The ship lost power and went down in minutes. Some men trying to get out of the ship in darkness from below deck ran into those like J.K. Suri going down to fetch their life jackets. The Khukri had only two exits and over 100 men crowding these two exit ports must have caused panic. In the melee they would have got crushed whilst the ship went down. Some were trapped as the aft hatch was locked. Yet the Captain helped each one he could see on the bridge to leave the ship. Commander Oomen, the tough and plump Malayali Engineer Officer may have decided to go down to the Engine Room like so many other dedicated sailors who are trained, by instinct, to rush to their action post, and suffered a watery death. Lt. Suresh Kundanmal, a fine 'Sword of honour' officer is reported to have jumped over the side after coaxing his Captain to do so too, but could have well got sucked into the whirlpool caused by the sinking ship.

All this is reported by survivors like Lt. Manu Sharma, another fine officer who has since left the Navy and settled in USA. His wife Rekha says he was extremely shaken when rescued back to Bombay, borrowing clothes and uniforms like all the others, and cautioned not to talk to anyone. All such happenings leave scars on people, and so it was for the rescued survivors of the Khukri. It was a shocked Navy, trying to cope with an unprecedented situation. Surviving officers and men wanted to talk, take things off their chest, and seek reassurance while they awaited the inquiry that followed. After all, warfare at sea has proved that the submarine with its stealth is still superior, and can only be killed after it has killed and shown herself.

The successful attack by a Pakistan Navy submarine, was possible because INS Khukri was doing only 12 knots. Lt. V.K. Jain, a bright Electrical Officer, who had researched on an attachment at TIFR (Tata) to improve the sonar performance of the 170/174 set was testing his new hardware on board. It is known that Captain Mulla did not favour this slow speed nor zig- zag to avoid submarines (SOP) but gave in to this young officer's request. One of those misfortunes, combined with the fact that this class of ship did not have a strong shipside and thus easily succumbed to damage. It is also possible that the Pakistan Navy submarine had tracked Khukri for some time, by keeping in company with some fishing craft which were earlier in the vicinity. The officers and crew were possibly not at their best alert whilst concentrating on the news bulletin, even though the ship's company was at defence stations. The crew was also not wearing life jackets continuously, because even in World War II this practice was not followed. INS Kirpan (Cdr. R.R. Sood) was in company and that ship also did not gain any submarine contact. This then was the fate of INS Khukri. The hit caused the few on upper deck, to be thrown out into the sea. The ship's Physical Training Instructor (PTI) held on to a piece of wood the whole night. Some took to life rafts, some lay in their life jackets awaiting rescue. (One recalls the famous story of "Kapok Kid" the navigator who was ridiculed for keeping his life jacket on at all times, but ended up the lone survivor of the Murmansk Convoy in World War One).

A major decision lay on the broad shoulders of the Captain of INS Kirpan, Cdr R.R. Sood (awarded the Vir Chakra, and later Rear Admiral). Should he pick up survivors, hunt the submarine or clear the area? He decided to clear the area, signaled the happenings as a witness, and requested the Flag Officer C-in-C Western Naval Command, Bombay for help. In the operation that followed INS Kadmatt (Cdr. S. Jain, later Flag Officer C-in-C Western Naval command) and Kripan arrived at the scene the next morning and carried out rescue operations. A total of eight officers and 61 men were rescued, whilst 18 officers and 176 sailors went down. A memorial was erected for them on the coast near Diu, and their memory is evoked every time a thoughtful Captain sails past the position where the Khukri memorial hostel was built at Bombay to house the widows and fatherless children of the ill- fated ship. The parents of Lt. V.K. Jain instituted the Jain Memorial Medal for excellence in innovation.

The reaction on the other ships in the fleet was naturally one of sadness. But it also acted as a warning. Anti-submarine warfare drills improved, torpedo evasion technique was practiced earnestly, life jackets and life raft release inspections and drills were exercised meticulously. Ships began to see themselves in a similar situation and attended to their damage control arrangements. It cannot be said that it was an expensive blessing in disguise, but it can be said that this event certainly did make its point, the Indian Navy now realizing what submarine torpedo attacks are all about.

While the Pakistan Navy achieved a kill through the sinking of Khukri, the three Indian Navy submarines of the F class deployed on offensive patrols failed to achieve any kills. The restrictions on submarines are many. They were banned by law to sink merchant ships. The London Naval Arms Limitation Treaty of 1930 declared that submarines "may not sink or render incapable of navigation a merchant vessel without having first placed passengers, crew and ships papers in place of safety." The Indian Navy was in the same dilemma in 1971 and had restricted its submarines to attack only on enemy warships that were positively identified. Since the chance of being sunk itself by a warship if she exposed herself, were high, it amounted to prohibition in a larger sense and inhibiting the freedom of a submarine commander in war.

The period after the war was traumatic for the families of those reported missing. Lt. Suresh Kundanmal's family got reports that many survivors had drifted away and that Suresh had been able to swim to safety after having given his life jacket to another. Astrologers too, assured the family that he was alive. Hope lived on for many. J.K. Suri's brother did not settle the family assets hoping his bachelor brother would return. Meanwhile, a polite message went out to all Captains at sea which ordered them not to emulate Captain Mulla's traditional Captain-goes-down-with-his ship attitude; but to save their experience to fight another day.

A few weeks after the war, some fine sailors from the Khukri joined INS Nilgiri, India's first Leander, as part of rehabilitation of the crew. The ship's company of the Nilgiri looked upon this as a superstitious omen, but when assured that they were experienced shipwrecked sailors who could possibly be of help in educating the ship's company of the new Nilgiri, welcomed them on board warmly like so many others of that ill-fated ship.

Incidentally, in the Falklands war, a total of seven warships were sunk, but all their Captains were rescued and lived to tell their tale. Admiral Nanda's message to his fleet Captains was propitious. Another Khukri has been commissioned, so that we do not forget.

THE KHUKRI IS NO MORE

I am Manu Sharma who served the Navy.
I knew the Khukri which also symbolizes Gurkha strength
And I was on her last voyage wherein served, Mahendra Nath Mulla the Captain who smoked His last cigarette as he went down.
The old man to the sea.
Thambe Ommen the ship's Engineer who tried his best
But the Arabian Sea engulfed him.
Young Suresh Kundanmal that fine personality
Who gave his life jacket to another, And lost his life without knowing it.
Joginder Suri who was the executive of the ship But saw his own execution for he could not swim. Also down went those smiling 176 Indian Seadogs The others whose names I remember not
But the Khukri I do.
They all lie some forty miles from Diu
Undisturbed till they are picked up.
And only a wreck marks that special danbuoy stave
As another Khukri rides India's waves.

Chapter 15
Forgotten Heroes - Roy Chou and Aku Roy

Should auld acquaintance be forgot, And ne'er brought to mind?
Should auld acquaintance be forgot.
And days o' auld Lang Syne. - Robert Burns.

Lt Cdr Jayanto Kumar Roy Choudhry - 'Roy Chou'

An unsung hero of the Bangladesh war, known as 'Navy Bahadur' for his Vir Chakra, is "Roy Chou" from the 14th National Defence Academy course, a close friend and course mate of the author, but who now lives modestly at Lebong in Darjeeling. Lt Cdr J.K.Roy Choudhry, a Bengali officer, was whisked away from his gunnery instructor job in Cochin in mid-1971 to work under directions of Capt. R.P. Khanna (NOIC Calcutta) and to join the Mukti Bahini. His family hailed from East Bengal. His aged father had been left behind in East Pakistan, when the rest of the family migrated to India during the partition and his family had fallen from zamindari riches. Roy Chou's brothers sent him to the Prince of Wales Military College at Dehradun, and then National Defence Academy. It was his boxing, athletics and football 'Blues' (NDA cadets who achieved high standards) from the National Defence Academy, Khadakvasla, that kept him in fine fettle in whatever he was achieving near enemy lines. He excelled in all games and showed his grit, and served as Gunnery Officer on INS Vikrant. When called up in mid-1971, to join the Mukti Bahini he was possibly happy to go to East Bengal, even though no immediate family remained there. It was a nostalgic return to his land of birth and he was there for a cause and to serve to his country, like many others.

He now speaks of the operations he executed with

Mukti Bahini sailors deep into East Pakistan, and when asked about the massive shrapnel wound in his leg, the reply he offers is interesting: "Oh that I got from my own Indian Air Force, as my prize for my service to the nation. Thank God they left me alive. Most of my East Bengali comrades died."

Roy Chou operated with Mukti Bahini as Captain of a requisitioned fishing craft Padma fitted out with 40/60 Bofors guns at Calcutta. The guns were incidentally supplied by a retired naval Commander Rao who was the legal agent of Bofors. Later Rao handed over to Win Chadha, who got entangled in the infamous Bofors scandal, for accepting winding up Agency charges, when Rajiv Gandhi banned arms agents. The Chadha family took refuge in Dubai, as Win's earnings were being linked to the Rs 64 crore bribe (commission) with the Hindujas to divert attention from Ottavio Quattrocchi of Italy, who died in 2013.

Twenty Indian naval divers and sailors, mostly Bengalis, trained over 400 young East Bengali naval divers, sailors and volunteers at Plassey near Calcutta, including Pakistan Navy submariners who had deserted from France. They were supported by BSF and Eastern Army Command to carry out attacks deep into Sector 10 of East Pakistan with limpet mines and grenades, as Mukti Bahini. They made many forays into Bangladesh and attacked ships evocative of the Second World War, in diver and commando like raids, sinking 200,000 tons.

Around 8 December, a squadron of three Mukti Bahini boats (Force Alpha), under Cdr M.N. Samant (Sammy) in INS Panvel (with Lt Cdr J.P.A. Noronha, both later decorated MVrC), Padma (Lt Cdr A.K.Choudhury VrC) and Palash (Lt Cdr Charlie Mitra who had made forays into Bangladesh with BSF craft Chitraganda), set sail from Calcutta. They were advised to display a yellow bunting cloth, four feet by four feet square on the ship's bridge top to avoid being strafed by the Indian Air Force and Indian Navy planes and to also fly a yellow flag.

All was well till the craft departed Hasnabad from the Indian side and arrived at Akram Point to enter the Pussur river, and at 2 am saw two merchant ships on radar trying to escape. The ships were out of range of the Bofors 40/60 mm, but the reporting led to the capture of Anwar Baksh and Baqir later carrying Baluchi troops and families to Karachi when they reached the open seas. There is the famous story of the capture of Anwar Baksh by a boarding party led by Lt Cdr Raz Bajaj when he killed a soldier on board who tried to attack him. He found himself ostracized later.

Task force Alpha led by Sammy crossed Mongla and Chalna early morning and neared Khulna to attack PNS Titumeer under the command of Commodore Gulberdin, in single column, when a formation of our own IAF Gnats appeared overhead and began to pull up for a diving run. No one realized the 'Snafu' (situation all f****d up); that the yellow bunting was helping the IAF to aim better on otherwise camouflaged boats. When all hell broke loose and their proficient aim, meant for the Pakistanis, was targeted on Sammy's force, it was Roy Chou who saw his boat Padma subjected to a strafing run with men on deck being killed even as they waved. Roy Chou saw his boat floundering and decided to beach his boat. Like Capt M.N. Mulla on INS Khukri, he ordered "Abandon ship" when all hope was lost. Forty died in the Khulna operation by Force Alpha.

Roy Chou was thrown overboard into the Pussur river, a tributary of the holy Ganga, and to his good luck INS Panvel sailed just past him, also manoeuvring in the melee to avoid the 'friendly' Gnats who reappeared. Someone recognized Chou, bloody and with shrapnel in his leg, saw he could not swim ashore, and rescued him. Roy Chou was filled with thoughts of some of his colleagues, now no more. He was hospitalized in the Military Hospital at Calcutta, where his wife had delivered a baby girl in the maternity ward not far away from his room a day before, but his thoughts were, "Why did this happen?" and "Where is Mitra?" He asks that even today. He remained melancholy and even the thought of his newborn daughter did not elevate his mood. During one of his breaks in Calcutta, his wife briefly wrote that Chou seemed to be enjoying his work, but she worried for him after reading the papers. He had left her behind in Calcutta, quite pregnant, and there were long stretches when Roy Chou was not heard of.

That ended Roy Chou's escapades but it came to light that in the fog of war, instructions like yellow bunting can get fouled up and the message did not reach the IAF Squadron of the Eastern Air Command at Shillong. Bunting is a naval term for cloth woven for naval flags. The story of President John F. Kennedy in World War II came true again. He always believed in double checking his minor instructions because of a theory he picked up in command of Patrol Boat PT 109, when it ran aground under his command in World War II. He ordered "Abandon ship" like Roy Chou did and was about to jump overboard assuming that he was the last remaining one on the ship. Just then the phone from his engine room rang, and his duty machinist reported, "Captain, I think we are aground". It was then that he uttered the phrase, "Some bastard down there may not get the message. Always double-check".

Anyway, Roy Chou was brought back alive to relate this tale and how he earned his well deserved Vir Chakra and the heroic actions of Mukti Bahini. Regrettably, like many others who toiled and risked their all in war, but could not pick up that 'good boy's chit' called the Annual Confidential Report (ACR). His name did not appear in the list of those promoted to Commander in 1974, unlike term mates who did get promoted. In war, tempers can get frayed. Roy Chou who was superseded for promotion promptly put pen to paper much against the advice that

John Hopwood gave in 'Laws of the Navy' on resignation: "For some shelved and forgotten, With nothing to thank for their fate, Save "That" (on a half-sheet of foolscap), Which a fool "had the honour to state." (The way a letter always began in the Navy)."

When this author contacted Roy Chou on the phone at Visakhapatnam where he was the Command Gunnery Officer and asked him to hang on for the next promotion list and withdraw his resignation as advised by the Chief of Personnel (COP) Vice Admiral M.N.Batra who had received a call from Admiral Chandy Kuruvilla, Roy Chou replied in a tone which many of his superiors and colleagues had heard as polite, but full of conviction. "Some give up their lives for a thing called pride (as a Rajput does). The least I can do is to give up the service I love for my pride, and what I did in 1971. Do me a favour and get my papers through." I tried to persuade him and said the COP wanted me to convince him to withdraw his resignation. He replied, "Hey, while all you guys were sleeping with your wives, I was saving your backside." Roy Chou is one of such brave mavericks, who fight against odds, and lead their men in the face of daily death in war. It is fortunate the Indian Navy had many such officers and men in 1971. In peace they are often forgotten, as is the way of the world with soldiers. This author visited Roy Chou at Lebong in Darjeeling and found him living on his paltry VrC allowance and some savings in a charming wooded house.

The author's research with the IAF could not locate the pilots who carried out the Gnat attack. However, when this author asked Lt Gen J.F.R.Jacob, the Chief of Staff Eastern Army Command, who played a stellar role in the 1971 war and the surrender, to comment on this incidence of 'Blue on Blue' fratricide fire by Gnats, said the task force Alpha had crossed the Bomb Line and Padma and Palash were targeted by the Gnats. Surely IAF pilots are not dumb and would have taken a closer look and seen no one was firing back and yellow buntings were the markers. "Some bastard did not send the message, or some bastard did not pass on the message", is what Roy Chou told me with no bitterness.

Statistics by an Air Force pilot: During the 1971 war on both fronts, the IAF flew a total of 11,549 sorties. Of these 6,609 sorties were flown by fighters, remaining by helicopters and transport. Of the 6609 fighter sorties, 3243 sorties were flown towards 'Close Air Support'. Fratricide was an accepted part of the battle, if it did take place. 28 planes were lost during Close Support, and 24 were lost during Counter Air over Pakistani targets, and only 4 were lost in Air combat and 15 were lost on Ground at Pathankot and Kalaikunda airfields.

Lt Cdr Ashok 'Aku' Roy

Another unsung hero of the 1971 war is Lt Cdr Ashok Roy (Missing in Action Presumed Dead) who served in and near East Pakistan from Calcutta with the Mukti Bahini before the 1971 war and later in the Western Sector flying a Breguet Alize on a Electronic Warfare sortie during the war, when he was lost. A very interesting question of the 1971 war which has not been answered with definite proof is how this fine young pilot Lt Cdr Ashok Roy went down in Alize No. 203 on a flight from Jamnagar to Bombay with Lieutenant Sirohi and Chief Aircrew-man Vijayan. Ashok had endeared himself to each and every one who had come in contact with him. He was an emotional, strapping red-faced 'Pathan' looking officer whose mother was an Estonian. He was the son of Brig A.N. Roy (later Major General) in the Medical Corps. This well-built six-footer was proficient in games, a powerful swimmer and an ace Indian Air Force trained carrier qualified pilot with high grading. He had done his stint on board INS Vikrant in the Cobra Squadron of Alizes and was transferred to an 'R' class destroyer that aviators are posted to gain sea experience.

Ashok Roy had been through many scrapes in life. In the late 1960's whilst in service his eyesight had started to weaken and he prayed to God to heal his eyes so that he could catapult off the deck of the Vikrant again. He had been advised by one and all to pray to God — something he did not normally do. Apparently God heard his prayers, for lo and behold, Ashok was back in AI SI medical category and back to the flat-top he loved. In another incident in a car race back from the Sealord Hotel to the naval base in Cochin, after a night out, as Aku was running out of the hotel, he fell into a ditch and broke his knee. Despite this, he raced all the way to the base, won the race and the prize — only to be admitted into hospital, plastered and immobilised. He was again advised to pray to God, to get back to his first love — aircraft. Aku was appointed as the Torpedo and Anti Submarine Officer (TASO) in INS Rana, and could be seen working on weekends coming to grips with the 144 Q Sonar set and Combined Anti Submarine Execises (CASEXES).

Suddenly in June 1971, Aku was not to be seen nor heard of. Later, one learnt that he had gone off to be with Sammy (Cdr M.N. Samant) and his band of some Bengalis and divers operating from Calcutta under cover and presumably engaged in planning on what to do with that 8 million influx of refugees into West Bengal from East Pakistan. All of a sudden, just before the war, an emaciated Aku turned up in Bombay and refused to talk about his exploits. He was pining to go on leave. Just then the war broke out and Aku was back to flying his beloved Alize, a flying machine that carries good ARAR French electronic warfare equipment, possibly the world's best at the time. His other colleagues were on the Vikrant in the Eastern Sector and that saddened him a bit.

This author learnt that Ashok Roy along with Mukti Bahini personnel had many times carried foreign exchange to East Pakistan and had gone all the way to Chittagong port on an undercover operation and attacked and sunk ships around 14 August, as reported in the media. On his way back, he was trying, along with Bengali refugees, to cross into India in South Tripura area near a place called Belonia, where the Battalion headquarters of the 4 Guards (1 Rajput) was located. He looked suspiciously like a Pathan and the Army team guarding the area caught him and beat and cursed him, hit him with rifle butts and hand cuffed him, as he could not say where in East Pakistan he stayed. JCO Subedar Makhan Lal interrogated him, and told him he would be kept in custody. Ashok then told them he was a Hindu, and lowered his trousers to prove it! They took him to Major Chandra Kant (later VrC and bar) and made him sprawl at his feet. Major Chandra Kant says that at this point, Aku asked to speak to the Major in private. Ashok told him he was sworn to secrecy, but he was a naval officer - Lt Cdr Ashok Roy from the National Defence Academy, and was returning from a secret mission. When asked names of his course mates, he rattled off names of Shivvy, Gilbert Menezes, John D'Silva whom Chandra Kant knew. Aku's repatriation was arranged. His father never learnt what his heroic son did in East Bengal but the VrC was a consolation.

Next heard, Aku was operating from Jamnagar from where the IAF were launching strikes. One day in December during the war, Aku, and Lt A.K.Dua in another Alize, took off from Jamnagar. Aku ordered his junior winger to proceed to Bombay and he himself went off to possibly investigate a target, or on some classified mission. Whatever it was, Aku was never heard of again. He was awarded the Vir Chakra and his citation reads that a Pakistan Air Force plane shot him down. Pakistan Radio did announce shooting down of a plane over the sea, but was Aku there? As asked of the MH570 in 2014, how did it happen? Was he shot down by a Pakistani trawler with anti-aircraft guns? Was he on a secret mission and taken prisoner? If he was shot down, surely Alizes can survive a belly-landing type of ditch, and Aku was a powerful swimmer. Did the Pakistan Air Force actually strafe him to death, a single-engined slow-paced aircraft at that? Was he surprised? Did he suffer engine breakdown? Did he trespass into enemy territory on an EW mission?

Somewhere in the 2500 square miles west of Jamnagar lies the answer to the questions of his family and friends.

An emissary from Pakistan informed Maj Gen. A.N. Roy that his son was seen with a broken leg in plaster in the Lahore jail along with some East Bengalis. When the General tried to arrange his son's escape at some cost to himself, Aku apparently wanted a slight delay. The story goes that Aku was rescued by the Baluchis along with the other pilots and kept in captivity and then in settlement

— for he did resemble the Baluchis. This mystery can be solved only by a co-operative answer by the Pakistani Defence Forces, for Sirohi was also not heard of. His wife, Priscilla, left India for the UK. Vijayan, the air crewman, is the other unsung hero. As time passes, memories also fade.

Lest we forget, this chapter is dedicated to Roy Chou and Aku, and the many others like them.

Chapter 16
Pakistan War Stories – 1971

The Pakistani naval raid in 1965 on Dwarka left the Indian Navy infuriated and humiliated. Admiral SN Kohli. The 1971 war has been pushed under the carpet, and we pretend it never took place. Pakistan recognized Bangla Desh only after March 1972. - Cmde Arshad Rahim, PN

This chapter is a pot-pouri of interesting snippets to encourage readers and researchers to delve further into the actions of India's and Pakistan's Armed Forces. Their wars have been futile.

Haider's critique. Air Cmde Sajad 'Nosey' Haider in his book, "The Flight of the Falcon", demolishes myths of Indo-Pak wars. In the 1971 war, Pakistan lost more than 72 aircraft, 51 combat types, admitting 25 to enemy action. It had F-6s, Mirage- IIIs, 6 Jordanian F-104s which were not returned to their donors. IAF lost 65 IAF aircraft, 54 were admitted. The IAF helicopters executed the Meghna Heli Bridge (Op Cactus Lily) on 9 December 1971, and airlifted troops of IV Corps from Brahmanbaria to Raipura/ Narsingdi over the Meghna, surprising the Paksitan army. Haider blames the splitting of Pakistan on the Punjabi cabal of Ayub Khan. He admits West Pakistan's "attitudinal problem" about Bengalis, and is critical of Bengali labour.

Haider theorizes that Mrs Gandhi's objection to Sri Lanka's facilitating the airlift of three Pakistani infantry divisions in 1971, was part of India's conspiracy to break Pakistan. Yet he sweeps under the carpet the genocide of millions of Bangladeshis by the brutal Pakistan Army, described in Gary J Bass' The Blood Telegram - India's Secret War based on US Consul Archer Blood' dispatches from Dacca from 4 April 1971 onwards (see The Tilt).

Haider labours to save the mauled reputation of the PAF after the 1971 war. He claims that the PAF held itself back to support a spectacular attack on India by Pakistan's II Corps. He claims that the attack never came because Gen. Tikka Khan and his coterie were hoping the American 7th fleet would come to Pakistan's rescue. Haider is bitter about Pakistan Navy's not acknowledging PAF support, but blames the "blue on blue" fratricide, of a PAF F-86 Sabre attacking a Pakistan navy ship, on the navy itself.

On corruption, Haider cites a US $ 890 million deal with France for submarines was inflated to US $1.2 billion for the kickbacks. Later, shoulder fired Mistral SAMs were hurriedly acquired on the pretext that an Indian and Israeli attack was imminent on the Kahuta nuclear complex, despite the fact that such missiles would be useless in such an attack. India too suffers the same affliction (HDW, Bofors, Scorpene, Tatra, AW -101 Westland Agusta deals).

The book describes the coup against President Gen Yahya Khan and a virtual mutiny in the PAF. Haider claims his friendship with Bhutto was betrayed and he was wrongly imprisoned but later let off in the "Attock Ahmedi conspiracy" to assassinate Bhutto. This was called a "Qadiani" conspiracy. In the light of the May 2010 massacre of Qadianis in their mosque in Lahore, one can imagine how much further Pakistani attitudes against Qadianis have moved in the years since Haider's trial was held. Haider's inspiration to write his book came after the attack on the Indian Parliament in 2001 when India executed Op Parakarma, and he saw the depths to which the country he loved and served loyally had fallen.

Pak Submarines. In 1971, East Pakistan Bengali naval officers were put on non-combat duties. Some were jailed in the West and others escaped, including the author's friend Lt Col Sajjad Zahir. Manpower was reduced by a third. Rear Adm M.N.Vasudeva relates how Bengali submariners, who deserted in France with Indian embassy help, were debriefed at safe houses in Delhi's Sujan Singh Park. Pakistan had India worried with its advantage in sub-surface forces, with 4 submarines and 6 Cosmos midgets with a torpedo each. The Daphnes were to patrol the west coast of India. Vice Admiral Tasnim met the author and he disclosed that on 3/4 December night, Hangor was at 50 metres depth, and had in his sight 8 IN ships leaving Mumbai, but with no orders to attack, a golden opportunity was missed. After sinking INS Khukri, Cdr Tasnim heroically escaped by diving and conserving battery power.

Pakistani Naval Strategy. The 1971 war reveals that Pakistan replicated the 1965 strategy of 'offensive defence'. It deployed its surface fleet along its shores for 'sea defence denial'. In 1987 in Ex Brasstacks, this author then as C-in-C Pakistan Navy under Lt Gen V.N.Sharma successfully employed the same strategy. A presentation was made to PM Rajiv Gandhi at Palam, with the Chiefs in attendance. Deploying Pakistani surface ships on a mathematically calculated cordon 150 miles from Karachi, and submarines in an offensive role off India, validated the belief that submarines are the most suitable platforms for countries with limited naval power for use against a superior force. Today India has depleted submarine strength which needs correction, but has excellent newly inducted P8is for maritime reconnaissance. Pakistan Navy has employed MESMA Air Independent Propulsion (AIP) in its Agostas.

The book, Sentinel s of the Seas, provides the Pakistani story of the riverine operations in the East, by Capt Ejaz R. Chaudhri, include actions by Sylhet and Rajashahi and its escape. The gunboats had directed Sqn Ldr P.Q.Mehdi's No 14 Sqn's F-86s in Op Barisal. Cmde Arshad Rahim's chapter on the 1971 war has excellent photos and proved invaluable for research.

From 'Bubbles of War' by Rear Adm Mian Zahir Shah: Vice Admiral A.U. Khan confirms Vice Admiral Ahmad Tasnim's story 'Repairing the air-conditioner', on PNS Hangor. After a major breakdown of the air-conditioning, it had to return to the dockyard to be repaired in 36 hours to prevent electrical short circuits, over- heating and deterioration of equipment. While repairing on surface, it detected an Indian warship on ECM at night, and Tasnim heard an urgent call, "Captain on the Bridge". LRO Bashir reported, "Sir, I've just picked up a ship transmitting on CCN to Bombay. Strength is strong. The ship is very close!" The warship switched off her navigation lights a mile away, which is fairly close at sea, and started challenging by flashing light. Tasnim made no reply, and curbed a submariner's instinct to dive - a dead give- away. He decided to 'charade a fishing vessel', vented ballast tanks to go down a bit, with only the sail showing, and with a sigh of relief, saw the IN ship turn away with two Osas, possibly changing stations. The episode lasted 20 minutes. Eight days later, Khukri was sunk ... in retrospect, thanks to repairs to its air conditioner!

Lt Hassan Asif (in 'Dead or Alive') was navigating officer of PNS Khaibar on 4 December and recalls that as the ship went down, he found himself in a group of 55 survivors in the water on that dark moonless night. By sunset next day, only 31 were left. The lifejackets of those who died were taken by those alive, who were rescued 14 hours later. Surg Lt Irshad had declared Topas Jogindar dead, but amazingly, on hearing a shout of 'pilao' he blew his whistle, and seemed to come alive, but later was seen as dead. Was it imagination? Steward Jan was floating past Asif on a plank; the pleading eyes of the dying man haunt him even today.

Commander M.Rafique, then a Sub Lt as DLO on Khaibar at the main switch board (actions stations), recalls the huge explosion forward of the funnel. Along with LO Lt Cdr Fazzal Ahmad (who did not survive) he started the

Emergency Diesel Generator. Able Seaman Adalat who was dead-beat in the water, wearily took off Khaibar's lifebuoy and handed it to Rafique. "Sir it is all finished for me. You have this now." With these last words, Adalat went to his watery grave. Labouring to stay afloat, Rafique was rescued but he let go of Khaibar's lifebuoy, and lost the souvenir that AB Adalat had given up his life for.

On 4 December, Lt Cdr Shaiq Usmani (later Justice Usmani) CO PNS Muhafiz, sailed 30 miles off Karachi. He ordered life jackets, but felt that a Captain puffing a pipe and wearing a life jacket would not look reassuring. A white light appeared on his port side at a thousand feet, and Usmani assumed it was an aircraft. Suddenly a Styx missile struck the funnel area with a flash, burning his skin and singeing his hair catapulting him high and then deep into the water with debris and flames. PNS Sadaqat, commanded by Lieut. Qayyum Khan finally rescued the survivors. Of the fifty, only three finally survived, including Usmani. His wife, who came to see him burnt completely black at PNHS Shifa, recognized him by his feet. Adm Zahir Shah saw a burnt pipe on the Judge's table, and with the Navy's help, collected such stories for the PN Book Club and published Bubbles of Water. Bravo Zulu Zahir.

Vice Adm S.T.H. Naqvi in 'The Lucky Captain' quotes Vice Adm Hiranandani's book "Transition to Triumph": "There were also reports that the Pakistan Navy on their own, fitted two midgets with external torpedo tubes for firing MK-44 torpedoes (actually E-5s). When one of them tried to fire against an Indian ship, the fire control system did not work." This is correct as Lt Naqvi commanded that 62 ton midget. One fine day on 6 December, off Kathiawar Coast in dog watch (1600-2000), the sonar picked up propeller noise and periscope broke surface. Naqvi sighted a Petya with side number obliterated at 1200 yards charging on, with no idea a midget was close. Naqvi ordered "Shoot!" Nothing happened. "Shoot! Dammit!"

he yelled, using more air pressure. The Petya came close, and Naqvi dived. On the Petya, Capt Gopal Rao or Cdr Tony Jain was the lucky Captain for the close shave he'd had with Naqvi's 'reluctant torpedo', as the angle of the midget at that moment prevented the torpedo from swimming out. The midget sat prominently at the roundabout in Karachi's Gizri area for some years, and the place is still called Submarine Chowk.

On the night of 8 December when the Vinash (with Jerath) carried out a missile attack, there were oiler PNS Dacca and minesweeper PNS Munsif off darkened Karachi. The sinking of Khaibar and sister ship Muhafiz, was fresh in their minds. Munsif was anchored between merchant ships and switched off radars. A tired EXO, Lt Jamil Akhtar, recalls he went to sleep. The steward shook Jamil shouting "Sir, Karachi is under attack!" Munsif came out unscathed and had a grandstand view of the four missiles fired by Jerath that night and lived to describe the attack in detail. Munsif first rescued the survivors of Dacca and thereafter from the burning MV Harmatton, when her tanks burst and a huge piece of burning debris flew in the direction of Munsif. A young sailor shouted "Missile! Missile!" Someone added "Abandon ship!" In moments, there were the sounds of a dozen men splashing in the water. Lt Akhtar got them back on board, especially Chief ERA Ashraf who always said, "Chees ye hai na jee" ("It's like this, you see"). Sub Lt Razaq Mirza on the darkened deck heard "Chees ye hai na jee. Sir, could you kindly chuck that life-buoy down?" Mirza smilingly replied, "Chees ye hai na jee, Chief Saab, you come back on board right now!"

On 8 December night, when the missile struck PNS Dacca, Captain (Retd) S.V.Safvi was a Sub Lt on watch. He saw a young OD jump, land unhurt on the steel deck and jump into the sea, clinging to the ship's side, screaming away that he couldn't swim, and would someone throw down a rope. Boats were lowered and the

OD survived the missile. Safvi calls him 'a born survivor'.

Adm A.U.Khan describes the painting of Hangor's attack on Khukri which is displayed at the Maritime Museum in Karachi. Cdr Tasnim, is giving orders to the Ops Room Team, asking to classify target in the early stages of the approach phase, and the team looks relaxed. On the left is the XO Khan himself, wearing headsets. The navigator is seen cross-checking target reports from the Sonar Operator, sitting next to the sonar console officer Lt F. Bokhari, who is working out target parameters - target course, speed and range on the self-illuminating tracing table. The Assistant Plotter with divider in hand is assisting him. This captures the spirit of the Ops Room of the Hangor.

After Hangor sank Khukri on the night of 9th December, the Indian Navy employed ships and Seakings to hunt the Hangor for 48 hours, and lobbed over hundred squids and depth charges, scaring Hangor as she was low on batteries and could not snorkel. Tasnim rigged Hangor for silence, switched off electrical equipment, creeping towards Karachi with oxygen candles and air scrubbers to revitalize the stale air. Movements of the crew were minimized to conserve oxygen. The Chief EA told Khan on his rounds, "Sir, lets go back home. I know these sasuras (referring to in-laws, but in this case Indians) intentions are not honorable." Khan replied, "Chief, we've sunk their ship, what do you expect ... we sank their ship!" Chief EA: "Yes Sir, but you are the EXO. Tell the Captain we have done our job, now stop playing this cat-and-mouse game with the sasuras and head home ... otherwise all that money I have hidden will be lost – forever!"

Zahir Shah's book has a story by Rear Adm S.A.Buquar about mining the Southern main approaches to Chittagong and the Karnaphuli River. A 1000-ton ship with a derrick was converted for mine-laying with Lt G.Z.Malik as CO. PNS Sylhet's Captain, Lt Sikandar Hayat Khan executed navigational directions, to lay moored mines at night

(Kutubdia island lights were doused) with Sylhet's TM 707 radar fixes keeping station at 7 knots while laying mines, each the size of a fat man - 35 mines per night for three days. On the final night, the crew fouled the derrick drill. A mine dropped between the ships. Sylhet heeled over to starboard, the outer side, and all hung on before she was righted back.

On 16 December, Lt Sikandar, and others gathered at Chittagong's naval base, heard the shattering announcement of Gen Niazi's Surrender on the 8 o'clock news on a transistor radio. Sikandar, in shocked silence, thinking of escape asked, "What about the minefield? Our own mines, meant to keep the enemy out, are going to turn to keep us in". A hushed silence followed. Buquar cheerfully told them he had made a tracing of the chart of the minefield. This became his ticket for a berth on board the Rajashahi's daring navigational escape out to sea, and passage to take asylum refuge at Penang (like Graf Spee did at Montivedeo after the Battle of the River Plate) with a full load of personnel. This escape took the Eastern Fleet by total surprise. Sikandar (as Cmde) in 'The Sacks of The Coins', writes that all treasury coins were put in bags with orders to Rajashahi to dump them at sea, which they did, but at Penang, a few bags were found. Not allowing finders-keepers, Sikandar cut the bags and dumped the coins into the sea.

Rear Adm R A Qadri recounts Hangor's first missed E-5 torpedo fired on Kirpan and the kill of Khukri. The sonar and torpedo morale boosting recordings are housed in the PN TAS school for every student to savour.

In a chapter, 'Between the Wars', in The Story of the Pakistan Navy, the re-vamping of the Navy with submarines and its air arm is described. Guy Toreman's The Pakistan Navy in Transition is informative with photos of all Pakistan Navy ships. It recounts how the Navy transited to the missile age with Harpoons and Chinese supplied C-802 missiles.

Chapter 17
Operation Lal Dora – Mauritius

Abridged and Updated from The Asian Survey, Vol1/2013 Routledge - David Brewster and Ranjit B Rai

"Mauritius is the only important island left in the Indian Ocean that is not in the pocket of any superpower... It would be sheer folly to dismiss the likelihood of a coup in Mauritius." - *Mauritius Times in 1978.*

The Indian Ocean of the late 1970s and early 1980s was a scene of superpower competition and intrigue, as a new frontier of the Cold War. The Soviet Union and the United States expanded their naval capabilities in the region and jostled for influence over Indian Ocean island states, for access to local port facilities and air bases. The withdrawal of the British Naval Forces from Singapore from 1975 where the cost of maintaining the Singapore Naval Base alone was 70 million pounds a year, left a vacuum in the Indian Ocean. US naval ships filled the vacuum, with a base at Diego Garcia. India strongly opposed the US military presence in the Indian Ocean as a threat to regional stability. The "intrusion" of the USS Enterprise led naval Task Force 74 in 1971 was remembered as an impermissible exercise in gunboat diplomacy. New Delhi strongly resented the US base on Diego Garcia, which gave the United States the capability to dominate the entire Indian Ocean and intervene in South Asia.

In this scenario, PM Mrs. Indira Gandhi grasped the importance of Mauritius which has a majority Hindu population from Bihar and a long economic, political and strategic security relationship with India, which a US diplomatic report characterized as Mauritius' "willing subordination" to India. A seminal turning point in the relationship occurred in 1983, when, in Operation Lal Dora, India came to the point of a full scale naval military intervention in the island to ensure that it stayed in India's strategic orbit, when a political crisis threatened to overturn a Hindu-led government. This led to plans for an Indian intervention in the island. At the last moment, India's military leaders hesitated, and disagreed over the command of the military operation, so Indira Gandhi turned instead to her intelligence services to achieve India's objectives.

The lessons cast light on India's thinking about its role in the region, its military decision-making processes, and what could be seen as an alignment of interests between India and the United States in the Indian Ocean Region. These issues are particularly relevant as currently the USA looks to further develop its strategic partnership with a hesitant India as part of its 'Pivot to Asia'. USA has supplied India the latest military technologies and proposed that India sign a Logistic Supply Agreement (LSA), a space cooperation agreement BECA and a communications security agreement CISMOA. The LSA was supported by the Indian Navy, MOD and MEA, but the Government has dithered.

For much of the Cold War, the growing influence of the USA and the Soviet Union caused considerable dismay in New Delhi. India saw itself destined to become the leading power in the Indian Ocean. However, it did not have the military capability to challenge the regional presence of either the USA or a "friendly" Soviet Union. The ideology of non-alignment to which India subscribed, held that the 'intrusion' of great powers (particularly Western powers) into any part of the developing world was inherently illegitimate and the primary source of insecurity among developing states.

Although India had a strategic partnership with the Soviet Union, it was also suspicious about Soviet activities in the Indian Ocean region, particularly after the Soviet intervention in Afghanistan in 1980. In the early 1980s, the Reagan administration increasingly saw India as a status quo power that could act as a security provider to the region.

Political instability in Mauritius Mauritius, in many ways is the "Little India" of the Indian Ocean, colonized by the Dutch, the French and then the British. Between 1834 and 1920, some 420,000 Indian indentured labourers migrated to Mauritius, mostly Bhojpuri speaking from Bihar, making up 70% of Mauritius' population. The rest is mostly French Creole speaking, and a small white French community. Although whites no longer control political power, the key Franco-Mauritian families called "Grand Blancs" exert considerable economic influence.

Early Mauritian political leaders took inspiration from India's struggle for independence and the Indian community clung tenaciously to the idea of 'Mother India'. Since gaining independence from Britain in 1968, Mauritius maintained a democratic system, dominated by Sir Seewoosagur Ramgoolam, leader of the Mauritian Labour Party, for 14 years. After the Royal Navy withdrew from the region, Mauritius swapped one security guarantor for another. India effectively assumed responsibility for Mauritius' security under a 1974 defence agreement, under which India transferred patrol boats and a helicopter to Mauritius and Indian Navy personnel effectively took responsibility for the Mauritian Coast Guard. Indira Gandhi considered Mauritius to be one of India's most dependable international partners and a potential safe haven for her family. Dilip Bobb in an India Today article "Blunting The Edge" on 1 September 1980, stated Mrs. Gandhi kept an IAF plane standby (for Port Louis?) at Sarsawa air base during the 1977 elections.

India had steadily supported Ramgoolam, but by the early 1980s it was clear that he would lose the forthcoming election to the main opposition, the Mouvement Militant

Mauricien (MMM), nominally led by Anerood Jugnauth, a London-trained lawyer of Indian descent. Its "ideological leader", was a firebrand socialist of French descent, Paul Berenger. The politically active Indian Mission in Port Louis facilitated several meetings in New Delhi between Indira Gandhi, Jugnauth and Berenger in 1980 and 1981. Mrs. Gandhi, sensing the reality of transfer of power, swung her support behind the MMM. That's real-politik.

In June 1982, the MMM decisively won the elections and Jugnauth became Prime Minister, with Berenger as Finance Minister. Indira Gandhi made a triumphant visit to the island, showcasing India's special relationship with Mauritius. India signed a Double Taxation Avoidance Agreement (DTAA), which saw the blossoming of the Mauritian economy with representative offices, as Foreign Direct Investments flowed through Mauritius (reaching about $41 billion till 2012). It facilitated 'round tripping' of Indian illegal moneys (hawala), as investments back into India from Mauritius, bereft of capital gains tax, till the Vodaphone case in 2012 put a full stop to that, with retrospective law entered into the Budget.

There was considerable friction between Jugnauth and Berenger, and disagreements over Berenger's imposition of economic austerity mandated by the IMF. Berenger trying to promote French Creole as Mauritius' national language angered Hindu leaders who had less economic and political power than the Franco-Mauritians despite majority in numbers. They feared Berenger's role could signal a return of the "Grand Blancs" to power. Berenger aimed to exclude high caste Hindus from power and establish military rule.

In early 1983, Jugnauth became concerned about Berenger leading a coup against him with the help of Libya and the Soviet Union. The Indian Mission in Port Louis kept a close watch on developments. According to one of Jugnauth's advisors, after the 1982 election both the United States and the Indians were feeding false intelligence to Jugnauth about Berenger's socialist links. In February 1983, Jugnauth met with Mrs. Gandhi in New Delhi, requesting military assistance in the event of a coup by Berenger. Mrs. Gandhi assured him of Indian support, telling him that, "Within five hours a contingent of my air force will be in Mauritius."

In mid March 1983, on Mauritian Independence Day, while Jugnauth was in New Delhi attending a Non Aligned Movement summit, Berenger arranged for the Mauritian National Anthem to be broadcast over television in Creole. On Jugnauth's return to Mauritius, Berenger proposed constitutional changes that would strip power from the Prime Minister. The MMM government disintegrated. Jugnauth was left with a small number of mostly Hindu followers.

New Delhi's concerns

New Delhi was concerned about these developments and worried for the welfare of the Indian ethnic population in Mauritius under a Berenger government that may favour the Creole and Muslim minorities and provoke a refugee exodus of Hindus. Of greater significance were New Delhi's concerns about the drift of Mauritius out of India's sphere of influence and the possible loss of Mauritius as the only unquestioning supporter of India's foreign policy in the Indian Ocean. New Delhi was concerned about Mauritius' links with Libya and the Soviet Union, which had been funding the MMM prior to the 1982 election. After the election, Mikhail Orlov, the Soviet Ambassador to the Seychelles, had secretly met Berenger to offer assistance in reorganising Mauritian internal security services and offered to supply patrol boats to the Mauritius Coast Guard, posing a direct threat to India's position there.

The United States indicated support for status-quoist Jugnauth against the socialist Berenger, particularly worried that a Berenger government might allow the Soviet Navy access to Port Louis and prosecute Mauritius' claims over Diego Garcia. General Vernon Walters, the legendary Deputy Director of the CIA, took a close interest in Mauritius, cultivating personal links with Harish Boodhoo and other Hindu leaders.

Plans for Indian military intervention: Operation Lal Dora

As the Mauritian political crisis deepened in mid-March 1983, Indira Gandhi ordered the Indian Army and Navy to prepare to intervene against a possible coup. Despite Mrs. Gandhi's promise to Jugnauth, Mauritius was well beyond the airlift capabilities of the Indian Air Force. Instead, the intervention plan, named Operation Lal Dora, involved the landing in Port Louis of two battalions from the 54th Infantry Division, the Indian Army's designated rapid reaction unit based in Hyderabad.

The intervention plan unfolded in a way that was typical of the lack of coordination between the Indian Army and Navy at that time. An advance battalion of 54th Division troops arrived unexpectedly at the Indian Naval dockyard in Mumbai after a 30- hour journey from Hyderabad with orders to board Western fleet ships. The Navy's Western Command in Mumbai, which had commenced planning for the operation, was taken by surprise by the Army's arrival and many crew were on shore leave. The troops initially attempted to virtually force their way onto INS Mysore, which was the largest warship berthed alongside, but were stopped by the Operations team of the Western Naval Command and staff of the Western Fleet Commander.

After negotiations between the Army and Navy, the troops were sent to camp at the sprawling Colaba Army base to await orders while some of the Army's equipment was loaded on INS Mysore and other ships, and fuel, victuals and medical supplies were ordered for the amphibious task force. An SCI tanker was chartered for the operations, which could also carry troops.

The Western Naval Command planned the naval operation. Having studied the recent UK operation in the Falklands, they believed that the Navy could be ready in 2 days to transport the troops from its main western naval base in Mumbai to Mauritius, followed by around five days sailing time. The Navy then had no specialised amphibious lift capability in the Western Fleet. The troops were to be transported on warships. The naval task force was to include:

- One or two modern Rajput Kashin class guided missile destroyers (INS Rajput D 51 and/or INS Rana D 52), carrying KA-28 Helix helicopters;
- Three or four Leander class frigates with Alouette helicopters, as well as MK-42C Sea Kings for slithering operations;
- A Deepak class naval tanker, carrying one helicopter;
- A civilian tanker requisitioned from the Indian state-owned shipping company (which had previously taken part in naval exercises with troops and a naval party on board) for replenishment at sea; and
- A survey and training ship.

Notably, the naval task force would have no fixed-wing air support. India's sole aircraft carrier at that time, INS Vikrant, was being refitted to induct new Sea Harrier aircraft. Despite the crucial role of fixed wing aircraft in the Falklands, the lack of air support seemed of little concern to the Indian Navy given that Mauritius had no air force, and Indian Coast Guard was there for support.

Disagreements in the War Room

While preparations were being made in Mumbai, senior

military and intelligence officers met with Mrs Gandhi in the War Room in South Block. Present at the meeting was Mrs Gandhi's Security Advisor, R.N.Kao, a former head of R&AW. The Navy was represented by Chief of Naval Staff Admiral O.S.Dawson, and the Army by Lt. General S.K.Sinha, then Vice Chief of Army, who was preparing to take over soon from the Chief of Army, General Krishna Rao, on tour in Vietnam. Dawson was close to Mrs Gandhi since his younger days when he was ADC to the Indian President and would receive Mrs. Gandhi's children at the President's swimming pool. Sinha had a more difficult relationship with her.

It became apparent that the Indian Army and Navy had quite different views about the amphibious operation. There were considerable disagreements between Army and Navy over command and control of the amphibious task force, which was to be commanded by Vice Admiral K.K.Nayyar. Admiral Dawson argued that the Navy should be in overall command of the operation, while General Sinha made the case for the Army. Mrs. Gandhi suggested that the Navy would be Force Commander at sea, but the Army would assume command once the landings took place (which did not please the Navy). Command and control and rules of engagement in the Indian Armed Forces have been neglected subjects.

The Navy was confident of its ability to execute the operation, even at some 4,600 km from Mumbai, with its capabilities to refuel and replenish at sea. It was familiar with Port Louis, having accumulated intelligence reports and photographs from numerous ship visits over the years, and from naval officers stationed there. It was not overly concerned about landing the troops, believing that troops could be briefed at sea for alongside landings and disembarkation. The Navy did not believe that troops would need to be landed on beaches, but expected that troops could be landed at Port Louis docks without an opposition, or at worst a semi- opposed landing at the docks. The Mauritian Coast Guard (commanded by an Indian naval officer) would also provide assistance if necessary. Nayyar however requested Rules of Engagement in the event of US intervention, no doubt remembering the Navy's experience in 1971 when it had been given clear Rules of Engagement in relation to the USS Enterprise Task Force.

However, General Sinha told Mrs. Gandhi that apart from the question of command, he had major concerns about the army's ability to conduct such an amphibious operation, and about the possibility of US intervention. Sinha believed that his troops were inadequately trained for amphibious operations. The Army's previous experience in an amphibious landing had been disastrous. In the closing days of the 1971 Bangladesh War, in Operation Beaver, a force of Gurkhas had been landed near Cox's Bazaar in East Pakistan to cut off an escape route for retreating Pakistani troops into Burma. The amphibious force had not been able to find the correct landing beach in time for high tide and several Gurkhas drowned when they were ordered to disembark with full equipment into deep water. The badly planned operation was widely regarded as a fiasco. Sinha, a Gurkha himself, was no doubt deeply aware of this.

Sinha was also very concerned about the possibility of US intervention in the operation. The USS Enterprise was still fresh in the minds of Indian military leadership, as was the presence of US forces at Diego Garcia. This preoccupation among some Indian military strategists is termed the "Enterprise Syndrome."

Sinha may have been sufficiently concerned about the possibility of US intervention to personally consult with US representatives about Washington's views on the Mauritian crisis. (It is worth noting that the Indian armed forces are notoriously kept compartmentalized from both intelligence analysis and political decision-making in New Delhi). According to B. Raman, a former head of the counter-terrorism division of R&AW, Indian intelligence later became aware that a "senior" Army officer leaked Jugnauth's request for assistance and the details of the War Room meeting to the US Embassy in Delhi, which later "affected his chances of rising to the top." Two months later, Mrs. Gandhi controversially ordered that Sinha be passed over in his expected promotion to Army Chief and he took early retirement from the Army. (Sinha then joined the opposition BJP party and subsequently ably served as Ambassador to Nepal and as Governor in North East and Kashmir). If Raman is to be believed, Sinha was passed over because of leaks over the Mauritius operation, and also because of his opposition to Mrs. Gandhi and Op Blue Star, the assault on Sikh militants in the Golden Temple in Amritsar. Sinha's father was an associate of Jaiprakash Narayan, who opposed Mrs Gandhi.

With the military commanders unable to agree on execution of the operation, Mrs. Gandhi put Operation Lal Dora on hold. Equipment was unloaded and troops were returned to barracks. The most obvious reason was the Army's lack of enthusiasm. It is also possible that Mrs. Gandhi shrewdly intended Indian preparations for the operation to act as a signal to relevant Mauritian leaders of India's determination to support Jugnauth as with Op Buster in Sri Lanka (see chapter on Op Pawan). Word was spread in isolated Port Louis that the Indian Navy was "surrounding" Mauritius.

Political intervention and the 1983 elections

According to one account, in place of Operation Lal Dora, upon the suggestion of R.N. Kao, Mrs. Gandhi decided to send N.F. Suntook, then head of R&AW, to Port Louis to deal with the crisis at a political level. Suntook delayed his retirement at the end of March 1983, by a couple of weeks for this undercover assignment. His abrupt disappearance days prior to his retirement, provoked bizarre media accusations that he had defected to Washington.

Suntook was assisted by Ambassador Prem Singh, well known for his partisan support for Jugnauth. Singh was later accused of having played a virtual pro-consul role in Mauritian politics. Suntook and Singh worked with Harish Boodhoo and other Hindu and Muslim leaders to swing their support and build a new Hindu coalition around Jugnauth. It is likely that financial incentives were offered. Berenger claims that he knew nothing of Suntook's role. The book Kaoboys tells the tale.

Jugnauth and his Indian backers were successful. On the day after Suntook returned to Delhi in April, Jugnauth announced the establishment of a new party called the Militant Socialist Movement (MSM), which merged Boodhoo's Parti Socialiste Mauricien with Hindu elements from the MMM. This new party, along with other opposition groups, had the numbers to form a new government. In the August 1983 elections, Jugnauth won convincingly.

The Aftermath

India's already extensive influence in Mauritius got consolidated. After the election, all major political leaders publicly acknowledged India's special role in Mauritius' security. Jugnauth requested the appointment of Major General J.N.Tamini, the Indian Army's chief liaison officer with R&AW, as the Mauritian National Security Advisor. Tamini occupied that post for more than a decade, to be followed by other Indian appointees with connections to R&AW.

Mauritius also took a distinctly pro-Western turn in foreign policy. Jugnauth backpedalled on Berenger's previous strident stance on Diego Garcia, saying "we have to accept the base is there." Mauritius continued its formal claim to sovereignty over Diego Garcia, but dropped demands for closure of the base and any appeal to the International Court of Justice. It lifted the embargo on the supply of labour to the US base. Relations with South Africa also improved. Jugnauth stated that Mauritius would be "realistic" in its relations with Pretoria, even though it opposed apartheid. Pretoria got a diplomatic presence in the form of a trade office.

The Mauritian crisis also presaged India playing a much more active role throughout the Indian Ocean, particularly after Rajiv Gandhi assumed office in 1984. As Admiral R.H.Tahiliani (who in 1984 took over as Chief of Naval Staff) commented: "We must take the responsibility that size imposes on us. Coming to the help of a small neighbour is a responsibility, but we have no intention of spreading our sphere of influence." This operation was a precursor to Op Flowers Are Blooming in Seychelles (chapter 18) and when Rajiv Gandhi sent peacekeeping forces to Sri Lanka in 1987, for Op Pawan (chapter 19).

Operation Cactus to stave off a coup in Maldives in 1988

On 3 November 1988, following a request for help to PM Rajiv Gandhi by the India-leaning Maldivian President Maumoon Abdul Gayoom, (its ruler for 30 years, and whose brother Yaamin Abdul Gayoom with 51.4 percent of the total vote has become President in 2013), India flew in a battalion of troops from the 50 Independent Parachute Brigade and 6 Para to the Maldives, 3,500 miles from Agra. Three IL 76s from No 44 squadron under Gp Capt Anant Bewoor, son of a former Army Chief, made daring night landings with tourist maps, at Malé's Hulhule airport to avert an attempted coup by Tamil mercenaries (Op Cactus). The Hulhule island was secured and boats left for Male just after midnight to rescue stranded President Gayoom. By 3 am on 4 November President Gayoom was brought to the National

Security Service building. In house searches, paratroopers captured some 30 rebels with ammunition and explosives. Seventy rebels were captured by the Indian Navy later.

Crossing the harbour, the boats fired rockets at an escaping ship, the MV Progress Light, fleeing to Sri Lanka with rebel leader Lutfi and 70 Maldivian hostages. The Indian Navy's INS Godavari and INS Betwa returning from a goodwill visit to Australia were diverted at high speed under Capt. S.V.Gopalachari. MV Progress Light was intercepted and shots fired across the bows to stop. The ship was boarded and taken over and the culprits were brought to book. A Maldivian minister thanked the Indian Navy for rescuing his mother-in-law taken as a hostage. The 6 Para remained in Maldives for one year, and on 3 November 1989, the helicopters IL-76s and ships returned to Hulhule for de-induction.

India consulted the US and the UK prior to this intervention. Margaret Thatcher commented, "Thank God for India. President Gayoom's government has been saved. We could not have despatched a force from here in good time to help him."

Lessons from Operation Lal Dora and Cactus

Operation Lal Dora illustrates lack of joint operational coordination and lack of communication between services that have long plagued the Indian armed forces. Issues of command remained unresolved. Some steps have been taken to address these problems, including the establishment of the Headquarters Integrated Defence Staff (IDS) in 2002. Yet there is still no Chief of Defence Staff (CDS) as a single point advisor to the government, despite recommendations, such as from the Kargil Review Committee headed by doyen strategist late K.Subramanyam in 2000, and Arun Singh and Naresh Chandra Committees. A lack of coordination in joint operations could significantly impact India's credibility as a major power, and be a major issue for India in coming years, as demands for it to conduct combined force operations grows.

Finally, the stories shed light on India's expeditionary military and Blue Water capabilities. Although the Navy was confident about an 'out of country' operation, it lacked proper amphibious capabilities. Troops were to be transported aboard warships and the fleet logistics train was thin, with no fixed wing air cover. Over the last decade, the Navy has attended to this. It acquired the amphibious dock ship, INS Jalashwa and other landing craft from USA on FMS economic terms. The aircraft carrier INS Vikramaditya is operating with the powerful MiG-29Ks. The 8 Boeing 737 P8 I maritime reconnaissance planes with AGM-84 Harpoons and Mk 48 torpedoes and new Italian multi purpose tankers INS Deepak and Shakti will provide reach. With the GSAT 7 satellite, the Navy is now a net-centric force.

The Army, bogged by fears of China, has to attain confidence to conduct amphibious operations, exercised annually. The Indian Navy is proposing to procure upto four large 20,000 ton multi-role landing ship dock vessels, and an amphibious warfare school at Kakinada on India's east coast. In 2011, the 54th Infantry Division (chosen for Lal Dora) was designated as a Re-organised Amphibious Formation. The Navy demonstrated its amphibious capabilities in Indonesia, Sri Lanka and the Maldives as part of the 2004 tsunami relief efforts. It is eager to learn from the experience of the USA in amphibious operations through bilateral exercises. As India stretches its sea legs in the Indian Ocean, with ambitions to go beyond into the Indo-Pacific, the need for these capabilities is only likely to grow. Regrettably, Op Pawan in 1990 ended after the humiliating withdrawal of Indian troops from Sri Lanka.

Sadly too, Rajiv Gandhi was subsequently assassinated by Tamil extremists in May 1991 in retribution for his role in the operation. India found that foreign interventions can sometimes carry a significant cost, if not taken up with a joint strategy. On the other hand, India's military strategies, and No First Use of nuclear weapons, smack of ambivalence, which is also a trait in Indian culture.

Chapter 18
"Flowers Are Blooming" - Seychelles 1986

India is 'the awkward grandfather of the region'. India would like to play a bigger role, but it has a complex, that people will say they are being imperialistic. India is a reluctant power groping for a suitable Indian strategy. – The original article by David Brewster and the author appeared in Naval Review, UK, February 2011.

With India's rise as a major power, many within and outside the country expect an expansion of India's role in enhancing the region's security. A K Antony, as Defence Minister from 2009 to 2014 has charged the Indian Navy, with being a major security provider in the IOR. This account of India's involvement in the security and stability of the Seychelles, depicts the early stages of India as a regional power, and its capability for prompt action based on intelligence inputs.

Over the last several decades, India has developed good security and cooperative relationships in the Indian Ocean, particularly with island or small littoral states. These include Mauritius with a special Double Taxation Avoidance Agreement (currently in rough waters over its re-negotiation), Seychelles and Madagascar in the southwest Indian Ocean, Oman and Qatar in the Gulf, the Maldives in the central Indian Ocean and Singapore in the East with Operational Turn Around (OTR) facilities, and officers posted there (SAFTI, RECAAP and FUSION Centre).

India is now seen as a key security provider to, and even a security guarantor for, several of these states. However, the history of India's strategic role in the Indian Ocean has not been the subject of a great deal of study. This chapter will recall India's previously undisclosed interventions in the Seychelles in 1986, which acted as a prelude to other interventions throughout the region, including India's foray in Sri Lanka in 1987 (Op Pawan), and the Maldives (Op Cactus) in 1988.

India's Role as a Security Provider in the IOR

With the retreat of the British from the East leaving behind a vacuum in the 1980s, India began asserting a broad security role in the Indian Ocean region.

The assassination of Indira Gandhi and appointment of Rajiv Gandhi as Indian Prime Minister in 1984 was followed by an unprecedented level of security activity by India. In South Asia, the Indian armed forces undertook a massive game of brinkmanship with Pakistan (Exercise Brasstacks – 1986) under the swashbuckling Army Chief, General K. Sundarji, which nearly brought India and Pakistan to war. In March 1987, the army began challenging China through a complicated series of deployments in the Himalayas (Exercise Checkerboard).

In July 1987, Rajiv Gandhi made a hurried and ill-fated commitment of peacekeeping forces in the Sri Lankan civil war (Operation Pawan). The intervention was intended to enforce a negotiated solution to civil war and guarantee political autonomy for Sri Lankan Tamils. However, Indian forces, which ultimately numbered some 80,000 Army troops and elements of the Indian Navy and Air Force, soon found themselves in a full-scale conflict with Tamil LTTE insurgents and began to suffer heavy losses.

India was also stretching its strategic and diplomatic legs elsewhere in the Indian Ocean, marking a major break from India's long opposition to military interventions outside of South Asia. From the mid 1980s, the Indian Navy's growing capabilities gave it new options. As Admiral R.H. Tahiliani, the former Chief of Naval Staff, commented at the time: "We must take the responsibility that size imposes on us, without having any hegemonistic aspirations. Coming to the help of a small neighbour is a responsibility, but we have no intention of spreading our sphere of influence". The statement reekss of ambivalence.

In 1986, the Indian Navy secretly intervened in the Seychelles to head off an attempted coup. In 1987, it began patrolling the Mozambique Channel to interdict the supply by sea of South African-backed RENAMO insurgents fighting the Mozambique government.

Seychelles as a Cold War battleground

During the 1980s, the location of the tiny Seychelles in the western Indian Ocean between Madagascar and the Gulf made it especially prime for US-Soviet rivalry. The United States had maintained a small satellite tracking station there since colonial times. To avoid over-reliance on its base at Diego Garcia, it now wished to establish a base in the Seychelles, which the Seychelles resisted. On the other hand, the Soviets wanted to evict the US from the Seychelles and establish its own a base there to match Diego Garcia.

Seychelles was led by a socialist dictator, President Albert René, who in a 1977 coup shortly after Seychelles' independence, overthrew the former President James Mancham. René was fond of Marxist rhetoric, but in practice would maintain a non-aligned stance similar to India's, by balancing the competing interests of the United States and Soviet Union. He maintained a publicly hostile stance to the white South African regime. René's one-party state was a magnet for international organised crime and the target for numerous coup plots.

In 1981, the South African security services (through a private company called Longreach) famously organised an attempted coup against René by a group of 44 white mercenaries led by Colonel 'Mad' Mike Hoare. The mercenaries took a commercial flight to Victoria, the Seychelles capital, in the guise of a beer drinking fraternity.

However, the plot was uncovered at Victoria airport when the mercenaries' bags were discovered to be full of weapons. A gunfight ensued, which ended when most of the mercenaries flew to Johannesburg aboard a hijacked Air India 707. This caused a major international scandal as the full role of the South African security services was revealed. The South African government was forced to pay a ransom for the mercenaries left behind in the Seychelles, and placed those that had returned to Johannesburg on trial. However, in the aftermath of this coup attempt, Seychelles' relationship with South Africa improved considerably.

The South African government undertook not to threaten Seychelles security and instead developed close security links with many in the René regime. Seychelles also improved its working relationship with the United States, although René continued, to some degree, his Marxist rhetoric. The Soviet Union continued to provide substantial military aid to the regime, including some 20 military advisers to the armed forces.

Despite its secret rapprochement with South Africa, in the following years multiple coups against René were planned by elements in René's regime, among Seychellois exiles in Britain, South Africa and Australia and by assorted anti-communists in Pretoria and Washington. Beset by plots, President René turned to India as a security provider, seeking a commitment from Indian Prime Minister Indira Gandhi to intervene against any coups.

René commented that India was "the awkward grandfather of the region. India would like to play a big role, but it has a complex, that people will say they are being 'imperialistic'... India should say 'we're not going to let that nonsense go on'." India responded cautiously. When Indira Gandhi was asked to give a public commitment to intervene in a coup against René, she declined, commenting, "We don't think it would be wise."

Nevertheless, in the following years India provided two

helicopters, training, and technicians to the tiny Seychelles Air Force. The Indian Navy also regularly sent an Indian naval vessel to attend Seychelles' Independence Day celebrations every June.

In 1984, the author as Captain attended the celebrations in command of INS Vindhyagiri, accompanied by INS Rajput under the command of Captain P. S. Das and the Western Fleet Commander Rear Admiral I.J.S. Khurana. The Seychelles Minister of Defence, Ogilvy Berlouis, with his gorgeous wife, was invited on board and he entertained Indian officers at his home.

Visiting ship's officers would familiarise themselves with the Seychelles geography and its leadership, to later provide intelligence reports. A Confidential Navy Order and a letter of proceedings of the visit, were standard procedures inherited from the Royal Navy.

India's intervention in the Seychelles

Although India was active in the Indian Ocean since the mid 1980s, India's security role in Seychelles crystallised in 1986, over a series of coup attempts against President René led by the Seychelles Minister of Defence, Ogilvy Berlouis. The details of these remain unclear, because more than one coup was being organised at the time. According to some reports, the Berlouis plot, codenamed Operation Distant Lash, involved some 30 mercenaries and 350 Seychellois (perhaps an overestimate). Some claim that it had the support of South African intelligence and of prominent anti- communists in Washington. Berlouis had been invited to the Pentagon in 1985 and was seen by some in the US security establishment as a future president of the islands, being an ambitious man with no ideological baggage, despite his tenure of a senior post in the René government. However, the Reagan administration was ambivalent about any moves against René, fearing that Seychelles could be destabilised by the installation of a new leader. Having mended fences with South Africa and the United States: after the 1981 coup attempt, René was increasingly viewed as someone who they could work with. In late 1985, René agreed to extend the US lease on the satellite tracking station.

Flowers Are Blooming: The Secret Operation

Nevertheless, in June 1986, Berlouis and his co-conspirators decided to move against René. Informed of an impending coup by either Indian or Soviet sources, Prime Minister Gandhi (who was also Minister of Defence) and the junior Defence Minister, Arun Singh, contacted the Chief of Naval Staff, Admiral R. H. Tahiliani, with a verbal request to provide assistance to René. Coincidentally, the Indian Navy had already dispatched the INS Vindhyagiri under Captain S. Ramsagar on a scheduled visit to Seychelles to participate in Seychelles Independence Day celebrations. It was decided that on arrival Vindhyagiri would report an engineering defect requiring an extended stay in Port Victoria. The Director of Naval Intelligence (the author) and Director of Naval Operations then briefed an Engineer Commodore P.N. Aggarwal (later Rear Admiral) who was sent to the Seychelles on a commercial airline with few key sailors to oversee the operation and ostensibly take charge of repairing the ship. A local engineering company run by an ex-Royal Navy officer was enlisted to make some minor repairs. An Indian Navy team of supposed 'engineering' sailors trained in use of weapons, was readied for dispatch to Port Victoria, although their presence was not ultimately required. The Indian Navy gave the operation the codename Flowers Are Blooming.

René repaired to the Presidential Palace under the protection of his 50-strong North Korean bodyguard, while the INS Vindhyagiri remained at Port Victoria for 12 days, making great use of its Sea King to provide public displays of helicopter commando 'slithering' and assaults. The ship regularly trained its 4.5 inch gun on power mode as a demonstration to the coup plotters. Also present in Port Victoria was a Soviet Turya class patrol boat, the Zoroaster, which was due to be handed over to the Seychelles. At one stage the Zoroaster left Port Victoria on patrol in response to a report that two Royal Naval vessels were to enter the port in support of the planned coup. By mid-June, the coup had been averted, the presence of an Indian naval vessel making a significant contribution. Seychellois authorities, with the likely assistance of Indian security services, arrested six men (but not Berlouis). As a former Indian intelligence officer, then in the Seychelles commented, the Indian naval presence 'served the purpose'.

Two months later, Berlouis made another attempt to unseat President René, which India again helped to quash. The plot was uncovered in late August while President René was attending a meeting of the Non Aligned Movement in Harare with Rajiv Gandhi and other leaders of non-aligned states. René may have been informed by the South African security services, whose strategy was cultivating all sides in Seychelles, with a view to cementing its own influence. According to another report, René was personally informed about the plot by Rajiv Gandhi, who had been tipped off by the Soviets. Gandhi lent René his own plane, Air India 001, to return to Seychelles early. On 6 September René, reportedly disguised as an Indian woman wearing a sari, was met at the airport by an Indian diplomat and taken to the Commissioner's residence. Berlouis and other plotters were tracked to the island of Praslin (famous for the Coco de Mer coconuts). Berlouis and four other army officers were forced to resign and Berlouis left for London. The Indian ship INS Godavari, which was returning to India from New York after taking part in centenary celebrations for the Statue of Liberty, was diverted to Port Victoria, although she only arrived on 24 September and departed several days after. It was reported that in October 1986, some 50 Soviet troops were landed by the Soviet amphibious vessel the Ivan Rogov, to provide additional security to René.

India's interventions cemented India's role in the Seychelles. In 1989, India established the Seychelles Defence Academy and continues to play an important role in Seychelles' security. India lost some of its assertiveness in the region in the wake of the Sri Lankan debacle, and its inability to decimate the LTTE. India in Mrs Gandhi's time, developed close security relationships with many states in the southwest Indian Ocean, including Seychelles, Mauritius, Madagascar and Mozambique, which form an important part of India's broader strategy in the Indian Ocean, but has not followed through on that start.

Operation Flowers Are Blooming was the first demonstration of the Indian Navy's capability to influence political events throughout the Indian Ocean, far from the navy's traditional area of operations in South Asia. It showed that the navy could be used to project power effectively, at long distance, and with relative discretion. The success of the Seychelles operation may have given the Rajiv Gandhi government confidence that it could execute low cost military interventions in its Indian Ocean neighbours, including its decision to intervene in Sri Lanka in July 1987 and its successful intervention in the Maldives in November 1988. That the Sri Lanka intervention was ultimately disastrous for the Indian Army, Rajiv Gandhi, and of course Sri Lanka, is a reminder of the risks involved in such actions. Politico-military planning, that is not well honed, is India's Achilles heel that needs repair.

Chapter 19
Operation Pawan - Sri Lanka 1987

Was PM Rajiv Gandhi's Op Pawan (the Wind) a policy move or an instrument for diversion from the Bofors scandal? As the PM is India's de facto Commander-in Chief, Rajiv can be called the strategist for Op Pawan. Did he promise LTTE head Prabhakaran some form of Eelam in their 'one to one' parleys in New Delhi? This remains a question for researchers. – Author

"Most battles are won or lost before they are engaged, by men who take no part in them, by their Strategists." - Carl Von Clausewitz (1832)

Overview of Pawan - India's failed mission

Hindu and Muslim Tamils in Sri Lanka, many stateless till 1988 in central Ceylon tea estates, have been treated by the Singhalese majority as second class citizens, disallowing them their language, from 1956 to 1987. In researching Op Pawan, one concludes, that the real pressure and repression of the beleaguered Tamils in Sri Lanka for Eelam (Independence) got aggravated in 1983, and Mrs Gandhi possibly handled it with Op Buster.

Operation Buster - What was it for?

PM Mrs Indira Gandhi, distrustful of Sri Lanka's promises since 1964 for a language, or citizenship to its Indian diaspora, or equal opportunities and governance in the North, kept that island neighbour in check with "a carrot and stick policy."

In 1971, Pakistan's President Yahya Khan believed his troops had only to kill three million East Bengali citizens and change successor genes, and the rest would eat out of West Pakistani hands, and so he needed to reinforce Pakistan Army forces in the East. Mrs Indira Gandhi had banned Pakistani aircraft from using Indian airspace from January that year. Khan reached out to Sri Lanka's President Sirimavo Bandaranaike, who unexpectedly allowed Pakistani troop carrying aircraft to refuel at Colombo, even as Indian Naval ships were patrolling off Colombo, and the airport was being guarded by Indian soldiers against left wing JVP extremists trying to topple her regime. Pakistan launched operation 'Great Fly-In' to transfer the 9th and 16th infantry divisions of the West Pakistan Army to Dacca in February 1971, using Pakistan International Airlines and Air Force planes, and aircraft lent by Turkey and Iran. Mrs Gandhi was not one who easily forgot or forgave a slight.

In 1983, an order came down from Naval Headquarters (NHQ) to then Vice Admiral R.H.Tahiliani FOC-In-C West at Bombay to co-ordinate with Gen R.S.Dyal, GOC-In-C Southern Command, to plan contingency in a special operation concerning Sri Lanka. This author, as Command Operations and Plans Officer, and a navigation sailor (Radar Plotter) with naval charts, parallel rulers, dividers and tourist maps flew with the Admiral to Pune. An Army Brigadier and a Colonel assembled the next day in the Command House to plan a joint operation to cut Sri Lanka in the North East into a separate state, as with Bangladesh. A sketchily planned operation (impressive on paper) was hurriedly drawn up and only three copies were made titled Op Buster. This author was not allowed a copy, and told it was merely an inter-service exercise in contingency planning, normal in all professional militaries.

Nothing happened for years but this author's hunch (after inquiries) is that a copy may have been leaked by Mrs Indira Gandhi to Sri Lanka, in her 'carrot and stick' policy. If this was her stick, she also used economic means to keep Sri Lanka on board. She died in 1984, and Rajiv

Gandhi, lacking finesse or experience, fell into the trap of President Jayawardene's machinations.

High Commissioner J.N.Dixit in his book Assignment Colombo writes, "Rajiv's focus of attention on Sri Lanka was refracted from 1986 and the first five months of 1987, due to rising levels of tensions with Pakistan following Brasstacks and the Bofors scandal."

By 1984, around 100,000 refugees had fled the Sri Lanka reprisal and were housed in 31 camps in Tamil Nadu.

The Indian Government, especially the Tamils and Malayalis in Government, and M.G.Ramachandran, the Chief Minister of Tamil Nadu, were very sympathetic to the cause of Eelam (Independence), and desirous of emulating a Bangladesh. Sri Lanka's Tamil rebel leaders - Velupillai Prabhakaran of Liberation Tigers of Tamil Tigers (LTTE, ex TNT) , Sri Sabarathinam leader of TELO (a strong militant group of ex-convicts with enmity towards LTTE), Balakumar and Rathinsabhapathy of EROS, Padmanabha of EPRLF who was killed later in Madras, and later Douglas Devadanda and Uma Maheswaran, leader of PLOTE, harboured hopes of Eelam (Independence). Many took up residence in Madras to direct operations of their cadres in Sri Lanka. The Sri Lankan insurgency had begun, and India's hand in it was evident, through its harbouring of Sri Lankan Tamils, and the training and succour offered by Indian intelligence.

The camps in Tamil Nadu became an arms transshipment cum training area for the groups along the coast, whose game plans were often in conflict. Indian intelligence agencies, as R&AW's B. Raman writes in his book Kaoboys, were under no particular control, and played a divide and rule game, and so did the two main political parties of Tamil Nadu, the DMK and the AIADMK, between groups (as they do even today with India's Sri Lanka policy). CM Jayalalitha banned training for Sri Lankans in Tamil Nadu, and laid claims on

Kachiteevu, an island of Sri Lanka by treaty. On 2 August 1984, a Tamil Eelam Army's bomb blew up at Madras International airport killing 30 persons. Their aim to lay the bomb on a Sri Lankan Airliner misfired. DG of Police Mr Mohandas sympathetically tried to blame the Mossad. The Sri Lankans involved were all rounded up.

As LTTE enjoyed the patronage of MGR (AIADMK), his opponent Karunanidhi (DMK) chose to back TELO.

Prabhakaran won over MGR, and began toying with larger ambitions on Indian soil. Internecine battles saw LTTE decimate TELO camps and Sri Sabarathiman its leader. The LTTE cadres were supported by R&AW. LTTE was to become the "Indian Army's Frankenstein" in Op Pawan. The Tamil fighters began ambushing the Lankan military and were superior in jungle and IED warfare and dreamt of Eelam (just like the Mukti Bahini in 1971, see chapter 7). Their writ ran large in most parts of the Jaffna peninsula.

Money from sympathetic Tamils and terrorist groups abroad, local tax collections and robberies, enabled larger military operations against the Sri Lankan Army (better known then for its cricket playing skills, but a professional force to reckon with today). Jane's Weekly reported that LTTE cadres were provided training by Israelis, and some reports say, Iran and Libya. The Indian Intelligence agencies, Research and Analysis Wing (R&AW - India's CIA) in Centre 22, and Intelligence Bureau (IB) in the South, provided training and possibly funds. Sri Lanka's leaders found themselves helpless to tackle the situation and looked to India to bring the Tamil groups to the negotiating table, for a settlement. Mrs Indira Gandhi was assassinated in 1984, and Rajiv had come into power, but his attention was elsewhere.

In 1985, two futile attempts were made to negotiate for peace and a resolution short of Eelam. Talks were held in Thimpu in neutral Bhutan, to get the Sri Lankans, the various Tamil groups, and India's representatives to settle. The LTTE bucked the talks. Rajiv, riding a crest with his election victory, surrounded by his cronies, many from his Doon school days, was livid. MGR had flown to the USA for treatment. His influence was waning. The Indian advisers on Sri Lanka were Natwar Singh, Romesh Bhandari, J N Dixit, Parthasarathy Sr. Dinesh Singh, P. Chidambaram, Ronen Sen of PMO's office, and the key Joint Secretary in MEA Kuldip Sahadev. They were all grappling with a Sri Lanka policy. Intelligence agencies were mired in their own secret activities and preferences.

This is when in1986, this author arrived with limited intelligence expertise to become Director of Naval Intelligence (DNI) at NHQ. Having held operational appointments in the Navy, including CSO (Ops) and Staff Operations in Western Naval Command, Western Fleet Operations and Director of Naval Operations, helped in appreciating the voluminous 'Under Office' (UO) notes the intelligence agencies generated. So did JIC briefings, and some sage advice by Royal Naval Staff College colleagues and Naval Attaches trained in intelligence, who were posted in Embassies. Having visited Sri Lanka on ships, (when their Air Force flew us from Trincomallee to Katunaikye in Colombo and to Annaradhapura for visits), and Op Buster, was beneficial.

Speaking a few languages is a total boon in India, as explained in my book, Indians - Why We Are What We Are (Manas, 1998). India's caste-ridden society thinks more with its heart, not its mind. India is more a society than a nation, as we do not have "One language that we can all Read, Write, Cry or Sing Together". I requested wives of officers in the Directorate to read and translate vernacular papers on defence issues at their homes (Tamil and Malayalam translations of vernacular magazines and newspapers helped), and offered them small stipends, which they refused. We cultivated a retired Chief Petty Officer who was employed in R&AW to exchange notes.

All this helped a lot in Op Pawan.

Between 16 and 18 November 1986 at Bangalore at the SAARC meetings, President Jayawardene massaged Rajiv's ego and asked for help to mediate. Prabhakaran, the LTTE supremo, was called, but his aim was Eelam. The Eelam struggle was single handedly taken on by Velupillai Prabhakaran of the LTTE, which later took on the mighty Indian Army on very professional guerilla battle lines, killing 1400 Army souls in three years, and LTTE also fell out with R&AW who supported EPRLF. In India, R&AW was running Sri Lanka policy to foist its own favourites, and harboured a mole. India Today reported on a Mr Unnikrishnan, a R&AW operative, who used to come to JIC meetings in slippers, and was arrested in Madras by the IB for being close to a Pan Am hostess, supposedly planted by the CIA. She had met this R&AW operative in Singapore, where he went often. It was when she rendezvoused with him in Madras, that the lid was lifted open. This is depicted brilliantly in the movie Madras Café.

The Indian Army had to bear all these machinations in Op Pawan in the confused times of Op Brasstacks, Khalistan uprising, Op Chequerboard, the Samba Scandal and Bofors. New Delhi kept buzzing and busy, which times are brazenly recounted by Tavleen Singh in her book Durbar, as she knew Rajiv Gandhi and Arun Singh's families who were her close friends. Mrs Gandhi in her time used economic and other pressure tactics to keep the Tamil pot under control but things were going out of hand.

Rajiv Gandhi's foreign policy advisers were enthused to make Rajiv a bigger hero than his mother, with international intervention like Mrs Gandhi did for Bangladesh in 1971. The Army Chief was Gen K. Sundarji, a brilliant, ambitious hard-drinking impetuous Tamilian, who acquired computer knowledge and would bully those not so endowed. The Army contracted an American company to scan and expand maps and charts on giant computer screens for Op Brasstacks at Delhi's Cantonment Parade Ground. Rajiv Gandhi appreciated computer presentations as he was also a computer buff and was assisted by a friend Suman Dubey and others. We in DNI commenced swift computerization under Cdr. Gupta. To see how South Block (MEA/MOD) in New Delhi worked then, was interesting and enlightening.

DNIs (Commodore rank) were expected to brief the Chiefs of Staff, in closed door weekly meetings on naval proceedings along with DAI (an Air Vice-Marshal) and DGMI (a Lt Gen.), where Gen Sundarji used to be present and would question. One had to answer carefully. M.K.Narayanan (a very competent DD IB and later head of IB and NSA to PM Dr Manmohan Singh, and Governor of West Bengal), invariably came early and always conferred on what was to be said and proffered useful advice, with his lifetime of experience in the Intelligence cadre and under varied political masters. I had observed Gen K.Sundarji's overbearing ways in the Army Ops room in planning and presentations. His Military Adviser (MA), was a brilliant officer, but a Lt Col (normally MA is a Brigadier) Shammi Mehta (later Lt Gen). He had the General's ear and wielded powers and issued instructions on his behalf. GOC-In-Cs and PSOs knew it.

In a brush with General Sundarji, I mentioned in passing in a briefing, that I had read his unclassified PhD thesis on Nuclear Weapons for India (loaned by then Brig Dipankar Banerjee of IDSA, later Maj Gen of Peace Institute USA). I did not know the Government had told him not to publicise the study. The General went ballistic, and asked for my source. I replied, "Sir, a good intelligence man never reveals his source." Sundarji called me 'Casey' after that. After retirement in 1989, he came with his wife, as K.Sundar and Miss Vani, and spent ten interesting days with us in Singapore, where I was the Defence Adviser, under some fine Ambassadors Yogesh Mohan Tiwari, K. Raghu Nath (later Foreign Secretary and Ambassador to Russia), Satish Chandra and Mrs Kaushik. I was accredited to the Phillipines and Thailand, a learning period of four years in ASEAN.

In those days, diplomats served under the constraints of non– alignment, though India had leased the nuclear submarine INS Chakra from Soviet Union to the ire of ASEAN, who looked to a region free of nuclear weapons (ZOPAN). In Singapore, Sundarji discussed Op Pawan and Bofors and issues threadbare. He phoned India Today from Singapore and told the editor he would give an interview on his return, to ask the Government to cancel the Bofors contract, as he had learnt his name was being maligned in the money-making trail being reported in the media. He followed through on this.

India provided support to the Sri Lankan Tamil militant groups including LTTE. During CNS Admiral Tahiliani's time in 1987, the Navy was asked if some naval limpet mines could be sent to a railway siding in Tamil Nadu, for a transfer. It is providential that the Admiral got advice that the mines, in the wrong hands, could be used against our own ships. He asked the Minister of State for Defence Arun Singh who the mines were meant for. They were evidently for the Tamil militant groups. This author met a Sri Lankan team in Chennai in 1987, led by the chief negotiator of the Liberation Tigers of Tamil Eelam, Anton Balasingham, who had asked for help of weapons from the Navy. I told him this was way beyond my brief, as I was only looking after intelligence for the Navy. The matter never came up again. Had the mines been provided to the LTTE, they could have been used against Indian naval ships operating in Op Pawan. The Navy was not touched.

The long Tamil uprising (1983-2009) finally was ended by the re-vamped Sri Lankan army in a vicious war pursued by President Mahinda Rajapaksha with his brother former Major Gotabaya Rajapaksha as Defence

Secretary, and Chief of Army Gen Sarath Fonseca (who revolted later). With Prabhakaran's death on 19 May 2009, the LTTE was decimated and the Tamil uprising in northern Sri Lanka obliterated. Thousands of Tamils were made homeless. Pakistan and China supported Sri Lanka with arms and aid, while India's role was ambivalent. India transferred an OPV Sarayu P-54 (now equipped with Chinese Yingi Y-82 anti-ship missiles and surface to air missiles) and India loaned two other OPVs from the Coast Guard in the 2000s to the Sri Lankan Navy. The OPVs were originally bought from Pusan in South Korea and 'copy built' in Indian PSU shipyards with financial assistance from ONGC. They were meant for patrolling the coast and Bombay High assets, but two were converted to fire Dhanush 300 km nuclear missiles. Their absence, among other factors, contributed to the deficient patrolling along the coast, leading to the 26/11 attack in 2008 on Mumbai by Pakistan's LET. These deficiencies are now being corrected in a programme called NC3I by the Cabinet Secretary for over Rs 2000 crores.

Op Poomalai followed by Op Pawan

On 2 June 1987, 19 boats with stores and kerosene, led by Dr. V.K.Moitra, Director of External Publicity, aboard Coast Guard vessel Kittu Chennamma, and Vikram under Cdr Bapat, left from Rameshwaram for Sri Lanka. The boats had orders to return at the slightest provocation. The Sri Lankan Navy vessel Edithri confronted the fleet near Kachitivu. Captain O.T. Samarasekara insisted that Dr Moitra come to his vessel to discuss the matter. Dr Moitra asked the Sri Lankan naval captain to come aboard Vikram or give permission for the humanitarian mission. Whether diplomatic missions were consulted is unclear, but the Sri Lankan Naval Commander denied permission and the Indian flotilla turned back.

Military intervention was ordered by Rajiv Gandhi on 5 June 1987, when five An-32 Air Force transport planes with journalists, accompanied by four Mirage-2000 fighter planes armed with Magic Matra 11 Missiles under Wing Cdr Ajit Bhavnani (later VCAS) from 7 Squadron transgressed Sri Lankan airspace and ADIZ, and air dropped 25 tons of food and medicine by parachute for the Tamils in Op Poomalai (Eagle Mission 4). The Jaffna area was cut off and was under siege by Sri Lankan forces in Op Liberation (Op Vadamarachi). The military offensive was carried out by the Sri Lankan military from May to June 1987, to regain the territory in Jaffna from LTTE control. The 1 Gajaba Regiment in the operation was commanded by Maj. Gotabaya Rajapakse. On 27 May, Dixit called on President Jayawardne, who writes in his book, Men and Memoirs, that Dixit had jotted points on the back of an envelope to convey Rajiv Gandhi's message to call off Op Liberation. J.N.Dixit in his book Assignment Colombo writes that JS Ronen Sen in PMO, handling Sri Lankan affairs, had conveyed the contents of the ultimatum. (It was Ronen Sen, later Ambassador in Israel, Russia and finally the USA, who contributed much to the success of India's nuclear deal).

The foxy President Julius Jayewardne then looked to India for help. His Army was besieged by the Tamil uprising in the North and the Janata Vimukti Perumuna (JVP), who were unhappy with the rate of Sinhalaisation, and ran amok in the South. Jayewardne was remembering when India sent armed forces to Sri Lanka to quell the JVP in 1971. Units from the Indian Army's Southern Command landed at RCyAF base Katunayake, joined by 5 Chetak helicopters from 104 Helicopter squadron. The Indian Navy deployed a naval cordon of ships led by INS Kirpan (Cdr. D.S.Paintal) off Colombo since the Royal Ceylon Navy had deployed its sailors on ground operations and harbor defence, which were later taken over by Indian and Pakistani troops and Indian Air Force helicopters. The UK also sent its forces in 1971.

President Jayawardne wanted Rajiv Gandhi to help tame the LTTE which was running all over areas in Jaffna, in bitter fighting against the cricket-playing Sri Lankan Army, as many called it. The Indian Government was looking for a diversion, as it was cornered in the Bofors scam. In parleys, Army Chief Gen K.Sundarji assured Rajiv that he could settle the LTTE boys in a few days, and military preparations to deploy 54 Div (340 Brigade at short notice) from Hyderabad, were set in motion. The author watched proceedings in hectic meetings in South Block at Deputy Chief level, and the Navy with Cmde Rollo Lewin earmarked operational ships to transport troops from Chennai. When Air Chief ACM Dennis La Fountaine said the IAF had limited capacity for the air lift of a Division, Rajiv Gandhi, an ex-Indian Airlines pilot assured the Air Chief, that all Indian Airlines flights on D day would be cancelled for the operation. I recall La Fountaine, who this author knew from NDA, where he was a very well-liked Divisional officer, say, "Well then, Bob's your uncle!"

Maj Gen Harkirat Singh, 54 Div Cdr, in his book, Intervention in Sri Lanka (Manohar, 2000) describes how First Secretary Hardip Singh in Colombo informed Prabhakaran that Rajiv Gandhi was waiting to meet him to discuss issues before an accord was finalized. Prabhakaran was delighted and he with family and other leaders of the LTTE were flown in IAF helicopters on 28 July from a spot in the Jaffna jungle to Palali, where IAF Avro-748s were positioned. He did not arrive at the appointed Jaffna University grounds, fearing a trap had been laid. From another site, Capt B. K.Gupta, Defence Adviser, escorted Prabhakaran, and the author was in touch with him. Prabhakaran warned Gupta that he held him responsible for staying safe, and threatened that Gupta's own family would be in trouble in anything happened. He had the Avro diverted to Madras, to meet Chief Minister M.G. Ramachandran, an LTTE supporter in more ways than one.

MGR provided refuge in Tamil Nadu to LTTE operators, and many say had money connections. Hectic messages were exchanged between Joint Secretaries Kuldip Sahadev (MEA) and Ronen Sen (PMO). Prabhakaran landed in Madras, and held talks behind closed doors with MGR who had lost his voice, and used an aide, who lip read him. Serious talks must have ensued.

On arrival in Palam Air Base on 28 July afternoon, I was part of the reception party. Capt B.K.Gupta and I were told the Navy's task was taken over by the MEA officials, who whisked Prabhakaran and party away. Prabhakaran met Rajiv Gandhi and no record has been released of what transpired. When Ambassador Ronen Sen was asked in 2013 about Op Pawan, when he delivered a brilliant talk to Delhi Gymkhana members, he replied, "It is too early to discuss this." Prabhakaran was housed in Room 318 at Ashoka Hotel where Gupta and I met the other LTTE members who kept guard outside his room. I was keen to meet Prabhakaran (an admired revolutionary leader who adored Netaji Subhash, Winston Churchill and Napoleon). With my smattering of Malayalam, I tried, but his guards would not allow anyone in.

On 29 July 1987, PM Rajiv Gandhi signed a hurried Accord with the Sri Lankan President in Colombo, negotiated by HC J. N. Dixit to preserve the sovereignty of Sri Lanka (Para A), and to devolve powers to the Tamil minority in the island republic forming a Provincial Federal Tamil state in the North East with a Chief Minister and elected council. Para F read "India was to provide military assistance".

Ranasinghe Premadasa of the UNP opposition party, who became President in 1989 and asked IPKF to leave, did not attend, showing his opposition. Premdasa was killed on 1 May 1993, during a Mayday rally, by an LTTE suicide bomber, a week before Defence Minister Lalith Athulathmudali was assassinated.

After discussing with his aides, Prabhakaran was awaiting another meeting with Rajiv Gandhi on 29 July, not knowing Rajiv was already in Colombo. Harkirat writes, "The Indian Prime Minister's visit was telecast live, and watching it, the LTTE leaders felt betrayed. After I reached Jaffna on 30 July, the LTTE informed me in no uncertain terms, that First Secretary Hardeep Puri should not be seen in Jaffna if he valued his life. I conveyed this to Dixit." The LTTE was a vicious organization and never forgave betrayal. Its cadres always carried cynanide suicide capsules. Capt Gupta was told to take a few days' leave. He was worried for his family, should anything happen to Prabhakaran. The Indian Navy had promptly sent ships to patrol, ready to return to Madras to embark troops if ordered.

During Rajiv's accord signing visit, Jayawardene asked Rajiv, who was embroiled in the Bofors scandal, for immediate assistance to subdue the Tamils. Rajiv readily agreed to the request to send troops to disarm the Tamils, and instructed New Delhi to send a military force. It was called IPKF - Indian Peace Keeping Force and the final brief Ops Order was hurriedly signed in the Army Ops room dictated by Army Chief Gen K.Sundarji and others, as the Chairman Chiefs of Staff Committee Admiral R.H.Tahiliani had just left for Moscow. Units of 54 Div moved swiftly under Maj Gen Harkirat Singh by air and sea.

On 30 July, after the accord signing, an ill omen occurred. A Naval Rating Wijemuni Vijitha Rohana in the ceremonial departure guard, assaulted Rajiv Gandhi with his rifle butt, at the President's House, Colombo, in an attempted assassination. Captain Gupta told me that the practice of removing firing pins from rifles at ceremonial functions, was on his insistence. Rohana's six years' sentence was later commuted by President Rajapaksa after just a few years, and Rohana contested a general election in 2000, and also became an astrologer. (In 2013, he predicted Narendra Modi would be India's Prime Minister in 2014).

From 29 July 1987, in two days, the Indian Army with an almost division-strong peacekeeping force landed by ships, air force and Indian Airlines planes, and forayed to relieve a beleaguered Sri Lankan Army and quell the Tamils and the LTTE. The mission was undertaken hurriedly with no planning or military aim, as India's Prime Minister Rajiv Gandhi was possibly seeking a diversion from what had come to be known as the Rs 64 crore '310 FH77 Bofors Howitzer Commission Scam', in which Sonia Gandhi's close friend Ottavio Quattrocchi, an Italian representing Snam Progetti was named for taking commissions abroad from AE Services (Major Wilson), though this could never be proved.

Monies were paid to Swiss accounts, which a Swedish Radio unearthed. Win Chaddha, the Bofors agent in India, got payment as winding up charges after Rajiv Gandhi had banned arms agents. He was charged and fled to Dubai with family. The Hinduja brothers were charged for receiving money, as Bofors had deposited amounts in their accounts, but they claimed the money had nothing to with the Indian Howitzer purchase. Hindujas were also the suspected commission takers in the HDW four submarine deal for the Indian Navy which went nowhere. The submarines were originally meant for Iran and Hindujas were their agents, but the Shah of Iran was removed and the Iranians cancelled the deal. Rajiv Gandhi was under pressure to explain Bofors. His close aide Minister of State Arun Singh later reportedly resigned over the Bofors issue. K.C.Pant was appointed Defence Minister on 10 October to defend Rajiv on Bofors.

Gen K.Sundarji had assured the PM that he would disarm the young LTTE boys easily, but the peacekeeping mission turned into a full scale war in Sri Lanka in a few months, with no holds barred on the LTTE's side. They refused to surrender their arms as per an agreement signed by Hardip Puri and LTTE Deputy Gopalaswamy Mahendraraja on 29 September. Seventeen LTTE cadre including two regional commanders, Pulendran and Kumarappa were captured at sea on 3 October by Sri Lankan Navy and brought to Palali. Rajiv Gandhi was preparing for a holiday in the Lakshwadweep and orders and counter orders to Maj Gen Harkirat took place, as Sri Lanka wanted them to be brought to Colombo. The captives committed suicide rather than be flown to Colombo. More and more Indian Army units built up, with tanks carried in LSTs and one each by IAF transport planes, and artillery were inducted into Sri Lanka. Ultimately three divisions were deputed. Most went in without adequate training for asymmetric warfare, or asking for the politico-military aim and rules of engagement.

Butchery of the Indian Army followed, achieved by LTTE suicide bombers, and IEDs by motivated sacrificing Tamils craving for a homeland of their own. The LTTE had funded shipping companies under a financier Kumaran Padmanathan (better known as KP) abroad, and daring LTTE leader Kittu. Later LTTE ship MV Ahat with Kittu was captured 340 nm south of Chennai in Op Zabardast by Coast Guard ship Vivek and INS Kirpan on 13 January 1993. MV Ahat was blown up by Kittu after its crew was told to swim to safety. Kittu was the LTTE's most important man next to Prabhakaran, after Karuna defected. Padmanathan (KP) was the LTTE's lifeline, its chief arms procurer, supplier and fund-raiser. LTTE had better communications and interception equipment than the Indian Army, procured from Singapore. They could intercept and check most moves of the Army patrols and blow them up with IEDs. A para drop into Jaffna Unversity on 12/13 October saw complete annihilation. The battle for Jaffna became bitter.

The Navy and the Air Force supported the Army to the best of their abilities. The Indian Navy transported the troops and equipment in naval ships and requisitioned vessels to and from India to Sri Lanka for Tricomalee and KKS. The Navy's rejuvenated Alizes with rockets at Goa, and helicopters fitted with guns. Operating from Ramnad airbase, it threatened the LTTE boats by firing. In return, the LTTE, so as not to invite the wrath of the Navy, never touched a naval ship. The Navy did not lose a man.

Naval officers and sailors and Marine Commandoes (MARCOS) took part in the Army Commando operations ashore and at ports of Kentisurai and Trincomalee. Lt Arvind Singh (MVC), a trained US SEAL was head of the Indian Marine Special Force (IMSF). Along with 10 Para Commandos, he executed daring tasks in Sri Lanka killing LTTE. Arvind with his team broke out from Jaffna Fort on 19 October and secured the area which resulted in the link up of 41 Brigade with 1 Maratha Light Infantry on 20 October 1987. On the night of 21/22 October 1987, IMSF team was tasked to destroy Guru Nagar Jetty and speedboats in the Jaffna Lagoon. Lt Arvind Singh and Leading CD1 C Singh were awarded the Maha Vir Chakra. Other Lts Anup Verma and Prakash Chandravarkar were awared Vir Chakras, emphasizing the role of the MARCOS.

The coordinated command and control of Op Pawan was diffused with a central node at New Delhi under COAS Gen K.Sundarji who used to overrule others at will, though GOC-in-C Southern Command Lt Gen Dipender Singh was the Overall Force Commander (OFC) at Pune. Naval operations were under Flag Officer Commanding-in-Chief Eastern Naval Command Vice Admiral S.Chopra assisted by term mate Rear Admiral P.S.Das from Visakhapatnam, and Air Force at Tambaram. An IPKF command was established at Madras with an ambitious Lt General A.S.Kalkat, with term mates Brig Ravi Ipe and

Nikkie Kapur (later GoC-In-Cs), who assisted the author as DNI. The left hand generally did not know what the right hand was doing and this author slept many nights in the Army Ops Room in a room provided to the Navy, courtesy DDGMO Brig Ved P Malik, to be able to brief CNS and Chairman Chiefs of Staff Admiral R.H.Tahiliani and PSOs with intelligence inputs. Tahiliani once informally let slip that Op Pawan was "Sundar's war". It was indeed so, and with Sundarji's forceful personality, the subject of Indian Armed Forces ad hoc command and control without a CDS has never been analysed to learn lessons, because the official papers of the wars have not been released.

The Henderson-Brooks Report on India's debacle in the 1962 war with China has been withheld by the Government, but in March 2014, the author of India's China War, Neville Maxwell released it. The document depicts a total political-military-intelligence disconnect as Op Pawan did.

A review of Op Pawan

For India's military foray into Sri Lanka in 1987, the strategy was solely left to PM Rajiv Gandhi who was also India's Defence Minister. His close confidant was Rhodes Scholar and schoolmate Arun Singh, his Minister for State for Defence. Rajiv's military commander was Gen. K.Sundarji, unlike in 1971 for the liberation of East Pakistan (Bangladesh) when Gen Sam Manekshaw as Chairman Chiefs of Staff Committee guided military strategy and tactics as a CDS (chapters 7-9). A hurried Joint Op Order was signed in a day before the Army left for Op Pawan. The Government did not involve Chairman COS. There is no written rule to involve him in operations. Gen Sundarji showed bravado and confidence to succeed, but did not. As of writing, this malady of co-ordination in command appears more complicated, with

India going nuclear with a large Integrated Defence Staff (IDS), a National Security Council Secretariat (NSCS), a National Security Advisory Board (NSAB) under a powerful National Security Adviser (NSA) in PMO, and multiple intelligence agencies.

India's Foreign Policy advisers of the time were Natwar Singh, Romesh Bhandari, A.P.Venkateswaran (who resigned when rebuked by Rajiv after his Pakistan visit to to discuss Siachen), K.P..S.Menon, and India's High Commissioner in Sri Lanka, J.N.Dixit, assisted by G.Parthasarathy, head of the Planning division in New Delhi, and Gopi Arora. The Intelligence agencies, the R&AW, headed by Mr Joshi and later Anand Verma, and IB under M.K.Narayanan and their band of many operatives, had a free hand with their machinations, as villains of the piece.

An analysis in hindsight of the events leading to India's actions in Sri Lanka needs to determine whether India wanted to obtain greater autonomy for Tamilians, or relieve pressure on the Tamils, or take on the LTTE, or other diffused aims, like maintaining the integrity of Sri Lanka, or preventing foreign interference. The CIA was a palpable bogey, as the USA had set up a Voice of America Radio station in Sri Lanka. Rumours were rife that it would lease tank farms in Trincomalee, for which India had bid. Pakistan was supporting the SLAF with training and small arms in the Zia Agreement, and so too the Israelis through Col Levy's team.

Cost of the Sri Lanka War

The government has repeatedly stated that the cost of the peacekeeping operation, actually a war, was negligible. A study of the cost of the Sri Lanka foray was calculated at $ 3 billion ($10 billion today) which included massive spending on use of fuel in foreign exchange, and logistics from hidden payments. Much military equipment was lost, and Indian Navy ships came in for expensive refits earlier. This author is convinced that the huge fuel bill of imports, military purchases, oil exploration costs and rupee rouble payments, for goods exported to the Soviet Union like computers but imported with FFE dollars, soared. India was left with just two months FFE reserves in 1991. The author as Liaison Officer to Finance Minister Dr Manmohan Singh, Commerce Minister P.Chidambaram and a large delegation in September 1991 in Singapore, witnessed India 's desperation to garner investment and funds from the Asean Tigers, after the IMF had sanctioned

$2.3 billion, and laid down terms to liberalize the economy. Singapore became an investor and a strategic partner over time, and the 'Look East' policy was born.

Singapore has a policy which believes that a benign strategic relation fosters trade. The Indian Navy has a navigating officer posted as instructor at SAFTI (Academy), a Naval Defence Adviser and an officer in the Information Fusion centre monitoring the Indo- Pacific and a Coast Guard officer at RECAAP. The Navy has Operational Turn Round (OTR) arrangements with Singapore and the navies have exercised in 20 SIMBEXES. The Singapore Army has armoured assets stowed at Babina for regular exercises. In Op Pawan, LTTE purchased much equipment from Singapore.

Conclusion

As long as records of Op Pawan and wars lie locked behind the portals of the MOD, at the mercy of termites, there is a lurking danger for politico-military decision-making in India. Trying to be part of the solution in Sri Lanka, India became the problem. India entered the scene with its powerful military in 1987, to decide who would be the hero and who the villain. It got enmeshed in ethnic Tamils, Muslim and Sinhala politics which could never be solved militarily, although a flamboyant Gen

Sundarji tried to. By 1990, like a poor actor, India left the scene and de-inducted its Army in the intermission. The hero and the villain are yet unidentified. Relations with Sri Lanka are tenuous.

Rajiv Gandhi succumbed to the blast by Prabhakaran's LTTE suicide bomber on 21 May 1991, cutting short a young life. An LTTE team with bespectacled lady suicide bomber Dhanu came to Chennai and thence to a public meeting. She carried a garland with liquid explosives. Dhanu dropped the garland as she came face to face with Rajiv Gandhi and knelt down, ostensibly to pick up the garland, or touch Rajiv's feet. Seconds later, Sriperumbudur, the birth place of Saint Ramanujam, was devastated by a deafening explosion that night. Rajiv's torso was torn to pieces. Retribution is what the LTTE called it! Questions arise which defy answers: Could there be a link between Rajiv's assassination and his promise to the LTTE or to LTTE's multi-million dollar arms shipments? Was Rajiv killed by the LTTE alone? Was it the brain behind the assassination, or just the hand? Was LTTE supremo Prabhakaran so naive as to risk a crackdown which was inevitable, or did he do it on behalf of some individuals or powers? Was there any link between the LTTE and Premadasa, who himself became a victim of a Tiger suicide bomber on 1 May 1993? If so, could it have a bearing on Rajiv's assassination?

This chapter is more a salute to the hapless Indian soldiers, who being caught in a web of rudderless policy makers in New Delhi under Rajiv Gandhi, were themselves trapped by Sri Lanka's shrewd leader Jayawardene. The Indian Army lost around 1,400 souls, and 3,000 were wounded, thanks also to the machinations of R&AW with proven moles, and the Indian Foreign Service who acted as bystanders, leaving the brandy sipping High Commissioner J.N. (Mani) Dixit in Colombo, a friend of Jayawardene, and his team of bright staffers in the mission (the Puris, who became Ambassadors), to dictate even military policy in Op Pawan.

Many books and two full length films chronicle this. Madras Cafe comes closest to the truth, unveiling the R&AW operative who was involved with a PanAm hostess. Today India assists and demands the rehabilitation of the displaced and poor beleaguered Tamils in the North. It desires the promised Federal Tamil state with an amendment to the Constitution with full police powers. PM Dr Manmohan Singh declined an invitation to attend CHOGM at Colombo in 2013. India has voted twice (abstaining the third time) in the UNCHR to have an international commission to go into the brutal war crimes in the war against LTTE, similar to the Nuremburg trials. Sri Lanka objects to foreign enquiry. It has a Reconciliation Commission to report on the war.

Sri Lanka's economy has improved and its links, including military, with China and Pakistan which assisted in the war, are strong. There are Chinese investments in ports and airports and a satellite station near Kandy. India has no deep water port. Colombo with third generation container vessels, and soon Humbantota, can handle 70% of India's containers for trans-shipment. Indian tourists to Sri Lanka have increased. India and Sri Lanka need to have shared destinies. As Jayprakash Narayan once advised Mrs Indira Gandhi: "Be an elder brother to Sri Lanka, not Big Brother."

India's planners must note that the island states including Sri Lanka are critical for India's Indian Ocean strategy, an area that Mahan said would be important in the 21st century. Dr K M Panikkar's 'India and the Indian Ocean' emphasizes: "The Indian Ocean will be one of the major problems of the future. America, China and Russia will have access to the seas in a manner totally different from what the Europeans had in the centuries that followed Vasco da Gama's arrival." The winds of change are blowing.

Chapter 20
Nuclear Sub INS Chakra-1 A Near Miss

At Independence, India's Navy had visionary seniors, many of whom were war hardened, and trained in the UK. Cdr S.G.Karmarkar (later Rear Admiral) had commanded British officers on INS Cauvery. He had pulled British naval officers chestnuts out of the fire in INS Kunjali, when sailors mutinied against them in 1946. The Indian Navy inducted 8,000 ton six inch gun cruisers (INS Delhi in 1950 and Mysore in 1958) and the 17,800 ton aircraft carrier INS Vikrant in 1961 with latest Breuget Alizes and Sea Hawks. The breed of officers that manned warships included many Anglo-Indians, Parsees and experienced merchant navy officers, who trained the younger lot for confidence in duties on the bridge and deck with integrity. They ensured care for the men they commanded in the divisional system, to play hard and work harder. They tolerated dissent, but once an order was given, it was to be obeyed. This is the hallmark of any great Navy, as maritime strategy and tactics, like foreign policy, are in continual flux.

In the 1980s, the Navy proposed that it should look to nuclear propulsion for its future. Project Advanced Technology Vehicle (ATV) for building a nuclear powered submarine as a technology demonstrator was born under DRDO and PMO. DRDO head, Dr Raja Ramanna, selected his London room-mate late Vice Admiral M.K.Roy to head ATV. Officers were deputed to Bharat Atomic Research Centre (BARC) for training. For practical training Admiral Gorshkov (this author was his Liaison officer for three visits) agreed to loan a nuclear submarine and convinced Defence Minister Dmertri Ustinov. A lease cum training contract for 670 Charlie class K-43 nuclear powered submarine was signed in the mid 80's.

The story of how the officers and men trained for long periods in facilities built for officers at Vtoraya Rechka, a suburb of Vladivostok, and the crew at the Bay of Ulysses, is narrated by Capt Alexander Ivanovich Terenov (who served on board and assisted in training for INS Chakra-2 too) in his book, "Under Three Flags", translated from the Russian by Admiral R.N.Ganesh, Chakra's first Captain.

The commissioning date was set in December 1987 at Vladivostok and invitations issued for the ceremony. A sudden change of heart took place to forbid foreigners on board. The order came from the highest in Moscow. The Indian crew was devastated. Captain Terenov suggests it was because of US pressure to deny Indians the nuclear boat. Russia had got close to the US with Gorbachov beholden to its President Reagan. After ten days, with NHQ too unaware of what had transpired, a dejected Capt Ganesh took a bottle of whisky to Terenov for counsel. Terenov, knowing how Soviet Russia worked, suggested that only if the Indian Prime Minister spoke to President Gorbachov would the impasse be bridged. PM Rajiv Gandhi was scheduled to visit Moscow two weeks hence. He met Gorbachov and all fell into place.

Twenty year old K-43 was hurriedly commissioned as INS Chakra S-71 on 5th January 1988 in minus 25 degrees C with minimum fanfare, a lunch by Ambassador T.N.Kaul and dinner by C-in-C Pacific Fleet Admiral G.A.Khvatov, and immediately sailed (just like the new Akula Nerpa INS Chakra did in March 2012). On sailing, the planes seized, precluding diving with frozen snow, which the crew ably chipped with axes. The passage was predominately executed under water to achieve high speeds, on orders from NHQ. An Indian Navy warship rendezvoused the boat near the South China Sea when she surfaced for the Singapore Straits passage. She was tailed and photographed and reported by Jane's Defence weekly. On 3rd February 1988, PM Rajiv Gandhi embarked Chakra off Vishakapatnam and dived with the officers and the coxswain, a key member of any submarine.

The book covers the tribulations of the commissioning of K-43 Chakra which operated on both Indian coasts with 63km range Amethyst (SS-N-7 NATO Codename Starbright) missile, and CASEXES (Ship cum Aircraft and Submarine exercises) and torpedo firings, with the fleet. INS Chakra suffered a fire in the switchboard at sea in 1989, when she sank from 40 feet to 200 feet, losing power. The emergency was superbly controlled by blowing tanks. The boat was refitted by the crew, Naval Dockyard Vishakapatnam and Zvezda technicians. The book describes how the three Captains R.N. Ganesh, S.C. Anand and R.K. Sharma along with professional nuclear submariners, operated Chakra safely for the three years of the lease, and demonstrated the capability of the Indian Navy to handle the most complex nuclear technology.

Capt Vinod Pasricha (INS Viraat) choppered in to witness a missile launch. Yet sadly, visits to the submarine by Indian naval personnel were restricted. Though involved in the arrival protocol, this author viewed Chakra from afar. The draconian Official Secrets Act 1923, an antiquated act held over from British, precludes learning. Gen K.Sundarji in 1987 tried to amend the Secrecy Act but a fiasco between the Army and R&AW over Pakistani army movements during Brasstacks, saw opposition by the powerful intelligence agencies. No Indian bureaucrat likes to release power. CNS Admiral Vishnu Bhagwat asked for more say in ATV spending and policy. In 1998, he was surreptitiously dismissed under Art 310/311, without pension and rank, and President's Pleasure was withdrawn by Defence Minister George Fernandes. No legal recourse is allowed. This author wrote the book, "Admiral Bhagwat - Sacked or Sunk" (Manas Publication) with JAG Brig R.P.Singh. The book, which recommends the removal of the draconian 311 article, was banned for military libraries by George Fernandes.

The Chakra was exploited for 72,000 nautical miles (133,000 km), and the reactor was active for 430 days with five missile and 42 torpedo firings. Terenov writes that the nuclear base at Vishakapatnam is 'as good as any in Russia', and pays tributes to the Indian Navy. However, Vizag is a busy port with a narrow channel which can be blocked.

It needs recalling that in 1991, NHQ had requested the Indian High Commission in Singapore to obtain blanket diplomatic clearance for an IN ship, stating exercises were being conducted in the Bay of Bengal. Through the good offices of CNS Rear Admiral Teo Chea Hean (currently Deputy PM and Home Minister) the unusual permission was accorded. Early on a Sunday, this author received an irate call from Joint Services Intelligence Directorate in Singapore inquiring for details of IN warships entering the Singapore Straits. I was dumbfounded and rang NHQ, who said, "No one is to know, no one knows." USA, UK, Australia, New Zealand and Malaysia at Butterworth had joint ANZUS Intelligence. So I rang Col John Kerry, the Australian DA, and asked him if he could offer me a cold beer. After small talk, I said, "John, lets see how good your intelligence is. Do you know which IN ships are in the Straits?" Kerry replied, "Your bloody nuclear submarine and an OPV are heading east." I informed my High Commissioner H.C.Tiwari. INS Chakra was on its way back to Vladivostok.

Admiral Nadaf (ex ATV and BARC) in a classified book has recorded ATV's history, but it was Chakra's operation that gave confidence to build a nuclear submarine and a miniature reactor by BARC. Admiral Roy was succeeded by Admirals Bhushan, R.N.Ganesh, P.C.Bhasin, D.S.P.Verma and currently Prabhakar. Bhasin cut steel on his birthday on 5 January 1998, at the expansive Ship Building Centre (SBC) with nuclear facilities carved out of the Naval Dockyard at Vishakapatnam. India's first nuclear submarine INS

Arihant, to be India's nuclear deterrent with 700 km Sagarika-B-05 missiles, was built at Ship Building Centre by DRDO in a Public Private partnership with Larsen & Toubro Ltd in a leased ship. As of writing in 2014, Arihant is awaiting sea trials, with its reactor purring. A longer range K-4 missile has been tested for future larger SSBNs.

Chapter 21
Views by General Muqeen Khan and other Authors

Many authors have analysed the events of the 1971 war, when India-Pakistan relations fell to their nadir. The current India Pakistan relations stand unimproved, so some airing of these views would help to appreciate the 1971 war and its aftermath. If past is prologue, then it behoves the powers that be, to revise the thinking that led to that past. This look backwards will provide the insights that have informed the prognosis for the future of the Indian Ocean and the author's suggestions in the Epilogue later.

Varying perspectives and ambitions of Pakistan and China

General Fazal Muqeen Khan In his book, "Pakistan's Crisis in Leadership", discusses the causes of Pakistan's debacle in 1971, which he terms as not a defeat, but a humiliation. Muqeen asserts that the colonial roots of Afsariat (bureaucracy), Daftariat (red- tapism) and Choudriat (boss-ism), were the contributing factors, along with the crucial lack of a war aim. The political conditions in the East caused the defeat. The reaction of Pakistani Jawans when ordered to cease fire was understandable – they wept! Hawaldar Md Khan summed up the mood in Punjabi, "Grandma first made the mistake of getting married (East Bengal), but she made an even worse mistake by seeking a divorce". Fazal Khan indicts General Hamid Khan (COS) as an indecisive man deep in intrigue against Lt Gen SGM Peerzada, the PSO to the President, whom he wanted replaced by Maj Gen Ghulam Umar Khan. The services, and especially the Navy, were victims of defections and treachery by East Pakistanis who leaked naval dispositions. The Pakistani Armed Forces were suddenly deprived of good Bengali officers and technicians. Pakistan was hurled into a war they could not win. President Yahya Khan's assessment, even after 21 November, 1971, was that there would be no war, assuming USA and China were fully behind him. The views of President Nixon and Kissinger are now in the public domain.

On the Pakistan Navy, Muqeem Khan writes, "The story of the Pakistan Navy is a continuous struggle to establish its role and attain its rightful place in the defence hierarchy of Pakistan. The importance of maritime power was never adequately appreciated, and little could be spared from the expenditures of the Army and Air Force to provide for the Navy. A low priority to the Navy was perhaps natural, as the men who had the overriding say in Defence matters had inherited a long and distinguished tradition in soldiering, and had all been soldiers. For them, the sea was remote. Under colonial rule, the British Royal Navy guarded India's sea frontiers as apart of its Imperial responsibility. There was no need to keep an Indian Fleet in being. The British Indian Army's influence in the Government of India was all pervasive and at times decisive. The Pakistani statesmen and soldiers took to this tradition without understanding all the implications of governing a Sovereign state, unique in its geography and under constant threat from the neighbouring country, separating the two wings of Pakistan."

The author observes that Pakistan since Independence has not cashed in on its geographic locale by getting nations to invest in its coast line for commerce as it has deep waters. Nor has it offered bases, even though it was part of Western Alliances. On the other hand, Chinese demonstrated its long-term thinking, in appreciating the warm water facilities Pakistan affords, along with its connectivity to Central Asia and Southern states of China. China employed a creeping technique into Gwadar and

Pakistan Occupied Kashmir(POK) and got Pakistan to cede 2,239 sq miles of the Shaksgam valley (J&K territory under Pakistan's illegal occupation, flanking Soltoro Ridge) in exchange for a legally binding international border settlement. To the detriment of India's claims in POK, it was inked in that India would have to deal with the Sovereign Government of People's Republic of China on the future of Shaksgam, should India succeed in its claims on POK. The border treaty was signed on 2 March 1963 by Foreign Ministers Chen Yi of China and Zulfikar Ali Bhutto of Pakistan. It is to Indian Army's credit that the ambitions of Pakistan and China to some day link up Baltistan with China via the Karakoram pass and Siachen were foiled in 1987 by the heroic Indian troops led by Naik Subedar Bana Singh who captured the 21,000 feet Quad-e-Nizam post in the area and renamed it Bana Post.

Revelations by other authors

In his book, 'Beyond NJ 9852-The Siachen Saga' (Penguin Press) Nitin Gokhale writes, "In Pakistan, Siachen is a subject that hurts, just like a thorn in its flesh. It's a psychological drain on the Pakistan Army. Pervez Musharraf had once commanded the Special Services Group (SSG) in this area and made several futile attempts to capture the Indian posts. This was one of the motivating factors, and one of the military objectives of the Pakistan Army in the 1999 Kargil war to re-capture part of the Siachen Glacier and cut off India's crucial communication links to this vital area. Pakistan failed and suffered huge casualties."

It is providential that when the cease fire line was being delineated between India and Pakistan on the basis of Accession of Jammu and Kashmir (J&K) in October 1947 and the Karachi Agreement of 1949, the cease fire line beyond NJ 9852 (Saltoro Ridge and beyond), where it abruptly ended, was worded to be as, 'running Northwards to the glaciers'. The credit for the wording is ascribed to Gen Thimmaya, and interpretations between India and Pakistan vary. In 1987 Pakistan signed the protocol to formalize the demarcation of the termination of the boundary with China at Karakoram Pass, implying the tacit Pakistani recognition of Chinese sovereignty over Aksai Chin which India claims, and is another indication of understandings between Pakistan and China. No wonder China treats Aksai Chin as its territory and large development of roads and infrastructure have taken place, should it need to move its military in to the area. Pakistani patrols boldly foray ino Indian territory, to test Indian reactions, as the Chinese did in mid April 2013, in a three-week long stand-off at Daulat Beg Oldi (DBO) in the Depsang plains, with a small platoon of Chinese troops supported by helicopters. The area is patrolled by the Indian Tibetan Border Police (ITPB) in normal circumstances and Indian Army was rushed there. This was finally diplomatically resolved by the National Security Adviser (NSA), Shiv Shankar Menon and the India's Ambassador in China, 1955 born Subrahmanyam Jaishankar (son of famous doyen strategist late K. Subrahmanyam) currently Ambassador in Washington DC. Incidentally Menon and Jaishankar were on the team that concluded India's nuclear deal with the USA, when Jaishankar was India's High Commissioner in Singapore.

Gen Sam Manekshaw and spymaster R&AW Chief R.N.Kao met Mrs Gandhi in April 1971. Kao knew Mrs Gandhi had told Manekshaw that she needed to go to war. Manekshaw visited BSF camps in mid 1971 and BSF gave Mukhti Bahini cover. When Col Osmany complained that the Indian Army under Maj Gen Jacob was overbearing with its orders. It was P.N.Haksar and Kao who intervened to allow a free hand to Mukti Bahini and gave it access to funds.

Young East Bengali University boys who witnessed rapes became Indian Navy-trained frogmen and, led by

Indian Navy as Mukti Bahini, sank 150,000 tons of shipping. India avoided keeping records for fear of being sued. Kissinger was clear that President Yahya Khan was to be supported at any cost. Commenting on Mrs Gandhi's November State Dinner hosted by Nixon, he says, "I liked the art of the Ballerina", when she said, "India hails the brave young boys of the Mukti Bahini". At the end of her visit, Nixon sniped, "What does the bitch think?"

Indian intelligence agencies looked to inputs from Mukti Bahini and media, such as Mark Tully's broadcasts. It was the New York Times' Delhi correspondent Sydney Shanberg's first war, when he travelled with Mukti Bahini in October, and reported, "The Mukti Bahini are taking the shit out of Pakistan. Luckily Pakistan could not find any Bengali quislings."

Edward Kennedy commented, "The Government of India as it saw this first tide of human misery begin to flow across its borders, could have cordoned off its land and refused entry, but to Mrs Gandhi's everlasting credit, India chose the way of compassion." By September 1971, eight million refugees were being looked after and Mrs Gandhi was clear - if the world did not act to liberate Bangladesh, she would do it."

General Mohammad Musa's views in his book, "Jawan to General", chides Yahya Khan. Musa asserts that on 21 November, India invaded Pakistan's Eastern wing. The tried and tested concept was that the onus for defence of East Pakistan lay in West Pakistan, but no action was taken from the Western wing for 12 crucial days. An air strike on some enemy bases followed on 3 December, by what amounted to only a show of force and three minor attacks against Poonch, Chhamb and Ramgarh. Only the Chhamb operation succeeded.

In the Combat (Paris, 27 December 1971) Geoyes Anderson lists the causes of defeat, and writes that the speed of the defeat and the collapse of the Pakistani Army surprised the West, as the Pentagon and a certain number of European Generals considered it to be the best in the Asian continent. However, this is not the first mistake of judgment US intelligence Services have made. India won in a fortnight due not only to her superiority in number of troops and fire power, but to more detailed planning, support by Mukti Bahini and better strategic and tactical organization, faultless cooperation of the three arms with MOD. Above all, he commends the discipline and dedication of Indian Armed Forces and the total confidence in their high command. The author once again stresses the need for joint-ness, a CDS and theatre commands to galvanize the power and strength of the fine Indian Armed Forces.

In A Nation and its Navy at War, it is written that on 15 December 1971, Mrs Gandhi seeing victory for a Bangladesh, and sensing a cease fire as unavoidable, promptly wrote a long personal letter to appease the US President on what India did and why it was done. "I am writing at a moment of deep anguish at the unhappy turn of events which the relations of our two countries have taken.

One such great moment which has inspired millions of people to die for liberty was the declaration of Independence by the United States of America ... This war could have been avoided if the power, influence and authority of all States, and above all of the USA, had got Sheikh Mujibur Rehman released ... Mr President, may I ask you in all sincerity, was the release or even secret negotiations with a single human being namely Mujibur more disastrous than waging of war?" President Nixon received the letter but declined to disclose its contents in DC.

The R&AW angle and Intelligence Accountability

The recently released book 'Mission R&AW' by former

R&AW officer R.K.Yadav has a chapter on Liberation of Bangladesh. Yadav says the Mukti Bahini was the brain child of R.N.Kao and has headings of events leading to the crisis such as Nixon's unhelpful role, the brutality of West Pakistani forces and genocide. He discusses how Kao used and funded Tiger Siddiqui and how R&AW operated the special Frontier Force under Maj Gen Uban from Chittagong hill tract for success. The book has a day by day account of the war repeats the details from 'A Nation and Its Navy at War'. Researchers could find Yadav's book useful to research the intelligence aspects of India in war. They would also do well to consult "Crusader or Conspirator? (Coalgate and Other Truths)", by the former Secretary, Ministry of Coal, P.C.Parakh, to glean how the Central Bureau of Investigation (CBI) conducts its interrogations. In his case he found they did not know the difference between a 'coal mine' and a 'coal block' and how the coal mining business works but grilled him for two full days. India's intelligence needs a professional revamp. The future can be India's golden era, if enlightened leadership leads India with reforms and accountability.

Yadav breaks the unwritten code that intelligence operatives hold to, to carry national secrets to their graves.

In his 523 pages, Yadav opens many Pandora's boxes, passport scandals and details of tenures of R&AW chiefs with revelations and achievements about India's Intelligence. He explains how India was dissuaded by USA from conducting a nuclear test, noting "In 1995, Ambassador Frank Wisner (whose father was in the US Intelligence SSG) met Indian Prime Minister Narasimha Rao and showed him some photographs of US satellites which detected that India was preparing for a nuclear test. He maintained it would harm Indo-US relations if India would not abandon its plan to conduct such a test. These details were revealed to the media later. Hence while conducting the nuclear test in 1998, India scientists (this author includes Adviser in DRDO K.Santanam, a former

R&AW nuclear specialist, and other satellite analysts) were wary of the US warning of 1995, and thus took all possible security measures to conduct the nuclear test in utmost secrecy so the US Government should not have wind of it." The Army vehicles carrying the six devices (five were used for Shakti tests in May 1998) from Bharat Atmoic Research Centre in Mumbai (BARC) were camouflaged and moved as for a routine exercise to Pokhran under cloud cover or when there was dust cover to avoid satellite detection.

Yadav adds, "After Admiral Jerimiah panel (set up to investigate the lacunae in intelligence from India) indicted CIA for its failure to anticipate and forewarn US Government on the Indian nuclear test at Pokhran, American media openly published reports of that fiasco. The CIA planned to detach its staff from the American Embassy in New Delhi and other organizations. The then CIA Director, George Tenet after testifying before the Senate Intelligence Committee, openly declared before media persons that he would directly examine the CIA's methods of collecting intelligence in India, and how collection and analysis of such intelligence was properly utilized to ensure such a failure like the inability to detect that nuclear test, did not occur in the future. Thereafter CIA started an intense recruitment drive for engineers, scientists, IT specialists, linguists, and other professionals, with higher perks and salaries in various desks of the CIA to work against India. It set about recruiting moles in Indian establishments at exorbitant cost, and they succeeded to some extent in this venture." Yadav in Mission R&AW goes on to claim that Rabinder Singh, a senior R&AW operative, became a CIA mole, like Unnikrishnan during Op Pawan. He was caught but he and his family were facilitated by CIA in defection to the USA, with copies of what looked like original documents.

Emerging security challenges converge at sea

In conclusion, Commodore Lee Cordner, a researcher from University of Wollongong, Australia, who spent three months in 2014 studying a Maritime Strategy for India in co-operation with IOR nations, confirms maritime security in the Indian Ocean Region (IOR) has become a central issue for regional and extra-regional actors.

The states' emerging traditional and non-traditional security challenges largely converge at sea as they impact economic, environmental, energy, human, food and national security. There are compelling drivers for enhancing maritime security cooperation in the IOR. As the major regional power and an emerging Asian great power, India's willingness and capacity to provide strategic leadership is critical. There is a sad lack of alignment between the Indian political and military establishments, combined with a demonstrable lack of political will for reform and increase in FDI to 49% in the Defence sector. This raises questions about India's strategic competence and its prospects or capability as a regional leader. India's strategic policy of ambiguity undermines regional trust and confidence. Regional actors look to India to provide strong, proactive and coherent leadership and engender a spirit of cooperation and shared destiny. India's strategic leadership presents an opportunity to meet any challenges currently posed by an enterprising China.

This has been the abiding theme of the book. While covering the many operations and the wars, its seeks to offer confidence to the nation of the capabilities of its small but dedicated Indian Navy in the immediate future, working in cohesion with the rest of the fine Armed Forces for long term national security. The book's constant emphasis is on the need to chart a revised co-operative diplomatic strategy, to upgrade the structure of the Armed Forces and its intelligence, and mobilize the nations' support to expand the Navy's capabilities to meet what Dr KM Pannikar observed for the long term, "It is a pre-requisite of India's freedom that she should share in the responsibility of guarding in the Indian Ocean ... as her interest in this area is predominant."

Shan No Varuna.

India's Maritime Perspective

By
Admiral Vishnu Bhagwat PVSM AVSM, Former Chief of the Naval Staff

The golden period of our history coincided with the centuries that India's trade and cultural influence climaxed in the West and the East. Accompanying it were not only extraordinary bursts of energy, but also an unbounded spirit of adventure to explore distant lands, for trade, trading settlements and commerce. Backing this were the skills, organization and capabilities of the peoples of the peninsula and the ocean /sea minded states in India that had the will and determination to support these organized, creative enterprises.

The concept of 'Strategic Frontiers ' was embedded in the consciousness of the Nation then, as it ought to be in our times— to know to what distances and seas/ shores and beyond we need to defend and enhance our interests and influence, not only in the geographical sense. The Navy is only one component of our strength and capabilities at sea, but it is also the leading one.

Much of the public discourse on this subject restricts itself to a conventional look at the threats (two threats), but unfortunately does not make a comprehensive assessment and projection of the global forces that are at work, which impinge and indeed influence and subtly or openly come in the way of 1200 million people shaping their own destiny and choosing their own autonomous path of development. Autonomy and sovereignty seem to be remembered in a limited and restricted way, only when the nuclear environment, potential and capabilities are discussed.

Despite our historical experience and the lessons that we ought never to forget, there is selective, even severe general amnesia, as though we had deliberately wiped out all historical memories. The forces of colonialism and imperialism that enslaved, looted and deprived us are forgotten, to such extent that their new aggressive capture/ prying open of markets, resources, oil, gas and strategic raw materials continues, blinding the ruling establishment by the allurements that are offered and accepted by the few subservient and appendages of these interests, rather than the policy objectives of the development of 1.2 billion people, with policies to enable the country to take off in every sphere - economic, scientific, technological and cultural. It is necessary even today to recall that, then as now, the imperialist powers /colonialists were leading sea powers with powerful fleets and hence the dictum 'Trade follows the Flag'.

Navies and maritime capabilities are not built with the capabilities of one or two countries in mind, either against country X or Nation Y, articulated with a jingoist mindset, within the framework of a bureaucratic apparatus, with decisions guided by a feudal mindset. Navies and the maritime capabilities of a State enhance the strength of a Nation in the broadest and most comprehensive sense, as a Navy is the mirror of the country's scientific and technological development, its reach and depth in research, its manufacturing industry , its capabilities in design engineering and innovation, and also in the frontiers of space and the ocean depths /seabed, and the morale of its people, and the country's acceptance in the comity of nations as a maritime trading power.

Our navy is fortunate that it has the support of ISRO, our most efficient entity in the public arena. However our efforts, organization and structures in the hydrosphere and ocean-atmosphere are lagging, due to the absence of a vision and perspective among policy makers. We have a very long way to go, as somewhere along the way, the perspective has been limited and warped. Several decades ago, the grit and persistence of a VK Krishna Menon laid the foundations of the shipbuilding industry and ancilliary manufactures, which was enhanced by our Naval Staff by forging relationships with a large number of quality suppliers in   large, medium and small scale industries, covering mechanical, electrical and electronics sectors. This has progressed with time over the last 5 decades, though far from adequately.

It was the late Prime Minister Indira Gandhi who gave directions to the Navy and the Ministry of Defence to build and acquire 'strategic platforms' and associated capabilities in October 1968.

Unfortunately this directive was not given the necessary priority in design personnel, materials and resources and, therefore, progressed in fits and starts, sometimes with ideological blinkers and prejudices, which retarded the progress that should have followed had we imbibed the ISRO model of Prof Satish Dhawan and Dr Bhabha's path in the Atomic Energy Commission (AEC).

Notwithstanding this lack of consistency and drive, the Navy, and for this the credit goes to the Leadership of the Service, including its Technical and Design cadres, that it continued its commitment to self–reliance or swadeshi, with few deviations. Still, we cannot rest on our laurels as we have several challenged ahead. For example, the Design Bureau and associated Bureaus still need to be expanded, and their field units in the shipyards and our dockyards further strengthened.

While the design and production of surface combatants up to destroyer and frigate class have reached world class standards, we have been seriously remiss in our capabilities to maintain our submarine strength over the last 25 years, and to expand the submarine fleet size. As a consequence, the submarine arm is the weakest link in the chain of maritime defence and offensive capability. This is a paradox and one can hardy find a satisfactory answer for an unsatisfactory delivery of our plans, except to highlight it as a major and serious strategic omission.

Every professional with a strategic understanding is aware that the submarines enjoy an unbeatable advantage that these platforms have in tropical waters over anti-submarine forces/ means of every kind. They are also natural stealth platforms, immune to electronic and space surveillance, detection and monitoring, which compromise the position and movements of surface and air combatants from the very start. The more we lag in this field, the wider this strategic gap and deficiency, the more we will surrender our potential advantage, and all the intellectuals and thinkers who make speeches extolling the virtues of sea power, and our reach and potential in the IOR in particular, are only day-dreaming or praying heavenwards, with no real intent to set right this situation.

Navies and sea-power and all its constituents are fundamentally a function of the Nation's economic strength and progress, as demonstrated by its financial muscle and reserves, the harnessing of her manpower resources, and the strength of her national industry, design bureaus and her science and technology, given a certain dedication and commitment of her political, military and scientific leadership and cadres.

The Soviet Union, China and India are roughly comparable as twentieth century phenomena. The USSR and China were historically essentially continental and land oriented nations, with the exception that in brief periods like Peter the Great and in 15th Century China, there were short bursts of oceanic energy, ship building, and State driven investments and priority. The Soviet Union in the mid 1950s accorded the highest priority to building comprehensive naval and maritime strength, backed by the State, as outlined by Admiral SG Gorshkov in his "Seapower of the State". It was fortunate that the Soviet Navy had an unprecedented steadfastness in the Gorshkov-Engineer Admiral Kotov team for 26 years. However even this great Navy that they built came to a halting slow-down, when the leadership signed its political capitulation in 1991 to imperial-capitalist, financial and strategic interests of global finance.

The Peoples Republic of China took a very early decision in 1950, despite the overwhelming predominance of the Red Army/ PLA, to accord the highest priority to the PLA (Navy) in resource allocation, and industry support. If today the Chinese Navy is growing in every direction, it is also because China is the fastest growing economy, already in the second position globally, with the largest financial reserves. To this, one has to add the decision making and strength of the Chinese Military Commission, unhampered by any generalist bureaucratic structures, but supported and advised by specialized Institutes. One can take it as axiomatic that the Chinese Navy, merchant fleet, its shipbuilding and ports infrastructure and design institutes will grow in direct proportion to China's political-economy and China's trading clout the world over. Analysts and strategists can huff and puff, make learned speeches and present papers in seminars and think-tanks to their heart's content; however without a similar commitment to overall national development in India, it will be difficult to keep pace, due to the absence of a drive for overall economic development in India, a healthy and trained work force, and bureaucracy which seeks to obstruct and contain the Navy's plans and perspectives. China will advance its maritime interests and sail its ships where it wants, so long as the Chinese economy continues to grow, and consequently expands its areas of strategic interests. To give just one example, India does not have the demonstrated capability to construct ports and infrastructure in friendly countries as China is doing.

Notwithstanding our natural advantages, there are major contradictions in India's quest for building its military capabilities as behooves our size and population. We limit our selves severely if the nation continues to be the world's top arms importer, and pay tribute to armament companies the world over, or use arms deals as an instrument of political or personal funding, as has happened in a few cases in the past. We have yet to pull ourselves by the bootstraps and not pay lip service to our oft-stated goal of self-reliance. Perhaps the time is now that the Navy too should consider establishing a new weapons and sensors design bureau as DRDO has not delivered in this vital area.

It would be worthwhile recalling three golden precepts: Unbalance potential adversaries, pursue military systems options which destabilize them, conventional and unconventional, and always try to maintain the initiative, technological and strategic.

The 1971 Operations are a classic example to remember. The major reason why we and the Liberation movement / forces succeeded in just 14 days was that the 'War of Movement', bypassing several military strong positions and towns, was conjoined with the 'Mukti Bahini' and the 'Jal Bahini' , and the whole people of the 'Bangladesh' to be. The Mukti cum Jal Bahini carried out a myriad of special operations on rivers, junctions, logistics, and were the de-facto eyes and ears of the Indian Army, Navy and Airforce at every stage. However, why did 95,000 soldiers and officers surrender in Dhaka? General Niazi saw the hopelessness of his situation, even as they carried out genocide until the end. Our Navy had not only blockaded the Western approaches to their one and only major port, but also cut off the sea lines of communications between the West and the East, and completely blocked the approaches to the East, as well as destroyed/damaged the ports and harbours. The Commander knew he had no option but to lay down arms, despite the dim chances that an aircraft carrier led armada could arrive in time to enable a diplomatic intervention and pressure. The level of synergy in planning and operations as well as the total support of the population led to this unprecedented achievement. It would be well to recall all this when we are dismayed at some of our equipment shortages, and not count our force multipliers, which then were the exceptional political and military leadership, people's total participation, and other psychological factors which came into play .

This has to be emphasized, as above all, we cannot allow a psychology of dependence and dependency to propel us to looking for help, strategic concepts and ideas, from those powers that may be well endowed today, but are really declining powers, whose record post the Second World War is far from shining. They can bomb and destruct, but have not been able to achieve victory anywhere, especially in our part of the world. It would be better to seriously introspect and analyze, shedding our coloured lenses to see the reality - that it is simply not in the interest of the people, or of our country, to entertain such delusions that somehow we can don the mantle of a 'Swing' State or a 'Balancing' Power, and in the process incline towards agreements /alliances or positions which can invite adventure, and entice us to provide 'cannon fodder' in some 'cats-paw' or proxy games, inducing self–destruct through adventurism, or being an appendage in a military pact not in our interests.

A belief in India and its people's destiny alone should be our beacon and indeed our maritime compass.

I wish term mate Ranjit's efforts all success!
Mumbai 21st February, 2014

India's Role in Regional Security

By
Lt. Gen. Satish Nambiar PVSM AVSM VrC

In an analysis of the security perspective of the South Asian Region, three factors that are a unique feature of the geography of the region merit particular attention. The most dominant factor is India's sheer size in terms of land mass, population and resources. The second is that of the states that constitute the immediate region, India shares common borders with all except the Maldives. Other than Afghanistan and Pakistan, none of the other states have common land borders with each other. The third is that only India has shared ethnic affinities with sections of the population of its neighbours; not discounting some shared ethnicity between Nepal and Bhutan.

An appreciation of this unique feature is vital for an understanding of the complex inter-state political and security dynamics of the region. There is a bilateral security dimension between each of the countries and India, but hardly any with each other. While that may be the price India has to pay for its geography and cultural history, it could also be viewed as a feature that provides a reasonable basis for evolving a cooperative security framework.

For almost 45 years after attaining Independence, India had largely been insular and isolationist. Totally subsumed with the situation in Jammu and Kashmir and the insurgencies in the North East, the Indian establishment allowed China and Pakistan to call the shots most of the time. China did so by supporting the insurgencies in the North East in the early years, and using Pakistan as a proxy to keep India totally pre-occupied. Pakistan on its part deftly exploited the situation within Jammu and Kashmir as also in other parts of the country to wage a low intensity proxy war that included support to terrorist groups. The success the two countries achieved in this context is underscored by what had become a paranoid obsession about Pakistan; a paranoia that took India down to the same level as Pakistan. In the process, an otherwise untenable Pakistani claim of parity with India gained credibility in the international arena. Fortunately, we have graduated since the mid-1990s to drawing comparisons with China.

Notwithstanding the challenges India faces internally, we need to be clear that within the international setting into the second decade of the 21st Century, given our size, geo-strategic location straddling the Indian Ocean, a population of over a billion people, our undeniable democratic credentials, significant capability in information technology, space research, a large reservoir of scientific talent, management expertise, proven military capability, and the large market for consumer goods and services, the country does have a role to play both regionally and globally.

However, it may be prudent to remind ourselves that there was much euphoria about India's economic growth potential and its capacity to be a player on the global arena. Actual performance was always contingent on getting our act together in terms of critical issues such as development of infrastructure (airports, seaports, electricity, roads, railways, water supply, etc), pursuit of policies that promote growth, increased attention to vital aspects like primary and secondary education and provision of basic health services, particularly to the less privileged sections of society, and eradication of abject poverty. This has been somewhat tempered in the last decade by a slow-down in economic growth, the unemployment situation largely caused by under-performance in the manufacturing sector, questionable exploitation of the demographic dividend, inability to provide adequate opportunities to the poorer sections of our society, indifferent health services to large such sections of our population, inability to root out illiteracy, and so on.

Even so, the fact is that India has an inescapable and vital stake in the happenings in the immediate neighbourhood, as instability and social upheaval in the region will have adverse 'spill-over' effects that will cause us security problems and generate stress within our society. Internationally, the situation today is that most countries, including major players like the USA, European Union, Russia, Japan, etc, would without doubt like to see India play a more pro-active role in promoting democratic values and contributing to stability in the region; as much because of the perception that India has such a capability, as because they would not wish to be physically involved. We must therefore, be prepared to use our economic and military clout in pursuance of the maintenance of peace and security in the region.

The fact that the trade routes through the Indian Ocean are vital for the growth of our economy, as also the fact that India straddles the Indian Ocean, imposes on us the responsibility to ensure the security of the sea-lanes of communication from the East coast of Africa and the Persian Gulf to the Malacca Straits. In recent years, this has been acknowledged by a number of major international players like the USA, the European Union, Russia, Japan, Australia, and so on. Our spontaneous and most effective response to the tsunami disaster a few years back, and firm naval action against pirates off the Gulf of Aden have reinforced this position. Our maritime capability must therefore be further geared to meet this challenge. The diplomatic challenge is to initiate effective coordination with other littoral Indian Ocean states.

On the economic front it would be prudent and most appropriate that we draw in our immediate neighbours. We must not only remove trade barriers but also encourage and assist Indian business houses to invest in these countries, to boost their own economic growth. This will need some imagination, innovation and finesse. Whereas in the case of the rest of Asia and indeed the world, economic moves are largely driven by market forces, the immediate region is influenced by a number of local issues that need to be factored into our calculations. As an incentive for positive economic inter-action at the regional level, India may well have to make a number of concessions in the initial stages.

If we are to play any significant role in regional affairs and be taken seriously at the global level, Indian diplomacy will need to move into high gear, taking into account the fact that in pursuing international relations, there is no place for righteousness and moral posturing; it is guided solely by sovereign national interests. In the immediate region, it may be useful to get off the high pedestal we have placed ourselves on, shed the patronising approach we seem to have mastered over the years, and evolve working relationships with our neighbours.

This will need to be structured around two basic planks: one, an appreciation of their needs and sensitivities; and two, a clear enunciation of our security sensitivities and their non-negotiable status. Whereas we should be prepared to bend over backwards to meet the requirements of our neighbours, and genuinely do so, it should be made clear that where our security interests are concerned, no compromises will be made - that we will go the distance to ensure this, even to the extent of application of economic and military power.

This process will obviously take some effort, primarily because we have to first undo the present lack of credibility in regard to our determination in pursuit of national security interests. Not too many countries take us seriously, because we have indulged in rhetoric rather than action all too often. Simultaneously, we shall need to condition international opinion to the fact that we are serious about developments in the region, and that we propose to do something about dealing with those that impact on India's security.

To that end, we may well have to regularly inter-act with other members of the international community including the more powerful ones, and coordinate our moves in consultation with them.

Epilogue - The Mental Matters

A Debate on India's Maritime Strategy

"While India 'appears' to have a naval strategy, it does not as yet have a maritime strategy. It will be sometime before the country graduates from being a naval power to a true maritime power." - Ambassador Shyam Saran, Chairman of India's National Security Advisory Board (NSAB) – 2014.

A good book aims to inform, entertain, and leave its imprint on the reader. This Epilogue now goes a step further by tabling concepts and views that invite debate.

In April 1942, the Japanese stood at India's Eastern border. The Royal Navy lay depleted. India's gates lay open, but the Japanese halted. India just did not form part of Japan's 'Mental map' of Asia which ended at Burma. Leaders' 'Mental maps' matter in geo-politics to define national interests for nation building and to script strategy. For example, the 'mental map' of Maharaja of Bikaner Ganga Singh (Mayo educated 1880-1943) was to improve the fortunes of his desert folk. The Gang Canal with water from river Sutlej head works was inaugurated by Lord Irwin in 1933. Ganga Singh raised a Camel Corps and served the British abroad with his troops. He represented India at the Treaty of Versailles (1919) and invited the French PM G.Clemenceau for a Tiger shoot. He represented India at the London Round Table (1930). Bikaner became India's premier airfield, and today Nal is IAF's forward base. Marwari havelis of Rungtas, Ruias, Oswals etc, testify to the wealth of Bikaner which Ganga put on the caravan trade route to Karachi, thanks to his 'Mental map', carried forward by his successors. The partition forced the Marwaris to migrate.

In the last century, Soviets and Americans divided the world into camps, leading to a cold war mentality. NATO and WARSAW blocs formed. India stood for non–

alignment, but Mrs Indira Gandhi's 'Mental map' to liberate Bangladesh in 1971 led to a mutual security treaty with Soviet Union as insurance before the war. India was obliged to vote with the USSR in the UN. That is realpolitik. Mrs Gandhi took her role seriously as a de-facto Commander In Chief and delivered India its only military victory. Leaders with 'mental maps' shape history. It was Chancellor Helmut Kohl's mental map that brought down the Berlin wall in 1990. PM Atal Behari's mental map made India a nuclear power in 1998.

Indian leaders avoided 'Mental maps'as they were influenced by Nehruvian 'non-alignment' and ahmisa (non-violence). National interests took a back seat. Naval brass crafted India's Maritime Military Strategy in 2007 and revised the Navy's Doctrine accordingly in 2009, without MEA or MOD oversight, and modeled them on UK's Corbettian and USA's Mahanian power play to control trade routes, influenced by US Naval War College (NWC) graduating Naval Chiefs. Yet, unlike USA, India faced land threats from the West and North, and was not industrialized. India became the world's largest importer of defence goods and services. FDI above 26% in defence was not allowed.

Warships built in PSU yards cost more, and took longer and still do take ages to build. No accountability is shouldered by the MOD's ordering authority, Defence Production. Infrastructure and training lost priority though the Navy inducted latest technology. The Navy neglected the man called 'Eye Ball Mark 1' and safety procedures, overly depending on technology. Pakistan took advantage of India's porous coast and feeble intelligence, and paralyzed Mumbai for 56 hours on 26/11/2008.

Course Correction of Maritime Strategy Is Called For

Albuquerque's strategy of diplomacy laced with power, holds lessons for India. In the 15th century, Pope Alexander VI divided the known world between Spain

(King Phillip and Queen Isabella the Catholic) to explore West of Cape Verde, and Portugal (Prince Henry) to venture East by inking the Treaty of Tordesillas. 'Mental maps' emerged. Both nations prospered. India's West coast and the Arabian Sea came under the Portuguese Governor Albuquerque till 1662, when Bombay was gifted to Britain as dowry, Princess Catherine Braganza having wed King Charles 1, to further Portugal's 'mental map' in Europe.

In democracies, political masters lay down guidelines for the bureaucracy to craft policies and strategies.

Economists engage with military to chalk strategies and doctrines, especially for the nation's security and maritime interests. The opposite was true in the 1980s when Ministers crafted corruption-prone policies, and compliant bureaucrats abetted corruption. The infamous Bofors, HDW, 2G, CWG, Coalgate and recently the TATRA and 12 AW-101 VIP helicopters scandals followed. PM Dr Manmohan Singh blamed 'coalition compulsions'. The bureaucracy stymied the Armed Forces. Nuclear policy became the preserve of scientists but fortunately India's Space Agency, away from Delhi in Bangalore, pursued its 'Mental map' for India's future in space.

With Arab Springs, uncertainty in Afghanistan, and fragility of Pakistan's 200 million, the future of South Asia is in flux. The unprecedented rise of China, with military and economic inroads into the Indian Ocean and the island states, challenges India. China's 'mental map' is to never let repeat the 100 years of humiliation (1849-1949) and to match the USA, regain its territories and waters in dispute with Sun Tzu-ian strategies. It supports its military with a $130 billion defence budget labeling its nationalistic fervor as 'Love for One's Country'. USA's mental map (per a Pew survey) acknowledging the economic rise of China, is determined to remain the pre-eminent military power, with reliance on innovation and seeks to become energy exporting with its shale gas discoveries.

India's Maritime And Strategic Challenges

Indian Navy's Order of Battle (ORBAT) stands aged and reduced since the 1990s, with less submarines and helicopters and OPVs. Its personnel policies were tweaked in 2013. A Navy Chief convinced Defence Minister Antony to exclude submariners and aviators from the top posts. Navy's legacy infrastructure could not keep up with the fast expanding technological Navy and attend to aging Soviet supplied ships, especially the submarines which need Mid Life Updates (MLUs) with the support of Original Equipment Manufacturers (OEMs) of Russia and Ukraine, The Government avoided responsibility to support the Navy's needs, culminating in some serious accidents.

On 26 February 2014 Admiral D.K Joshi, US trained Naval Chief from the Naval Academy (Navac) resigned citing 'moral responsibility', which was accepted with no succession plan. This left the Navy with no head for 56 days, after which the second senior most Vice Admiral Robin Dhowan was named the Chief of Naval Staff. His tenure began with a call for professionalism, training and safety as lodestones for the Indian Navy on his watch.

The "Asia-Pacific" is gaining importance as its economies thrive. USA's 'Pivot' in the East is America's cat's paw to remain engaged in the region, with China's inevitable rise in mind. USA's mental map is changing to accept itself as 'the first amongst equals'. PLA(Navy) ships and nuclear submarines have ventured into the Indian Ocean. China's 'String of Pearls' now surrounds India.

India takes reactive actions when forced to with less long term thinking. China's amicably priced sale of 2 Song 039 submarines to Bangladesh, and support to Pakistan should concern India. Its security planners should shape India's maritime strategies with clear 'mental maps'. In

2014, China's President Xi Jinping enunciated a Maritime Silk Route (MSR) for the IOR and beyond with Sri Lanka as its first member, and has asked India's NSA for India to join.

India is fortunate. Its maritime geography juts into the Indian Ocean like a spear, with Andaman and Nicobar islands guarding the Malacca Straits, and Lakshwadweep islands as India's Western outposts. Oxford don Dr K.M.Panikkar in The Influence of Sea Power on Indian History' calls it India's trump card. Geography and geo-politics change the fortunes of nations. Pannikar recommended maritime strategies on Albuquerquean lines for India, and needs re-visiting. Mahan's and Panikkar's predictions on the importance of the IOR to the world in the 21st century ring true.

A view by India's NSA Shiv Shankar Menon on 'India's Strategic Culture and International Relations (IR)', was provided on 11 December 2013 at Jawaharlal National University.(JNU). "There have been those, like George Tanham, who deny that India has a strategic culture. My view is that this is an impossibility for a self conscious culture and civilisation such as ours, with our heritage and sense of our own importance and role. Just as saying one is apolitical is itself a political choice, saying that India has nostrategic culture is only to say that it is different from the strategic cultures one is used to. Sadly many have picked up Tanham's refrain. India has shown remarkable consistency in the manner of her engagement with the world, across different stages of her development, under governments of divergent political persuasions, and in very varied international circumstances. The record has been remarkably consistent."

Lee Cordner an Australian researcher in India commented, "India has a strategic culture; it comprises ambivalence, is surely secretive, and consists of centralised control by the civilian bureaucracy. It is a mix of pragmatism and Nehruvian socialism. India has grown in stature and needs change." The author leaves it to the reader to ponder over NSA's explanation. India's 65,000 strong Navy as a tool for India's diplomacy, but is not involved in maritime policy formulation, or the armchair Planning Commission, or the Shipping ministry, or DG Shipping for Port State Security Control, or advising on UNCLOS 1982. The Ministry of Earth Sciences has taken pole position.

China's rise is altering the balance of power in East Asia, forcing states to look for new security and economic partners and investments beyond the immediate region and Africa. India is a nuclear power with a no first use (NFU) policy and the BJP in its manifesto has stated it will re-visit India's Nuclear Doctrine if voted into power. The doctrine certainly deserves operational direction.

This Epilogue initiates debate to chart India's 'mind plan' and strategy for its rise as a strong maritime power! David Brewster and my retired naval golf foursome, Vice Admiral Bhasin 'India's Rickover' and builder of India's nuclear submarine INS Arihant, Rear Admiral Talwar who hawks yeast, and Cmde Bajwa who oversees Navy's non-public millions, offered their wisdom of decades of salted life, over hundreds of hours on the green.

Jai Hind!

"Prabhavasakti (power of the military and treasury) is more important than Utsahasakti (power and personal and energy), and Mantrasakti (power of counsel and diplomacy and friendship) is more important than both". Kautilya from Arthsastra - On Strategy.

Appendix 1

Other Operations of the Indian Navy

Operation Muffet 1992

The first ever overseas deployment of the Indian Navy was between December 1992 and October 1993 for Op Muffet, to support UN Search & Rescue (SAR) and 'Humanitarian Relief' operation in Somalia. India joined the UN Op Restore Hope with a brigade of 2000 troops and 3 Indian Navy ships, INS Deepak (fleet tanker), INS Kuthar (Corvette) and INS Cheetah, under Cmde Sampath Pillai. Offshore Patrol Vessels (OPVs) - Sukanya, Subhadra, Sharda and Suvarna were also deployed. OPV Sukanya participated in SAR of MV Remorra Bay carrying sugar to Somalia after losing radio contact off Merka. INS Sukanya also carried cargo to Mombassa twice for aid agencies.

Operation Shield and Bolster – Somalia, 1994

Op Shield from 6 to 11 December 1994 was to de-induct troops from Kismayo. INS Ganga, Godavari, Shakti and 2 Sea King helicopters escorted the Indian Army's 1 Bihar Brigade out of Somalia after their tenure ended. India had chartered merchant ships and an airliner for de-induction of troops and equipment. The Sea King Helicopters provided evacuation support for rearguard surveillance and close weapon support. INS Godavari had hospital facilities onboard. The Marine Commandos (MARCOS) provided close weapons support from both land and air. The task force later sailed to Mogadishu for Operation Bolster on 12/13 December to de-inducted troops. It received air cover from Sea King helicopters on the coast and till the final UN chartered flight left the airport.

Operation Madad, Operation Sea Waves, Operation Castor, Operation Rainbow and Operation Gambhir

Op Madad was a Humaitarian Relief and Disaster Relief (HADR) response by the Indian Armed Forces in aid of the 2004 Indian Ocean Tsunami. The operation focussed on the East Coast of the mainland and Andamans, after launching aerial survey within one hour of the Tsunami, IN and Coast Guard SAR units were dispatched to help the administration. Naval divers cleared the approach channels to Indian ports to enable merchant ships to aid the situation. IN amphibious vessels and landing craft also delivered aid to affected coastal communities that were cut off due to the tsunami.

Concurrently Ops Sea Waves unfolded in Andaman & Nicobar Islands, which were the closest to the tsunami epicenter. IN and CG assets at the Port Blair naval base were deployed for SAR. The navy delivered aid to survivors on remote islands who had been rendered homeless and IN vessels and aircraft were deployed for tsunami rescue and relief in neighboring Maldives (Operation Castor), Sri Lanka (Operation Rainbow) and Indonesia (Operation Gambhir). The alacrity and operational readiness of the Navy was applauded, as it was sailed while US Navy was still in preparation.

Operation Sukoon - Evacuation of Indians from Lebanon

OP Sukoon was conducted amid one of the largest deployments of Indian Navy ships overseas. It was also one of the largest evacuations by any Navy. At the outbreak of hostilities between Israel and Lebanon in 2006, about 12,000 Indians resided in Lebanon. A month prior to Op Sukoon, a detachment of 11 ships had sailed from Mumbai for exercises in the Arabian and Red Seas followed by overseas deployment to the Mediterranean. Seven out of these eleven ships returned to Mumbai from the Red Sea, and Task Force 54 (TF 54) comprising INS Mumbai, Brahamputra, Betwa and Tanker Shakti proceeded for an expeditionary international deployment in the Mediterranean crossing the Suez Canal, and split into two groups for calls. INS Mumbai and Brahamputra steamed towards Haifa in Israel, and INS Betwa and Shakti called at Alexandria in Egypt, and to Tripoli in Libya and the other two sailed to Izmir in Turkey. The evacuation of Indian nationals was discussed in Delhi and the anticipation built up that Task Force 54 may be used. The Task Force finally united in Athens, Greece, coinciding with visit of FOC-in-C, Vice Admiral Sangram Singh Byce. The ships sailed Athens on 13 July began monitoring Israeli communications, Notice To Mariners (NOTAMs) for navigation in the sea blockade declared by the Israeli Navy around the coast of Lebanon. The blockade was 70 nautical miles in length and 58 nautical miles in width (appr.130 km by 111 km).

After one Indian citizen was killed during Israeli attacks in Lebanon, the Government made urgent plans for the safe evacuation of Indian nationals from Lebanon. The Indian Mission in Beirut was in contact with the Indian nationals in Lebanon through various Indian organizations and arrangements made for them to leave Lebanon. At 9.30 a.m. on 17 July, when home bound, just short of Great Bitter Lake in Suez Canal, where the south bound convoys anchor, to allow the northern bund convoy, Rear Adm Anup Singh Fleet Commander Western Fleet FOCWF) received a message to turn back for Op Sukoon.

In an ops meeting of the senior officers and the Captains of all the ships, FOCWF issued detailed orders for logistics and armaments for a probable evacuation of Indian nationals from the war zone, with all the possibilities regarding security, immigration, food, first-aid, accommodation and transit of the evacuees. To turn around mid-way in Suez Canal is a task because the width does not allow a U turn, as ships pass through Suez in a strict column. Traffic is only one way and controlled by Egyptian port authorities, piloted by the Egyptian port officials. The Navy sought diplomatic clearance for reverse transit with the first north-bound convoy on the morning of 18 July, and was approved. The transit began by 6 a.m. and after 12 hours through the Suez Canal, the Force headed straight towards Beirut skirting the large blockade box. Having monitored Israeli Navy communication constantly and established its first contact with Israeli Navy directly on 19 July, Operation Sukoon got underway.

The Israeli Navy asked the fleet to enter the blockade area on its western extremity in order to enable the usual identification by their ships. Shakti was left outside the blockade area to patrol south of Cyprus. Three ships INS Mumbai, Betwa and Brahamputra entered the blockade gate at 3.30 am on July 20. A Lebanese pilot was sent to Mumbai at 8.30 am to guide the ship into the docking areas. INS Mumbai sent one of its vanguard boats to lead her to the harbour escorted by a Lebanese gun boat at 9 am, and berthed at the jetty, fully secured by Lebanese Army soldiers who were patrolling with their guns. Within minutes, a convoy of ten buses of 50 Indians each arrived. INS Mumbai established checkpoints and ships facilitated security control, immigration and baggage control for all the evacuees, to the surprise of local Lebanese as well as international media who had earlier covered some of the Western Navies in similar evacuation. INS Brahamputra and Betwa remained on patrol, and finally sailed out of Beirut at 7.40 pm in the evening at high speed to Larnaca in Cyprus. When the ships reached Larnaca in the early morning, all the evacuees were taken straight to the airport from where they were airlifted to India.

A second evacuation of 887, including 784 Indians, 41

Nepalese, 57 Sri Lankans and 5 Lebanese were transported safely to Larnaca airport by INS Mumbai, Brahmaputra and Betwa and once again airlifted by Air India on July 24. The third evacuation was completed on 27 July for 374, and the final one by Betwa on 29 July for 411 evacuated, including 82 Indians, 324 Sri Lankans and 5 Nepalese, bringing the total to 2280 people to safety that included 1764 Indian nationals. 65 tonnes of medicines, clothes and food were also transported to Beirut on 1 August by Betwa with swift turn around. Officers and sailors were non-stop Action Stations for more than 36 hours at a stretch on an average. The ships had to go through troubled waters each time, establish protection measures for safe movement and undertake careful navigation to avoid the danger of mistaken identities.

Ladies and children were accommodated in sleeping cabins and over 1000 full meals - breakfasts, lunches and dinners, prepared for the evacuees. The Beirut sealift was a mammoth evacuation, termed as the largest since Dunkirk in the western media.

Operation Blossom - Evacuation of Indians from Libya

Around 8000 Indian citizens in Libya needed to be evacuated due to the 2011 protests and violence against Gaddafi's military rule. Indian Navy deployed INS Aditya, Mysore and Jalashwa (ex USS Trenton), an 18,000 ton amphibious LPD bought for HADR for $ 70 million. The ships arrived off Tripoli on 10 March, 11 via the Suez Cana, and Jalashwa entered Tripoli harbour and embarked 150 stranded personnel stranded at Tripoli, while Mysore remained on patrol outside the harbour. The evacuees were disembarked Malta's Valetta Harbour where INS Vikrant had worked up in 1961The ships returned to India on 28 March 2011.

Operational Deployment of Eastern Fleet in S.E.Asia – 2011

IN ships INS Delhi, Ranvir, Ranvijay, Jyoti and Kirch sailed for overseas deployment to the South China Sea and Western Pacific in March - May 2011. The fleet called at Singapore, Subic Bay, Vlapostok, Manila, Ho Chi Minh City, Bandar Sera Begawan – Brunei, Kota Kina Balu - Malaysia and Jakarta. The ships participated in Bilateral Exercises with Singapore Navy (SIMBEX) and US Navy and PASSEX with host navies to enhance Navy to Navy cooperation.

Operation Rahat

Operation Rahat was one of the largest civilian rescue operation carried out by any Air Force around the world, using helicopters dubbed as the Himalayan Tsunami. The rains affected 1.6 million and 4,200 villages by 16 June, 2014. In Uttarakhand major landslides occurred at 110 places, washing out or damaging 154 bridges and 320 roads with loss of life of many poor people. While IAF flew 2,137 sorties and airlifted 18,424 people, both Army and the Navy were also involved in the rescue operation. The Indian Navy contributed marine commandoes (MARCOS) and divers trained in Special Operations to help in underwater rescue wherever required.

Appendix 2

The Future Indian Navy in the 21st Century

"The raison d'etre of of Indian Navy's existence is succinctly encapsulated in the theme. 'Indian Navy – Maritime Power for National Prosperity'. Our mandate is unambiguous."

- Admiral D.K.Joshi Former Chief of Naval Staff (2012-14)

The world has acknowledged India's economic trajectory, and as the country continues to progress on the path of sustained growth, there is a acceptance that the maritime domain will be a key facilitator of India's growth and security. 90% of India's increasing trade by volume and 77% by value is transported over the seas. Over 85% of India's energy needs of oil are either imported or produced from offshore fields. Consequently, India's economic growth is linked to the seas.

The Navy has issued many documents to further the Navy's strength from the current and 135 ships which includes 2 aircraft carriers, the 50 year old INS Viraat till 2016, and the newly inducted 45,000 ton INS Vikramaditya with MiG-29Ks, 30 Large Combatants, a depleting strength of 12 conventional over 20-year old aging Submarines (4 HDW & 8 Kilo) and two nuclear Submarines, INS Chakra on lease and home built Arihant, awaiting sea trials at Ship Building Centre (SBC), which will provide India's nuclear deterrence with K-17/B-05 700 km missiles.

The Navy has 10 medium Landing Ships Tank, 4 fleet tankers, 9 survey ships, 30 OPVs and corvettes and a grey line of platforms, and over 220 aging helicopters, Israeli UAVs, MR Dorniers 228, 5 IL -38s, 8 TU-104 and soon 8 latest P8i Boeing 737s (3 have arrived) with MK 84

Harpoons and Mk 48 US torpedoes. The Navy's main armament includes the 299 km supersonic BrahMos missiles and Israeli Barak AA systems with AMD radars and Russian Shtil AA. It is one of the leading navies in the world with a well trained component manpower and has plans to upgrade platforms and achieve a strength of 160 modern platforms, 3 aircraft carriers and over 400 aircraft by the 13th plan (2017-22), in its capability based strategy. 36 platforms are on order on Defence PSU shipyards including a 37,500 ton aircraft carrier INS Vikrant at Cochin Shipyard Ltd and 7 ships at ABG and Pipavav Defence and Offshore Engineering Co Ltd private shipyards, listed below with details of Request for Proposals.

The Navy's goals are anchored on India's Martime Military Strategy (2007) and Doctrine (2009) and based on Navy's Vision Document, the Maritime Capabilities Perspective Plan 2012-27, the XII Plan document, the XII Infrastructure Plan and 30 year Submarine Building Plan (1999) document for two line submarine building. Only one was set up but the construction of 6 Scorpenes by DCNS of France (Armaris terminated and Navantia's contract ended) at Mazagon Docks Ltd (MDL) Mumbai under MOD's Defence Production has lagged by five years depleting the Navy's submarine Order of Battle (ORBAT) due a flawed contract exceeding original ROM costs.

The warships built in Indian PSU yards are invariably 50 to 100 % over estimated costs with inordinate delays as most designs and weapons fits are not frozen on order of the platform due to a dilatory Ministry of Defence and a Defence Production Department and the DRDO. This needs correction as the Navy has to learn, that best is the enemy of the better. A booklet on Shipbuilding (which is not subsidized in India) has also been issued. Request for Proposals (RFPs) and Request for Information (RFIs) are listed with ships on order.

The Coast Guard is also competent and has an

ambitious expansion plan and operates 75 ships and 45 aircraft and helicopters. Currently 50 ships and small Interceptors including total 20 OPVs and 12 FPBs are on order in private yards. India's economic growth has slowed and the Navy experienced a slew of accidents in 2013-14, which could hamper the expansion to enable consolidation. The Navy has a new partly complete base at Karwar, the home base for INS Vikramaditya and is progressing another South of Vishakapatnam in Project Varsha for submarines as a forward operating base. The Navy's new Naval Academy near Calicut is over stressed with a larger intake than was envisaged, the Naval War College has been established at INS Mandovi at Goa and a Nuclear Engineering Training School set at SBC Vishkapatnam. Navy needs manpower and needs to establish Rashtriya Indian Naval Military Colleges (RINCs) in rural areas to tap talents as the Army did from IMC.

The Future Ships on Order and Planned
(from Media and Navy briefings)

India's naval strength is being augmented by 43 Ships on order. Around 20 more will be ordered soon. The status is listed to achieve 15 Year Building Programme target of 160 platforms and 400 aircraft and helicopters by 2022, to possess a credible nuclear deterrent and amphibious capability of One Division. The latest Defence Procurement Procedure (DPP- 2013) recommends "Make in India', 'Buy and Make in India', and 'Buy' precedence as order of the day by MOD and import contracts mandate 30% minimum offsets to induct technology, which has not succeeded thus far.

- 1 Aircraft Carrier INS Vikrant (37,500 ton) at Cochin Shipyard Ltd (CSL) for MiG-29K operations A futuristic 65.000 ton aircraft carrier is on the Drawing board at Naval Design Directorate NHQ with Naval Tejas planes or other carrier based. RFIs have been issued for Nuclear, Electric or Gas Turbine propulsion, which proposals are being evaluated.

- 6 Project 75 Scorpene conventional Submarines under construction at MDL. All hulls ready in two yards East and West. First boat due in 2015/16, 4 years behind schedule and 25% over cost already. An RFP is long awaited for 6 Project 75-I (India) submarines with Air Independent Propulsion (AIP), to emulate nuclear submarines endurance. The tested underwater launched BrahMos missile may be included in the RFP. DRDO with L&T tested hydrogen fuel cell at DMRL Ambarnath near Mumbai, or imported.

- 4 Project 28 ASW Corvettes, 3 launched at Garden Reach Shipbuilders and Engineers Ltd (GRSE) at Kolkutta. First to commission 2014. Composites for mast are from Kockums Sweden as the Corvettes became top heavy.

- 3 Type 15A improved Delhi class BrahMos fitted 7,500 ton INS Kolkutta Destroyers with M/F multi Functional Elta radar and MR Barak SAM, and Zorya Ukraine Gas Turbines at MDL. First to be commissioned in 2014.

- 2 Naval OPVs under construction at Goa Shipyard Ltd (GSL). Two delivered and 5 on order at private Pipavav Shipyard on USA Alion design at $ 110 million a piece, long delayed.

- 6 Catamaran Australian Transport Co design survey vessels at Alcock Ashdown Bhavnagar with Konsberg Huggins-1000 Under Water Vessel (UWV). First of class INS Makkar under trials. The Yard is facing financial difficulty and has suspended deliveries, thanks to untenable LI (lowest bid) syndrome in MOD and ordered on a rudimentary shipyard on the Kutch coast by Minister Antony in Gujrat for political reasons. L&T has not received dues, and construction reported stopped.

- 4 LPDs RFP issued for 2 to be constructed in

private yards in competition , who will get the design which will be transferred to PSU yards HSL for 2 LPDs.
- 5 Tankers and 2 DSRV fitted submarine support vessels RFI issued and for other equipment.
- RFI for Submarine mine laying and Hovercraft.
- 2 - 3000 ton Training Ships of revolutionary merchant navy design at private ABG Shipyard at Surat. Exchange Rate Valuation challenging all private shipbuilders.
- 2 Additional Nuclear Submarines (Aridhaman) at Ship Building Centre (SBC) Vishakapatnam reported under construction in Private Public Partnership (PPP) with Larsen and Toubro Ltd (L&T) in leased yard. DMET Hyderabad is supporting for testing equipment prior fitting and for indigenisation.
- Over 100 Fast Patrol Vessels (FPBs) and Miscellaneous Interceptor Craft including order for 50 Interceptor boats from Solas Marine Sri Lanka, Larsen & Toubro Ltd , Pipavav and other PSU and Private yards with Ferries, Tugs etc.
- 7 OPV for Coast Guard at Goa Shipyard Ltd.
- CG and Navy are inducting more Dornier-228s, UAVs, Dhruv helicopters. 8 Kangnam Korean MCMVs contract has been cancelled and is expected to be retendered.
- Midget submarines will be inducted.
- Naval Aviation. 8 P8i MR Aircraft due in two years (3 Arrived) to be based at INS Rajali in Tamil Nadu and 12 ASW multi role helicopters selection process complete. MOD to select from Sikorsky's Seahawk S 70 or NH-90s Europe as NHI under inquiry. Remaining Seakings MK42 B are aging. 57 Utility Helicopters RFI issued.
- 6 MRMR aircraft and UAV RFIs issued.

The postscript to this chapter is that the Defence Production Secretary, who moves as Secretary Defence in many cases in MOD, is never questioned on delays and cost over-runs in PSU shipyards which get involved in legal cases rather than negotiating and getting hardware inducted. Control over DRDO projects in MOD is most unprofessional and more political.

The Navy has more in common with Ministry of External Affairs for diplomacy, foreign policy makers in PMO and National Security Council controlled by the powerful National Security Adviser (NSA), with authority as PM's adviser, but no responsibility. The Finance Ministry juggles funds, while the over worked Ministry of Defence (MOD), neglects informing NHQ in its dual filing system. Secrecy abounds in actions with regular leaks to the media. The MEA, realizing it is losing hold on IOR island nations, has formed a new division in late 2013 under a Joint Secretary for Sri Lanka and Maldives but has excluded critical Maldives, Mauritius and Seychelles. This needs rectification and must be strengthened with naval expertise. Navy needs representation or direct liaison in Ministries of Earth Sciences, Shipping and Petroleum for energy security. A Fleet Auxiliary of tankers and cargo ships needs to be set up. Andamans & Nicobar and Lakswadweep shipping service should be run by RFAs on semi commercial basis. Government must open up FDI to defence upto 49%, and rethink indirect and wide technology offsets. The L1 policy needs tweaking. All these suggestions are in the national interest, if India's Navy is to deliver.

Appendix 3
Simla Agreement and and the Hamoodur Report

THE SIMLA AGREEMENT (1972)

The Simla Agreement shows how close India and Pakistan came to a peaceful settlement on Kashmir, by respecting their territorial occupation, and conditional to release of POWs . However, a wave of terrorism was unleashed on India and accelerated from 1989. The Kargil war followed in 1999, a year after both nations went nuclear. Trade and transit is still not allowed. Pakistan loathes India's influence, and its interests in Afghanistan.

The text of the Simla Agreement signed on 2 July, 1972 between the Government of India and the Government of Pakistan through their leaders, is reproduced below.

The Government of India and the Government of Pakistan are resolved that the two countries put an end to the conflict and conformation that have hitherto marred their relations and work for the promotion of a friendly and harmonious relationship and the establishment of durable peace in the subcontinent, so that both countries may henceforth devote their resources and energies to the pressing task of advancing the welfare of their peoples.

In order to achieve this objective, the Government of India and the Government of Pakistan have agreed as follows:

1. That the principle and purposes of the charter of the United Nations shall govern the relations between the two countries.

2. That the two countries are resolved to settle their differences by peaceful means through bilateral negotiations or by any other peaceful means mutually agreed upon between the two countries; neither side shall unilaterally alter the situation and both shall prevent the

organization, assistance or encouragement of any act detrimental to the maintenance of peaceful and harmonious relations.

3. That the pre-requisite for reconciliation, good neighbourliness and durable peace between them is a commitment by both the countries to peaceful co-existence, respect for each other's territorial integrity and sovereignty, and non-interference in each other's internal affairs, on the basis of equality and mutual benefit.

4. That the basic issues and causes of conflict which have bedeviled the relations between the two countries for the last 25 years shall be resolved by peaceful means.

5. That they shall always respect each other's national unity, territorial integrity, political independence and sovereign equality.

6. That in accordance with the charter of the United Nations, they will refrain from the threat or use of force against the territorial integrity or political independence of each other.

Both the Governments will take all steps within their power to prevent hostile propaganda directed against each other. Both countries will encourage the dissemination of such information as would promote the development of friendly relations between them.

In order, progressively, to restore and normalize relations between the two countries step by step, it was agreed that:

1. Steps shall be taken to resume communication, postal telegraphic, sea, land, including border posts, and air links including over flights.

2. Appropriate steps shall be taken to promote travel facilities for the nationals of either country.

3. Trade and cooperation in economic and other agreed fields will be resumed as far as possible

4. Exchange in the fields of science and culture will be

promoted.

5. In this connection, delegations from the two countries will meet from time to time to work out the necessary details.

In order to initiate the process of the establishment of durable peace, both the governments agree that:

1. Indian and Pakistani forces shall be withdrawn to their side of the international border.

2. In Jammu and Kashmir, the line of control resulting from the cease–fire of 17 December 1971 shall be respected by both sides, without prejudice to the recognized position of either side. Neither side shall seek to alter it unilaterally, irrespective of mutual differences and legal interpretations. Both sides further undertake to refrain from the threat or use of force in isolation of this line.

3. That withdrawal shall commence upon entry into force of this agreement and shall be subject to ratification by both countries in accordance with their respective constitutional procedure, and will come in to force with effect from the date on which the instruments of ratification are exchanged.

Both governments agree that their respective heads will meet again at a mutually convenient time in the further and that in the meanwhile, the representatives of the two sides will meet to discuss further the modalities and arrangements for the establishment of durable peace and normalization of relations, including repatriation of prisoners of war and civilian internees, a final settlement of Jammu and Kashmir, and the resumption of diplomatic relations.

Signed on 3 July, 1972 at Simla.

President Zulfikar Rehman Bhutto, Islamic Republic of Pakistan, and Prime Minister Mrs Indira Gandhi, Republic of India.

Ranjit B. Rai, Joseph P. Chacko

THE HAMOODUR RAHMAN REPORT
- The Military Aspects abridged

A commission headed by then Chief Justice of Pakistan Justice Hamoodur Rahman was set up wih a wide mandate in December 1971, mainly "to prepare a full and complete account of the circumstances surrounding the atrocities in the 1971 war including the circumstances in which the Commander of the Eastern High Command surrendered forces under his command and laid down arms". The two other members were Justice S.Anwarul Haq of the Supreme Court and Justice Tufail Ali Abdur Rehman, Chief Justice of the Sindh and Baluchistan High Court, and Lt Gen Altaf Qadir as the military adviser.

The Commission submitted a preliminary report in July 1972 and its final report in November 1974 after examining the Pakistani prisoners of war released by India in 1972. It had chapters on Moral aspects, Alleged atrocities by the Pakistan Army, Professional responsibilities of certain senior army commanders.. It is reported that 12 copies were made. Bhutto kept one and 11 were lost or stolen, but parts of the report surfaced over time.

When Bhutto read the report he was shocked and he feared the people of Pakistan would rise in revolt if they came to know how they were served by their General and martial law leaders. Perhaps he also thought the Commission's findings on martial law and its recommendations would cause widespread demoralization in the Pakistan Army. According to a leading Pakistani journalist, the only remaining copy of the report was found from under Mr. Bhutto's bed, when he was arrested for trial leading to his execution. A photocopied version was smuggled out of Pakistan.

The Commission's report, according to media reports, including a story on 1 October 1988 by the Washington correspondent of the Times of India, J. N. Parimoo, makes it clear that the war on the West Pakistan front was started by Pakistan and not India. American policy makers and their friends in Pakistan had tried to create the impression that India wanted to extend the Bangladesh war to West Pakistan and that it was India that had opened the second front on the West Pakistan side. The Commission blames Pakistan's military leaders for unduly delaying the attack on India from the West Pakistan side.

On Criminal Conspiracy

The Commission had recommended that Gen Yahya Khan and a number of senior army commanders like Gen Abdul Hamid Khan, Lt.Gen S.G.M.Pirzada,.Lt.Gen Hassan, Maj.Gen Umar and Maj. Gen Mitha, be publicly tried for being party to a criminal conspiracy to illegally usurp power from Field Marshal Mohammed Ayub Khan on 25 March 1969, and to maintain Gen.Yahya Khan in power, if necessary by the use of force. They did try to influence political parties by threats and inducements to bring about a particular result during the elections of 1970, and later, persuading some of the political parties and the elected members of the National Assembly to refuse to attend the sessions of the National Assembly scheduled to be held at Dacca on 3 March 1971.

They brought about a situation which led to a civil disobedience movement, armed revolt by the Awami League, and subsequently to the surrender of troops, and the dismemberment of Pakistan. The officers should also be tried for criminal neglect of duty in the conduct of war both in East Pakistan and West Pakistan.

Disgrace and Defeat

Justifying public trial, it said, "These Commanders have brought disgrace and defeat to Pakistan by subversion of the Constitution, usurpation of power by criminal conspiracy, their professional incompetence, culpable negligence in the performance of their duties, and physical and moral cowardice in abandoning the fight, when they had the capability and resources to resist the enemy."

It referred to the shameful defeats in Rajasthan and Punjab. It recommended that Lt Gen Irshad Ahmed Khan, commander 1 Corps, be tried for criminal neglect of duty in the operation of his Corps, such that nearly 500 villages of the Shakargrah Tehsil of Sialkot were tamely surrendered, thus seriously jeopardizing the army offensive in the South. It recommended that Maj Gen Abed Zahid, Former GoC, 15 Division, be tried for the surrender of 98 villages in the Phukilan salient in Sialkot district and that Maj Gen B.M. Mustafa, former GoC, 18 Division, be tried for willful neglect because his offensive plan, aimed at the capture of Ramgarh in the Rajastan area was militarily unsound and badly planned, resulting in a severe loss of vehicles and equipment in the desert.

Immediately before the Bangladesh war, Pakistan's friends, including the US, China and Iran, warned President Gen Yahya Khan, that they would not be able to help Pakistan if it went to war with India. Yet Pakistan hoped till the eve of surrender that China would intervene, and kept urging it to. This illustrates Pakistan's dependency on China, which now has control over Gwadar port in its String of Pearls, its weiqi (Go board game) strategy to ring India with friendly ports. China provides arms, nuclear help and calls its friendship with Pakistan 'higher than the mountains, deeper than the seas', as its nuclear submarines and PLA(N) warships test waters by deploying assets in the Indian Ocean. India's shatranj chess-board responses lack long-term strategy.

Top left to bottom right: Lord Mountbatten supervised the Partition and the splitting of the Royal Indian Navy assets. **Cdr S.G. Karmarkar** (later Rear Admiral) was the first Indian officer to command British officers. The Pakistani officers who led the attack on Dwarka. An artist's impression of the Dwarka raid. Pakistan CNS Vice Admiral Muzaffar Hassan.

Bhutto's reluctance to accept election results led to the Mukti Bahini's struggle. Mrs Gandhi with President Nixon, who tilted towards Pakistan, ignoring the refugee problem. Sam Manekshaw provided concerted leadership. The ill-fated *Ghazi* takes a periscope check. PNS *Hangor* that scored a hit on INS *Khukri*. Defence Minister Jagjivan Ram consoles

Prime Minister Rajiv Gandhi aboard INS *Vikrant*. His Op Pawan provided lessons for offshore military operations. Current naval assets need a revamp and an astute strategy for a nation hoping to exert its presence in the Indian Ocean Region. The author with his wife presenting an earlier book to President Venkataraman.

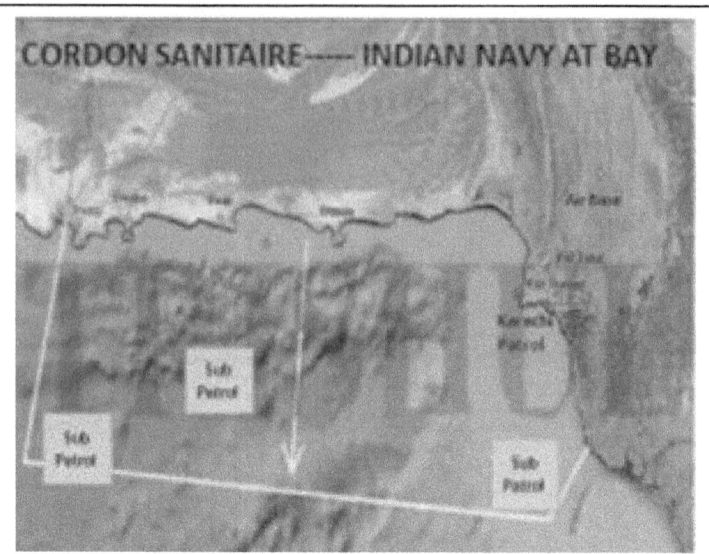

The defensive Cordon Sanitaire employed in Ex Brasstacks

(See Chapter 3)

ABOUT THE AUTHORS

CMDE Ranjit Bhawani Rai (Retd.) served in the Indian Navy, commanded four ships and the Naval Academy. He served twice in the NHQ as the Director of Operations and later Intelligence. He also served as Defence Adviser in Singapore. Leaving Navy prematurely, he attended IIM (Ahmedabad) for Shipping Management and was the rep for Waterman Shipping Corp USA (1993-2004), when India liberalized and shipping thrived. After US flagged ships withdrew to war in Iraq, he took to writing, broadcasting, and conferences. Author of four books, his avocations are TV commentary, golf and supporting his wife's inbound tourism activities.

Joseph P. Chacko is a defence journalist, enterprenuer and the publisher of Frontier India, a portal publishing news and current affairs. He specializes in defence and strategic affairs. He holds an M.B.A in International Business from the Maharishi University of Management, Iowa, USA.

www.ingramcontent.com/pod-product-compliance
Lightning Source LLC
Chambersburg PA
CBHW071251160426
43196CB00009B/1244